D0592496

CAST
THE FIRST
STONE

John M. Murtagh
CHIEF MAGISTRATE, CITY OF NEW YORK

Sara Harris

McGraw-Hill Book Company, Inc.
NEW YORK / TORONTO / LONDON

4374

Horsford

We are grateful to Edward H. Schmidt for his many able and constructive criticisms.

306878

CAST THE FIRST STONE

Copyright © 1957 by John M. Murtagh and Sara Harris. All rights in this book are reserved. It may not be used for dramatic, motion-, or talking-picture purposes without written authorization from the holder of these rights. Nor may the book or parts thereof be reproduced in any manner whatsoever without permission in writing, except in the case of brief quotations embodied in critical articles and reviews. For information, address the McGraw-Hill Book Company, Inc., Trade Department, 330 West 42d Street, New York 36, New York.

Library of Congress Catalog Card Number: 57-8015

HQ
1454
.M8

Published by the McGraw-Hill Book Company, Inc.
Printed in the United States of America

To Mary and Arnold

It is well to inquire—what is the city's responsibility in regard to the problem? Is it the responsibility of government to change the public's morals? Can this be done? Manifestly, there is a point beyond which morality must be left to religion, the home, and the school. The late Mayor William J. Gaynor once observed that "the business of government is to maintain law and order and outward decency." To this I subscribe. I believe the concern of the police and the courts should be (1) to prevent scandal by the open and notorious activities of prostitutes; and (2) to rehabilitate those who are emotionally disturbed and socially maladjusted and who are still capable of rehabilitation. We must still look primarily to the church, the home, and the schools to discharge the responsibility for teaching morality.

The prostitute has never been understood by our courts. Indeed, she is still an enigma to science itself. The nature of her emotional instability, its causes, its cure, are all matters beyond the knowledge of science, let alone the law. Because of this lack of scientific knowledge, indeed, the degree of her moral responsibility is essentially a matter that must be left to the Lord Himself. Is it not therefore incumbent that we approach the problem differently than in the past?

From a report on the Women's Court and the problem of prostitution by Chief City Magistrate John M. Murtagh to the Honorable Robert F. Wagner, Mayor of the City of New York, dated February 14, 1955

Preface

This book is a portrayal of the weird world of prostitution. It is a story of a world right around the corner from our own, and yet, in mores and standards, as distinct and separate a place as though its location were Mars instead of New York, U.S.A. It is a story of twisted, tortured people. It is a story of blatant degradation. It is, if you will, a sordid, shocking, gruesome story, and it has little trace of hope or uplift or joy. Sordidness and ugliness are the concomitants of prostitutes' commonplace, everyday routines of living. Here are people narcotized to accept hurts, humiliations, abasements as their daily portions. Here are people who know little or nothing of hope or joy or uplift. Truly, if we attempted to endow them with such knowledge, we would be writing our stories, not theirs.

Why, then, have we chosen to tell the story? Because we agreed, when this book was conceived, that there was need of an *honest* story about prostitution. All too often the problem of prostitution is either referred to in off-color stories or ignored altogether. It is our hope that this book may help bring the matter out in the open where adult Americans with a concern for the moral and social welfare of the community can discuss it intelligently.

All the characters can be seen almost any day in New York City's Women's Court. The incidents all occurred and have been occurring for generations, not alone in New York but throughout the world. In this area of activity, what is true of New York is certainly true—with minor variations—of every other city in America. We chose to do the New York story only because we have been in a unique position to record it in all its ramifications and in all its details.

The book is first and foremost an attempt to penetrate the world of prostitution and to understand how prostitutes and pimps became the people they are today. The reasons why a sociological writer would want to undertake such an assignment are doubtless plain. What could be more challenging than digging for the roots, deep in the community pattern, which have produced such people as prostitutes and pimps?

While a judge's motivations may not be so obvious, they are just as intense. Any sincere judge who is administratively responsible for courts which deal with sex offenders must be struck by the fact that our laws are based on false assumptions and unimaginative cruelty. Prostitutes are dealt with as though they topped the list of dangerous public enemies. Every day we send out plain-clothes officers who have been trained to inveigle women into offering them a good time just so they may arrest them when they agree—hardly a legitimate moral standard to use for tracking down immorality. Periodically we engage in "vice crackdowns" which never have accomplished anything and doubtless never will. And yet after the women are arrested, virtually our only answer is a period of confinement in a penal institution calculated to make more certain their further degradation. But no matter how a judge regards the law, his responsibility is to administer it, not to change it. In the long run, the only ones who can change the laws of a community are the people who live in it.

And so we have written this book as honestly as we know how—with faith in our readers and hope in our hearts.

JOHN M. MURTAGH
SARA HARRIS

Table of contents

A woman in my business should never have children. But you keep thinking that you're not going to be in it all your life. When you start out you don't think that you're going to do it all your life. The years just seem to slide by—and before you know it your time is almost up and actually—you didn't do any living at all. Because this isn't living, really. It's just existing from day to day. It's no kind of life for anybody.

From a taped interview of a
prostitute, December, 1956

ONE / There is no horror

Prostitutes, from the very young beauties to the shabbiest old fleabags, say that you can measure women in the "business" by the kinds of operations in which they engage, or the streets they frequent, and the places in which they solicit. They say you can appraise the pimps, the men the girls love and support and take orders from and call their own even though three or four other girls may be calling them theirs, by the girls themselves.

The aristocrats among prostitutes are expensive call-girls who work for fancy fees and keep their pimps in luxury. They live in sumptuous apartments or better residential hotels on New York's fashionable East Side, have good street dresses and striking evening clothes, never do their own work, and consider it a point of honor to buy their pimps new Cadillacs every year. There are some young girls among them, but they are mostly women in their late twenties and early thirties. A few are beauties, but the majority, while attractive, are hardly ever the ravishing creatures most of us imagine. In fact, once you get to know them, you are inclined to agree with the prosecutor in the celebrated Jelke case who, questioned about the looks of call-girls, said:

"Why, I have plenty of friends whose wives are prettier than most call-girls I know. I think it's amazing, the glamour some men manage to attach to women once they know there's a price on them."

Amazing or not, there are call-girls who earn between fifty and a hundred thousand dollars a year. They have customers who pay a hundred, two hundred, or three hundred dollars for a couple of hours with them and go higher for a full night. Some commuting businessmen, called *matinees*, reject the night hours altogether and come afternoons between two and four-thirty, so that they can be on the five-fifteen and five-thirty trains headed for Westchester and Connecticut.

Expensive call-girls are not easy for most men to meet. Public-relations men who have good names and addresses are not inclined to share them with strangers. And night-club personnel who know women and telephone numbers must be closemouthed until they are convinced that prospective customers are not police officers in plain clothes. The same goes for knowing cab drivers and hotel employees. Chances are that if a call-girl is easy to meet she is not, as her boosters boast, "top-drawer stuff."

Many call-girls who are not top-drawer are as attractive as the ones who are, but lack of contact or self-confidence keeps them from succeeding as well. Their fees are more modest, twenty to a hundred dollars, and their business is quantity rather than quality.

After the call-girls come the house-girls. Houses today are not the elaborate affairs that they used to be. A few are lush and pretentious, but most are simple and small. They consist of a madam, usually a former prostitute, and one or two girls who change from week to week. House prices begin at seven dollars for five or ten minutes with a girl and range up to fifty or a hundred for a night.

A step or two beneath the house-girls in the prostitutes'

hierarchy come the women who solicit their own men out of the exclusive night spots in the Fifties and Sixties on the East Side. They work all the spots, no matter how respectable and whether or not the owners approve. For what recourse do the owners have if they don't happen to like them? Suppose one spies a couple making a date, how can he be sure that they are not old friends who have run into each other?

So a girl with a fresh face can make the rounds of respectable places. There are enough of them in New York to take a long time to go through them all. And afterward, when she begins to lose her bloom and the people who do not want known prostitutes in their spots drive her out, there are other clubs that are as elegant and expensive, only not so bluenosed. There, for a price, bartenders and waiters will put men in touch with her. She knows, of course, that, even in this world, familiarity breeds contempt and that some night, bound to come sooner or later, she will be as unwelcome here as she was in those other spots.

So what? The East Side is not the only place in New York. Plenty of joints on the West Side in the Seventies and Eighties and Nineties. The customers there are neither so rich nor so generous, but then, they are not so demanding either. And, she still is not streetwalking for her living.

Call-girls, house-girls, and night-club prostitutes regard streetwalkers as the lowest women in their business and in the world.

Certainly they look an unappetizing group. There are plenty of young girls, including teen-agers, among them, but they are girls who have never learned to value either their youth or themselves. The older ones are mostly homely and dirty, with messy hair and bad complexions. Some of them look as if they had not bathed or changed their clothes in weeks.

Although there are individual streetwalkers who cruise their tricks in other places, there are four principal areas that are known streetwalker hangouts—Times Square, especially along 42nd Street between Seventh and Ninth Avenues; Harlem, especially 125th Street between Third and Eighth Avenues; Chinatown, and Coney Island.

Forty-second Street is the busiest and best known. Everybody has heard of its streetwalkers: out-of-towners looking for flings as well as native New Yorkers. It cries loneliness in its way and prostitutes make capital of the cry. They hang around the one-arm joints where people eat standing up, a fifteen-cent slice of pizza pie that drips tomato sauce, a frankfurter or a burger (also fifteen cents) washed down by a soft drink that costs only a dime. They haunt the doorways of the small bookshops featuring collections of true pornography and science shrewdly presented as such to people who do not know the difference—Krafft-Ebing's *Psychopathia Sexualis,* for instance.

The deluded would-be readers invariably complain, "The good parts are in *Latin,* for God's sake. Who the hell can read Latin? You got to be a college professor to get your kicks these days?"

The girls grab the window-shoppers as soon as they assure themselves they are not officers. They pet and stroke them and whisper words to make them feel they don't have to be college professors at all.

"I know things the writer of them books never thought about, mister. Try me out and see for yourself. I'll do anything you want."

Maybe they ask for twenty dollars once they have aroused a man's interest, but they will keep going down until they hit ten, or five, or less. Some of them try to spur him on to a better contribution with the moth-eaten streetwalkers' joke that has been told along the street for more years than most of them can remember. It is supposed to have originated in Harlem and is usually told with an accent.

"It's jus' plain up to you, mister man. Y'all gimme any amount y'all wants. Five, ten, twenty dollars is all alike to me. But not to y'all, because I does my business thisaway. For a five spot I'm just aroun' an' lets y'all do your own work. For a ten spot ah helps ya out some. But, honey, gimme twenty an' y'al don' need to do nothin' 'cept hang on."

The 42nd Street habitués have heard the joke over and over and have quit believing in it, so the girls save it for outsiders now and never tell it to the crowd that sits around the cafeterias all day and all night. This is the crowd that spends dollar after dollar for a little companionship, and makes profitable such institutions as the "New York Academy of Chess and Checkers Canteen— Games Arranged—10¢." The girls never bother the alkies and cokies of the street with their joke, but save it for the others who do not belong and are out looking for a different kind of titillation.

"Honey, gimme twenty...." They all say it pretty unvaryingly, the young and old, the fat and skinny, the blue-jeaned kids with their pants faded and tight from many washings (they like faded jeans along the street), and the pregnant women in their last months who tell their tricks that everybody knows that "girls get more *passionate* at a time like this." You would be surprised at the number of men, good husbands to their wives and fathers to their children, who go with them and keep goading them on to displays of what they choose to regard as the peculiar passion of pregnant prostitutes.

"They're dogs, those men, dirty rotten dogs," says twenty-nine-year-old Marsha Green in her eighth month. "But I should worry. I'm not married to them, thank God, and I don't want nothing they got to give except money. I see them one time or maybe a couple, so why should I care what I do with them? You wouldn't believe it, would you, but I been making more money ever since this baby started in showing. Tricks who never gave me a tumble before think I'm something special now. Fools. I can name you plenty of times when I seen them turn down cute young chicks and take me instead. Not just me, old hags without no teeth in their mouths."

Talk to the toothless ones if you want to get the surprise of your life. They will tell you about men, not necessarily 42nd Street habitués either, who choose them, as Marsha Green says, over the younger, prettier girls, wanting them, not despite their unattractiveness, but rather because of it.

"All kinds of wacks in a bag of tricks, you know," Maria Elena Blaine says matter-of-factly.

Maria Elena knows whereof she speaks. She is sixty-two and has operated along the street for many years. She and the other old ones come out in their greasy clothes, still smelling, some of them, from last night's nausea, and stand in front of the Times Theatre, which shows films like "Teasecake Burlesque" and "Strippers and Zippers" and features such performers as Miss Misty Ayres and Miss Lili St. Cyr. They watch for the men who come out of the movie, alert to be the first to grab them. Or they stand beside the shops that display tricks, toys, and souvenirs in their windows, and they draw men's attention to the tricks and souvenirs—the Jokerino Jumping Pens, guaranteed to open and fall apart as soon as you begin to write with them, the naked women that are cigarette holders, the electric bow ties, the nutcrackers that consist of two shapely female legs, the Adams Spiders, advertising themselves as "A Realistic Imitation of the Black Widow Spider; Creates A *Real* Scare and Can Be Used For Jokes Without Number," and finally, last but not least, the ultimate in conversation pieces, the suggestive ash trays labeled "He" and "She."

"Yessiree," old Maria Elena says, "trick stores can be a big help to a girl like me. I do most of my cruising around the Times Theatre. Guys come out hot and bothered and ready for anything, and I tell them to try me because old stuff knows more than young stuff does, and before they say yes or no I say, 'Daddy-o, you want to see some funny tricks to make you a hit at a party?' Then I take them past the trick store for a laugh to break the ice and I say, 'What do you want to do, go into a hall some place and save three bucks or get a real bed in a hotel?' "

Looking at Maria Elena, you would think she might have a hard time gaining admission to a hotel, especially if she claimed to be the wife of a sailor, who looked, let us say, young enough to be her grandson. But she has never run into any difficulty yet. The Times Square area is crawling with shabby hotels, the least respectable of which have girls, many of them teen-age narcotic addicts, who are available to guests along with their rooms. The most respectable of them accommodate women like Maria Elena and their escorts, no questions asked.

"They're hot-bed hotels," Maria Elena explains. "They make believe they're renting to you for the night, but they know they ain't. If I come in with a trick and say I want a room for tonight, they know I'm going to use it for an hour or less. The hotel guys like us prosses better than legits. They can make more money off of us. Me and the other girls like them, too. The hotels is one reason I keep working the streets and never go no place new. I don't expect I ever will, neither."

Maria Elena, along with the other Times Square habitués, believes that here is their mecca. They have a profound and unswerving loyalty to "the street." But such loyalty is not unique with them. Streetwalkers from other places also have it.

The girls who walk the narrow streets of Chinatown,

for instance. They say Chinese tricks are more approach-
able than whites and kindlier lovers. They say they like
everything about their Chinese tricks, the way they gamble
in the small smoky rooms behind their restaurants, not
silently, as white men do, but sociably, noisily, for small
stakes rather than large ones, and then, after the games
are finished and the night is almost over, the girls like
the way the Chinamen politely solicit their services:

"You come be my *me-me,* ha?"

Me-me is the Chinese word for sweetheart.

Another thing distinguishes the Chinese from other
tricks—sometimes he goes mad over a girl. When that
happens he wants her every night and he does not want
to take her for a price any more. He says he does not like
to exchange money for affection with one he loves. So she
tells him all right, and she fishes for gifts instead of money.
The gifts are worth five or ten times what she has been
charging, but he does not care. What he does not know,
of course, and doubtless never will, is that her pimp takes
all her gifts away.

Even if he does not fall in love with a girl, there is,
according to the Chinatown prostitute, an innate gentle-
manliness about all Chinese men. She has been to bed
with plenty of them and she ought to know. She would
not dream of walking any streets except those in Chinatown.

Nor can the Coney Island prostitute, young girl or old-
timer, imagine herself anywhere else. She claims Coney is
such a happy place of swing and jump, of fire-eaters and
snake-charmers and belly-dancers and tattooed folk.

Prices are low in Coney Island because competition is
keen ("too many freebies around wanting to give it away"),
but the ones who are oriented say a dollar here or there
doesn't matter one way or another, and you can always

make up in number what you don't get in price. Coney prostitutes are a crowd of opposites: many girls in their early teens and many women in their fifties and sixties. Business thrives all year round, but the summer months are the golden months. In June, July, and August older women may take many men on for fifty cents apiece, "any way you want it," while some younger girls service twenty, and even thirty, men a day at two to ten dollars each.

"But you got to be terrific to get a ten spot in Coney," says fat, blond, sixteen-year-old Carole Loomis. "You got to be hotter than a Nathan's hot dog."

The vast majority of Coney Island prostitutes do not patronize hotels.

"Under the boardwalk's good enough," Carole says. She believes that some of her tricks, and more particularly some of the tricks who patronize "them beat-up old hags we got around," looking as they are for dirt and dross, get greater titillation from "under the boardwalk" than they could if they had to take their girls in ordinary hotel beds.

Some women use the same places under the boardwalk every day. After a while they grow possessive and feel as though other prostitutes who come there are impinging on their squatters' rights. Sometimes fights occur and occasionally girls cut and beat each other up over a particular piece of beach.

"Get outa here before I cut ya in the face."

"*You* get out of here before I cut *you* in the face. I found this beach before you were born."

"So what do you think, you're Christopher Columbus or somebody? It's a free country and I never heard of you paying no rent on this beach either."

"If you don't get off my beach, I'll break your head open."

"You 'n' how many cops?"

Sometimes a girl does try to break another's head open or cut her in the face, and often succeeds, so that the defeated one lies screaming until she attracts the notice of some kind outsider who calls the Emergency Ward at Coney Island Hospital to come and get her. Or a friend finds her and tells her other friends, and then a real feud begins between the two enemies and their supporters.

"Oh, yes," Carole Loomis repeats, "Coney's the place all right. I mean if a girl's going to go in business, where else'd she rather be?"

Many girls would rather be in Harlem than Coney Island or anyplace else, white girls as well as Negroes, provided they are older in their business than Carole Loomis and shrewder in the ways of their world. For the wiser ones, who are onto a few of the motivations of their tricks, know that many white men come to Harlem expecting a special something they do not understand themselves, hopeful of experiencing new erotica beyond the ken of downtown. They have seen them there on 125th Street, these white men from higher places, sometimes brash but more often timid, walking with heads down and fear on their faces. They come to Harlem, of course, in search of Negro women, but sometimes, once arrived, they find that, despite themselves, something in them really prefers white after all. Then they will jump at the chance to take the first white woman they see. She might be one they would never give a tumble to downtown, and if they do not want to pay for a hot-bed hotel, they will go into a hallway with her; and, such is the nature of the beast, being prepared for erotica, they persuade themselves they are finding it here and invest their plain white women with some of the mystery Harlem itself holds for them.

It is the mystery of strange sounds and smells and signs

and places: ordinary houses and shops and stores bearing peculiar names they can memorize for the amusement of their timid friends who would not dare this trip themselves. Glamor Inn. Ritz Restaurant. Hi-Hat Bar. Paris de France Beauty Salon. All the so-called tonsorial parlors, plain old barbershops really. And the spiritual establishments and store-front churches, one or more on every block. See Me Today. Be Successful Tomorrow. Spiritual Healing. Religious Consultant. Domestic Problems.

And the girls, white and colored, who stroll along 125th Street with swinging breasts and hips. They come in twos and threes, talking warmly together but keeping their eyes peeled for a likely prospect. Once they spy him they decide between them which one is to have a try with him. The chosen one attempts to sell herself first, and if rejected, begins to laud her girl friend instead.

"Look at her, daddy-o. A doll from dollville. Try her out. I won't be insulted if you want her instead of me. Or maybe you want us both together. Her and I's alreet together. Well, what I mean, alreet. Or maybe you don't want me at all. Maybe you want my girl friend and her friend. Like I told you, mister, I'm not one to get insulted. Just tell me what you want and I'll try to help you get it."

You can be sure when you see girls working so cooperatively that they are "wives-in-law," feeling bound to one another because they happen to be connected with the same pimp, *sweet man* to them.

"It's like being in a family," they explain, not knowing why there should be any question about so logical a procedure. "Say you and your sister were in business together and you couldn't get a trick to go with you, wouldn't *you* try to get him for your sister instead of letting some strange chick who's not related to you get her hands on him?"

So they work together as families, these Negro and white girls and their pimps, Negroes too, nine times out of ten, until some hostile cop, dressed in plain clothes so he will look like a trick, takes them off to court and tries to make them inform on their pimps. But the girls won't rat on their daddy-o's. They'd rather go to jail. After they go off, the other wives-in-law seem sad for a while. But there is something else they keep down deep inside their hearts; they are glad, too, especially if the ones who are picked up happen to be important to their sweet men, if they are their "head chicks" instead of just one or another of their "barnyard hens." Of course, they play up the sorrow and beat down the joy. They cry about how their family is disrupted, and, along with more objective folk, accuse the police department of being discriminatory in Harlem.

Ginny Jones's plaint is a typical one:

"Damn cops come uptown all dressed like plain tricks in lumberjackets and torn shirts and with Band-Aids on their faces, so a girl'd think they'd been in some kind of a bar brawl or something. Then when they make a pass and a girl says 'O.K.,' why they take her right down to jail. Shoot, whyn't they try to get them some nice white meat from downtown oncet in a while instead of picking on us all the time? We ain't the only whores in the world, but if you looked in the jails sometimes you'd think we was. I just can't figure why the cops think dark meat's so special they got to pull it all off the streets. I tell them dark meat's all the same as white in the dark, but I think they can't believe it. I know white tricks can't.

"What's the matter with white folks? They're always talking about how fine their white ladies is. O.K., whyn't they stay with them then, instead of rushing up here for a brown girl? I used to have a sweet man in the down-town clubs who'd find white tricks and say to them, 'What does a hot-natured fellow like you want to be bothered with them anemic white chicks for, when you can come with me and get you some *dark meat?* You want real loving, then you got to get you some *dark meat,* boy.' Well, man, those downtown tricks come running, thinking us colo'd folks got everything so special here, hotter girls, hotter clubs, hotter everything. Suckers."

They are suckers, of course, the white men who come to Harlem with their naïve expectations, and everyone who has anything to do with them is oriented to "take them for a ride." The night clubs, mostly owned by whites, advertise their shows as "the torridest" and their belly-dancers as "the shakingest" and never have any trouble getting men, who have seen hundreds of hotter shows in the downtown places they frequented before they found Harlem, to believe their lies. And the white peep- and stag-show operators have fellows out to tell downtown tricks that Harlem peep shows are the wickedest ever, when all the time they know that they cannot compare for lasciviousness with some of those produced downtown. Along with the club men in Harlem, they laugh up their sleeves at the unshakable faith of the downtowners.

In a way, expensive prostitutes may be the ones who have the loudest laughs on downtowners. For they, without lifting a finger sometimes, are the main profiteers from what they know to be the biggest lies of all.

One of them is Jean Ford, a college graduate, tall, slender, her skin the color of *café au lait.* "It's fascinating about these tricks who come uptown. A colored girl who plays her cards right and isn't too bad-looking can practically write her own tickets with them. They seem to feel that, because some of us have remote ancestors who lived in Africa once, we are primitives at heart when it comes to sex. Actually, most of them are a lot more primitive than we are. Sometimes their good wives are, too. Catch them believing it, though. And we don't tell them. Why should we? Let the innocents hold onto their prejudiced delusions so long as they're willing to pay for them. Besides, I doubt we could disillusion them if we tried.

"I try once in a while, just for the hell of it. I go with some drooling idiot for two hundred dollars or so, and, instead of putting on the big passion play he has every right to expect for his dough, I lie in bed like a stick of wood. Now, I've got enough white friends in the business to know that any white whore who doesn't put on a sensational act for a two-hundred-dollar baby could, as we in the business say, expect to have her block knocked off. But me, I don't have to lift a finger to keep a white trick sure he's getting something special. And when I do make half the effort a white girl does, well, heavenly days and honest to Betsy, if you wouldn't think I was handing him the world in a nutshell.

"It isn't just the sex, either. It's the fact that being with me makes him feel like a gay dog. I take him to a joint or two, strictly tourist, and I say, 'White Boy, now you can see for yourself the way us poor niggers lives and loves.' Once in a while I get a trick I like for some reason, and then I'll take him to a real joint and watch him purr like a pussy cat."

By a real joint she means one of the many afterhours clubs around Harlem that cater primarily to prostitutes and pimps. They open their doors around 10 P.M. when the pimps, having kissed their girls good night and sent them off to "get some fish," come in to do some early drinking. They talk a lot together, addressing each other by the nicknames that are *de rigueur* in these places—Fu Manchu, Streamline, Black Percy, Sporting Dave, Tubby, Satinhead, Fruit, Sleepy, Lord Buddha. They gossip about their girls or about coming events that concern them all, the glamorous Pimps' Ball, for one, which is held every April at a downtown hotel. They compete a lot, especially when it comes to fancy clothes. They also take care of their business, bartering and exchanging their girls when it seems wise. They sit all night, dozing occasionally, until the girls start coming in in the early hours of the morning and their true social life begins. They leave each other then and take tables with their girls, talking and drinking with them instead of each other. Sometimes pimps, when they feel inclined, kiss and pet with their favorites and the girls never fail to be delighted by the attention. Then, before anybody has suspected how late it has gotten to be, one pimp or another looks down at his jeweled watch and announces that it's two o'clock in the afternoon by golly, and he, for one, is going to take his little chicks home to beddy-by. So the women and men leave together, arms around each other, and the men pick up their Cadillacs and Lincolns and drive their chicks to where they live.

Why do girls become prostitutes? How do they learn to live with the hurts, the humiliations, the debasements of their lives? What are the roots of the psychic misery that has driven them into such weird paths? The following six stories are drawn literally from hundreds. They do not begin to give all the answers—nothing could—but they may shed light on some of the forces behind a life and existence whose real horror is that for the prostitutes themselves there is no horror.

TWO / Hincty little ofay

NAME: *Mary Stewart*

AGE: *18*

MARITAL STATUS: *Single*

EDUCATION: *Grammar-school graduate*

Mary Stewart appears quiet and demure, quaint, in fact. Her long blond hair, worn in a braid around her head, makes her look older than her eighteen years. So does her erect stance. She carries herself very straight.

"Hincty little ofay" was what the habitués of Monkey's afterhours bottle club used to call her during the first few months she lived up in Harlem with Bible John. Bible John is a tall, handsome pimp who spouts the Bible like a preacher and runs a series of illegitimate businesses behind the façade of a righteous-looking, religious-objects store.

Hincty little ofay is Harlemese for snooty little white girl. Mary Stewart loved the label. She reveled in it. She was only sixteen when they began calling her that, a lush, ripe sixteen with a figure that the colts at Monkey's called a "coke frame—streamlined like a Coca-Cola bottle."

When she walked into Monkey's at two o'clock in the morning, leaning on Bible's arm, she in the tight black dresses Bible liked her to wear, and Bible himself in the off-green suits, a little tight around the buttocks (and why shouldn't they be tight? A man has as much right to show

16

his figure as a woman has), and yellow shoes and gray fedora hat, they made a striking couple.

Some of the men would whistle at Mary and some would give her long, hungry looks.

"Hey, Bible," one would say, "when you going to start passing this chick around?"

Bible only smiled to himself and held onto Mary's arm. She loved the way he held her arm so tight it hurt.

"Not ever in your territory," he would say. "And what do you know about that?"

Bible John made Mary think she was wonderful, and the leering men and the jealous women at Monkey's always sealed the illusion for her.

How she loved Bible for making her aware of the blessings she had never counted worthwhile before—her youth and her white complexion. Before Bible had come into her life and gone to the trouble of instructing her about herself, she had never thought that being young and white was anything special. For Mary, to be young had been to be sensitive to how different you were from other girls and to be easily hurt and miserable most of the time. But here at Monkey's, to be young and to be white were unique assets that made her infinitely desirable. To be young at Monkey's was to be feted there and to be white was to be right.

Bible's friends, all sweet men like himself, used to kid their white girls with the phrase "white is right."

"Yessiree," they used to say. "Brown is down. And white is right." Of course, their voices always sounded mocking, but Mary was one who could see beneath the mocking tones and know how much of a premium all these men placed on the color of the skin they pretended to make fun of. If not, why then should they regard her as such a precious one here?

Oh, there were other white women at Monkey's who came, as Mary did, with their colored sweet men, but they never managed to catch the same kind of attention. Most of them were older and few of them had "coke frames."

There was Betty who had a double chin and blamed her homely red complexion on Monkey's King Kong. She went around telling people that all she had to do was stop drinking Monkey's poison and her skin would grow as flawless as Mary's. She never did stop drinking long enough to prove her point, though. Mary thought she might have been right at that, because Monkey's King Kong certainly did pack a tremendous wallop, and there was no telling the effects it could have on people. Bible never let her drink too much, just enough to get that pleasant glow she sought after work every night.

Sally was a Monkey habitué, too. She was Betty's wife-in-law, a woman of about thirty-five. She had brown hair and eyes and a fair skin. She might have been attractive except for a slash on her face that extended from her eye to her mouth. She had once told Mary that her sweet man, Pal, had cut her.

"But why?" Mary had asked. "Why would he do that?"

"Because," Sally had answered, "I deserved it."

Mary had said, "Nobody deserves to get their face all cut up. After all, our face is our fortune."

Sally had held her hand to her head. "I did something terrible."

"What?" Mary had asked.

But Sally had been unable to tell her for a long time. Finally, she blurted it out. "Jeez, kid, I went and called Pal a nigger. Jeez!"

Mary used to be frightened every time she looked at Sally. She made up her mind that she would never commit the crime Sally had, no matter what. And yet, when she

reflected, she could almost understand why Sally had done
the terrible thing. Sally must have felt, as she did herself
sometimes, that it was a comedown for a white girl to live
with a black man. But was it? Really?

Maybe it was a comedown for some white girls who
hustled for their sweet-men and gave them all their money
and then had to share their attentions with five or six
wives-in-law. Mary could be proud indeed because she was
one girl who didn't have to get along with a single wife-in-
law, not to mention seven, as that sweet daddy called
Jo-Jo had. And Jo-Jo was an ugly man, too. She sometimes
wondered what his girls saw in him. He used to spend one
night a week with each of them. Why, Mary wouldn't even
be surprised if the girls didn't know which one he regarded
as his main chick. Probably told Chinky that she was, and
then Rita she was, and so on right down the line.

Mary thought she might die of jealousy if Bible ever
did as Jo-Jo did and got himself a full stable. But he
never would, as long as Mary stayed with him and remained such a productive hustler. It was really a great
compliment he was paying her. After all, before she'd
come to him, he'd had a stable bigger than Jo-Jo's. Sometimes he'd had eight or ten or twelve girls. And now he
was making do with her alone. She, of course, was considered one of the top, if not the very top, of the Harlem
hustlers. Her tricks paid well, twenty-five to a hundred
dollars, and she took six or seven a night. Sometimes she
took more than seven, if either she or Bible had a project
that warranted it.

Her mink stole was one such project. Bible had presented
it to her after they'd been together for about four months.
Her mother and father would probably say it wasn't a
present from Bible at all but one from herself to herself,
since her money had paid for it. But she had a different

point of view. What difference whose money? Bible had
thought up the idea of the mink all by himself. She hadn't
had to nag him. The other girls had to nag their men for
everything they wanted. You wouldn't catch them buying
mink stoles just like that.

Little Mary in a mink stole. If only her mother could
see her in it. But she'd have to see her on Bible's arm if
she saw her in the stole. And she might die if she did. She
might lie right down and die. After all, she'd hated
Negroes all her life. Not that she'd ever known any
personally. She'd just formed an idea about them—based
on nothing. She used to say there was a smell about colored
people that made her sick. Well, she was mistaken. Take
Bible. No smell about him to make you sick. He was the
cleanest and best-smelling man in the world.

But what would Mary's mother say if her daughter were
to tell her, "My sweet man's a black man and he's got
the nicest smell in the world. Not like Pa! Talking about
smells, Ma, when did Pa take his last bath?"

Sometimes, watching Bible sleeping in his pink silk
pajamas and with the pink sheet tucked beneath his chin,
she would think of her father and mother lying in bed.
Pa was such a filthy man. Poor Ma. To have to be with
him all the time. No wonder she was so sickly and always
had been ever since Mary could remember. Poor Ma. Why
was she such a dumb cluck? Why hadn't she learned as
early as Mary had what a woman's body was for? Not to
be abused by a man but to be used to get what one wanted
out of life. Now Ma's body was all dried up, though. No
man would pay for it. Pa had used it, that's why. Pa. She
could spit on Pa.

Mary Stewart feels contradictory about her mother. She
loves and feels sorry for her sometimes, and at other times,

when she recalls her life at home, she dislikes her with a conscious desperation. But her feeling toward her father is clear. It is unadulterated hatred.

"One time he went and raped me," she says. Just like that. Expecting no shock. She says it as easily as she says everything else about herself. "I was thirteen years old. Ma was in the hospital, gone there to have her fourth kid she didn't want."

Mary had been out all day after school had let out. She had come home around eight o'clock, uncomfortable because she had forgotten she was supposed to fix her father's dinner. He was sitting in the little room with an open bottle of whisky.

"The drink was running down his chin. He looked so dirty. I guess he never shaved in God knows when. His whiskers were just terrible. I wanted to ask, 'Why don't you do right and be like other fathers? You could shave once in a while. It wouldn't kill you.' What was the use of talking to him, though? He'd only laugh or slap me around. When I was younger, he used to knock me down if I got fresh to him once in a while. So I said to myself, 'What should I talk to him for? Let him drink himself silly if he wants. I should worry and get sick and die?' So I walked right past him to get to my room."

He stopped her. "Where you going?" he asked.

She said, "To a ball."

"Where you going?" he repeated.

"I'm going to bed," she said.

"What's the matter with you, anyways?" he asked.

She said, "Nothing."

He got up from the couch and walked over to her and grabbed her by the shoulders. "Why don't you give your old pa a little kiss, honey?"

She hardly knew what she was saying. "No."

He said, "Don't you 'no' me! What's the matter with you, girl? Who's the one puts the bread in your mouth?"

"You, Pa," she said, even though it was not true.

"All right, then, do what I tell you."

She held her face up for his kiss. It was awful.

"After he got finished with me, I ran straight in my bedroom. I forgot there wasn't any lock on the door. There used to be one before. But it got broke off. Well, what was the use of worrying when there was nothing I could do anyways. So I laid down on my bed without taking my clothes off and tried to get some shut-eye. But who could sleep with him right in the next room? So I laid awake and wished I was a boy. Then the old man would be ascared of me all right.

"Out in the living room I could hear him singing some sort of a dirty song. Then all of a sudden I didn't hear him any more. I thought, oh, oh, what's going to happen now? Maybe he passed out or something. You wouldn't hear me crying if he did. Nobody else in the family'd cry for him, neither. Except maybe Ma. The only reason is because she's the kind of woman is always thinking about what are the neighbors going to say."

She heard her father get up from his chair and begin walking toward her room. She cuddled under the blanket and closed her eyes tight. She began to count his heavy footsteps. One, two, three, four, five . . . ten. He stumbled. Good. Maybe he'd fall. No such luck. She counted the steps again. One, two. And now she could hear him standing at the door. He rattled the knob. She wasn't a child who knew how to pray but she asked God to help her.

Now he stood by her bed. His whisky breath nauseated her. He bent down toward her. He said, "Mary."

She pretended to be asleep and snoring.
"Mary," he said.

The next morning he was ashamed of himself. His old
bravado was gone. There were tears in his eyes when he
looked at her, but Mary was not moved.

"Him and his phony waterworks he could turn on and
off. He said he was sorry for what he done to me. Yeah.
Yeah. He was so sorry he came back three times before my
mother came home from the hospital."

Mary found herself daydreaming about her mother's
home-coming.

"I thought Pa'd go back to her once she got home and
leave me alone. Besides, I wanted to tell her about Pa. I
figured maybe we could get closer together if I told her
and she'd take all us kids and go away some place. Kick
Pa out. He wasn't any more good to her than he was to
us. She sometimes told me she hated him. So what'd she
go on staying with him for? I asked her one time and she
said, 'If I left Pa, honey, how'd I support you and the
other kids?' I really laughed because Pa never had supported us. All he ever did was make the relief people tell
us we couldn't have an allowance like they'd give us if
he wasn't hanging around the house drinking everything
up. Ma always supported us herself, cleaning people's
houses. Why'd she have to go and tell me Pa supported us
for? Such a big lie. I wasn't one of the neighbors she was
ashamed to have know the truth about us. Her and her
neighbors!"

Sometimes Mary thought the neighbors were the domi-
nant influences in her mother's life, more important than
she and her brothers and sisters.

"I'd ask her, 'Who counts more, Ma, your neighbors or your family?' She'd say, 'Mary, that's silly.' I'd say, 'Silly or not, who's more important?' She'd say, 'Sure, my family's more important. What kind of mother would I be if they weren't?' I'd say, 'O.K., if your family's more important, act like it.' She'd say, 'Don't go getting fresh now, Mary.' But she'd do what I wanted. Except when I told her about Pa. She wouldn't do anything about that dirty old man. Gee whiz, she wouldn't even listen to what I had to say about him."

Her mother was sitting in the old rocking chair and holding the new baby, who had been named Robert Taylor for the movie star.

"Ma," Mary said, "I got something terrible important to tell you."

"Yeah?" Her mother went on rocking Robert Taylor. Her stringy blond hair, neither short nor long, fell into her eyes as she rocked.

Mary spared no details when she told her.

Her mother buried her face in Robert Taylor's neck and made little cooing sounds.

Mary said, "Did you hear me, Ma?"

Her mother brought her buried face up out of Robert Taylor's neck. "Do you swear to God, Mary?" she asked.

"Yes," Mary said, "I swear to God."

"God would strike you dead if it's a lie you're telling on your father."

"But it's no lie." Mary began to cry.

Her mother cried, too. The tears ran down onto Robert Taylor's head. She got up and placed him in his crib. Then she came back and sat on the rocking chair again and pulled Mary onto her lap and held her close while she rocked back and forth. She kept on crying and calling her "baby."

Mary liked being in her mother's arms. She felt close to her. She felt warm and protected. She still remembers the wonder of the feeling.

"I just wanted her to keep on rocking me and holding me. But she stopped before long and told me to never mention one word against my father again as long as I lived. She said if she ever heard me say anything she'd slap me one. After a while I found out what was bothering her. The neighbors. She said they better not find out about Pa and me, or she'd never be able to hold her head up among them."

Her father stopped coming to her after her mother returned. Sometimes, though, she heard the two of them arguing in their room at night, her father calling her mother "a cold, cold iceberg, grr."

She spent as much time as she could outside her home. She joined a girl gang that called itself "The Seven Snappy Steppers" and took a blood vow to be true to her "sisters."

"I guess the time I was with the Steppers was the happiest in my life. We did everything together. We walked with our arms around each other. We practiced the walk so we'd really be fancy steppers, like our name said. Other girls were jealous and wanted in. We told them no no. Seven was what we started out and seven was what we intended to stay. I used to think we'd stay seven fancy steppers after we got married and had kids of our own. I got the idea of making the kids we had 'Seven Little Junior Steppers.' It was great, but I knew it couldn't last the way I liked it. The Rattlesnake Rowdies made it their girls' auxiliary. There were seven of them, too, one boy for each of us girls."

Mary's boy was named Shorty.

"They called him Shorty because he was tall," she said. "Six foot two and a half inches. He was ashamed of his

height. He walked sort of stooped over, dragging his feet
along after him. I told him he ought to become a fancy
stepper, keep his head up high, but he laughed and said
he might touch the sky. We laughed a lot together when
we were alone. He told me he liked me. But he'd be a
different fellow when the other boys were around. Then
he'd act like I was dirt.

"One night I was down in the clubhouse with my blood
sisters when Shorty came in. I don't remember why they
all had to go home and him and me stayed together. We
sat down and he told me he loved me. He did! 'I love you,
Mary.' I felt so good. Nobody ever loved me before, except
maybe my blood sisters in the Steppers. But they all got
boy friends after the Rattlesnakes took us in and they
loved their boy friends better. So I had to love Shorty
better. I began to love him like anything after he said he
loved me."

Lying on the clubhouse couch with Shorty, she felt fine
and wonderful to be making him happy—not dirty the
way she had felt with her father—until the next morning
when she ran into him and some other Rattlesnakes.

She said, "Hi, Shorty."

He did not answer.

She repeated, "Hi, Shorty."

He looked right through her, straight at her and right
through her, just as though last night had never been.

"Look," she said, "yesterday you slept with me. Today,
you won't even say good morning."

He said, "The guys got important things cooking. Be a
good girl, huh? Take a walk and don't bother me no more
till I tell you."

Remembering it all, she says she was so humiliated she
wished she could die. But today she smiles at her story

and says, philosophically, that she has relegated the hurt to its proper place.

"That's men for you." She shakes her blond head knowingly and fingers her mink stole. "They're all alike, except my Bible. If my sweet daddy was like the rest of them, I'd cut him all up just like I cut Shorty. I did cut Shorty. I was such a silly kid then, all I wanted was revenge, and I didn't even care about what would happen to me after I got it."

She took a sharp knife from her mother's kitchen, went down to the clubhouse, found Shorty, and began to slash at him. Somebody called a policeman, who took the knife away from her and brought her to the station house.

Three weeks to the day before her fifteenth birthday, Mary Stewart was adjudged a delinquent and sent to a Training School for Girls.

"I'm glad the judge sent me up," she says today, "instead of putting me on that crazy probation."

She considers the Training School with its finely kept grounds and attractive cottages where the girls all have small but private rooms a nice place to live. Nor has she any complaint about the school's vocational, educational, or recreational programs. They were all all right in their way, she says, even though a little naïve in their assumptions that Training School sophisticates would become beauticians, or bakers, or typists, or housekeepers, when they were released.

"It's hard to talk about the program or the place now," she says, "because they left me kind of cold. I mean I went to classes and to gym and every place, but I wasn't with it. Only thing mattered to me was the racket. Boy, it was sure something! I got invited in after I was there three weeks,

and by Big Bertha, Bible's sister. She was head pop. Not
very pretty. Homely, in fact. For a girl. But she would've
been a swell-looking boy.

"I always tell her that. I say, 'Bert, you should've been
born a boy.' She says, 'Yeah. But should have been and
was is two different matters, tootsie doll.' She's still a pop
at heart. She says any time me and Bible decides to call it
quits, she'll be glad to take me on as close as we used
to be in school. She says, 'Bible's my own loving brother
and I wouldn't go poaching on his territory, but after
all, you belonged to me before he got you. Right?' I tell
her, 'Sure.' I'm really lying though. Being with Bertha
was always different for me than being with Bible. I
never liked it, but I was afraid not to go when she asked
me."

Mary's induction into the racket and her homosexual
relationship with Big Bertha began, as she says, some three
weeks after the gates of the Training School had first
closed behind her. She had been through the periods of
hospitalization and cottage isolation that all new girls are
subjected to, and this was her first night in the cottage
that was to be her home during her entire stay. She had
met her housemother, a kindly-looking fat woman in her
forties, and her fifteen cottage mates. But their names and
faces were blurs to her.

"When I got into bed, I tried to remember one girl from
the other, but I couldn't seem to. So I stopped trying and
went to sleep. I don't know how long I slept but it was
still dark when I woke up. There was a big tree near my
window and the wind made an awful lot of noise when it
blew through. But it was hot, anyways. I tried to go to
sleep again but I couldn't."

She kept hearing small noises at her door. "Like somebody was picking my lock. I really didn't think anyone was, but I said 'Who is it?' anyways."

A husky voice she couldn't place answered, "Me."

"Who's me?" she asked.

"You'll find out," the voice said. "Just hold your horses, kid."

The sounds continued, slow and scrounging. Mary lay in bed staring at the ceiling, wondering what would happen to her, when the sounds stopped and the door finally opened. "What do you want?" she asked.

The voice said, "Pipe down before you jimmy up the works."

"What do you want to pick my lock for?" Mary asked again.

"Because I want to give you a little loving, baby," the voice said. And then the scrounging stopped, the door was open, and Mary had her second glimpse of Big Bertha, head of all the racket pops.

She was a dark-brown hulk of a girl with nappy hair and muscular arms.

"I hated colored people then, and I was scared stiff when I saw Bert. She said she wanted a little kiss from me. Then she got me in a bear hug. I felt terrible, but I knew I couldn't stop her, so I just stayed still and let her do what she wanted. After she got finished—she didn't do no more than kiss and hug me the first night—she said I better not tell anybody, if I knew what was good for me. She said the racket ruled at school and everybody was afraid of her and the other pops. She said, 'Looky now, if you went and told anybody what I done this minute, they'd tell you they don't believe you. You know how come? Because if they believed you, they'd have to do something. They're too scared us pops might cut them up if they did.'

"I found out Big Bertha wasn't kidding me. Everybody was scared stiff of the pops in the racket. They were tough operators." Mary, once she had been initiated, drifted into the racket more or less easily.

"Being with Big Bertha was no tougher than being with my old man, and I got to like it after a while. She *was* the head pop and all the other moms thought I was hot stuff to get her. None of them minded her being colored, so pretty soon I got to where I didn't mind either. Except I didn't want to go the limit when we first got together. Kissing and holding hands, O.K. Bertha said kissing and holding hands was a big deal for the birds, not for her. So what could I do? I said all right, Bert, do what you want. Listen, why not? What's a girl's body for, except to help her get things a little bit easier? Being with my old man never killed me, did it? What'd I have to lose? Nothing, if I told Bertha yes, but plenty if I told her no. She could leave me flat. Then I wouldn't belong to anything. Who wanted to be a crazy old lone wolf? Not me. Everybody picked on the loners. I didn't want them to pick on me. I knew they'd be afraid to, me having Bertha for a pop."

After Mary had "gone steady" with Bertha for a few weeks, they decided to marry. Marriage is a natural accompaniment of the pop-mom relationship at the Training School. It happens all the time when two girls decide they want each other forever.

"When Bertha said I was the only mom for her and she wanted to marry me," Mary says, "I told her fine. We had the wedding behind the laundry. My friend on kitchen assignment brought some cookies she snitched. All the girls said I was a gorgeous bride. I said, 'Nay,' but they said, 'Yea, yea.'"

Today, Mary believes her wedding to Big Bertha to have

been one of the bright spots of her life. It gave her status and a feeling of importance to have the head pop pick her for a bride.

"Sure it was kid stuff, but I didn't know it then," she explains from her present vantage. "All those girls thinking I was so great made me think, well, gee whiz, maybe I am great. After all. That's why I got a soft spot for the crazy old school. That plus all the things I learned while I was there."

She learned how to "roll lushes" and the technique of "boosting" merchandise out of department stores by rolling it up so small that it could be placed between the legs so nobody could suspect there was anything there.

"I also learned about my own trade. We always talked about hustling. We used to play the Hustlers' Game. A girl made believe she was working the street or she could be in the bar if she wanted. Another girl was supposed to be a bull. She pulled all the tricks bulls pull. The girl who was doing the hustling had to figure ways to spot the bulls, and say nay. What a hot game. I learned plenty: like what you got to do before you begin to talk price with a trick is feel all over his body to make sure he's got no gun on. Another thing's to make sure his hands are rough if he claims to be a worker. Bulls in workers' clothes usually forget to do anything about their hands and so they're soft and white."

Mary Stewart, by the time she was ready to leave the Training School, thought she knew every trick of hustling that related to women customers as well as men. For she had learned, through Big Bertha primarily, but not entirely, that there were places in Harlem and elsewhere in New York where women came for thrills with other women. Bertha said many women customers were wealthy and paid higher than men did. She had excellent contact among

madams who placed girls for work with women and she
would introduce Mary. Pretty as she was, they would all bid
high for her services and she could write her own ticket.
Big Bertha wouldn't be surprised if she earned between five
and six hundred dollars a week. Mary gasped at the idea of
that much money; but, still, she wondered deep in her heart
whether she couldn't do as well with men as women? Or
better perhaps? And even deeper down she wondered
whether she wanted to prostitute at all.

She had her answer on the night she met Bible. It was a
stifling June night, her third night home. She had taken
the subway to 125th Street and walked four blocks to
the 129th Street address Big Bertha had given her. She
stopped at the door, surprised at the shabbiness of the
tenement building. If Big Bertha's stories about her
contacts were true, why, Mary wondered, didn't she live
more prosperously? Maybe she wasn't as trustworthy as she
had seemed at school and Mary would do well to turn
around and go home. She almost did, but found she
couldn't. Something forced her up the three flights of creak-
ing stairs. She hesitated in front of the door for a while,
but then she knocked extra loud as a cover-up for the
timidity she was feeling.

Bible came to the door. He took her hand and pulled
her into the living room. It was small and dimly lit. Two
sagging couches, an old easy chair, and a lamp table were
the only furniture. Big Bertha sat in the easy chair and a
wizened white man sat on one of the couches. But Mary has
little recollection of either of them. She imagines Big
Bertha kissed her and introduced her to the white man,
who turned out to be a contact for taxicab drivers, but she
is not sure.

"The only one I saw was Bible. The way that man looked
at me. Wow!"

She'd never been looked at like that before, except by the pops at school. Who were pops, when you came right down to it? Just girls like Mary. And you couldn't be moved when their eyes devoured you. When Bible looked at her though. . . .

"I'll eat my hat, honey-girl," he said, and his voice was a song to Mary, "if you ain't the prettiest chick I ever seen."

She didn't want to do it, but she found herself blushing. She tried to summon some gay remark but none came to her.

"Baby," he said. "Baby doll." That was all. And his tone turned her into a fairy-tale princess. "I never seen a prettier girl."

Mary grew to know Bible well in the following weeks, and, when he invited her to his home one night, she was happy to go. He lived on Riverside Drive, and his apartment was as different from Bertha's as it was possible for two places to be. The building was clean and well kept and his rooms were spacious. There was a large living room, its walls painted slate gray; the furniture was bright red and mustard; there were a kitchen and two good-sized bedrooms. Mary told Bible this was exactly the kind of place she'd pictured him in, and she could hardly wait to start exploring every nook of it. He said he'd be glad to show her around but that he'd have to outfit her with some new clothes first. She laughed at that, because she knew that nobody could buy new clothes at midnight. But Bible could. He went to the telephone and made a call to somebody named Gloria Ann.

"Listen, Baby. I want you to hie your little self down to my pad and bring everything you got in size nine."

Mary was flattered that Bible knew her size without asking. She thought none of the women out home would believe her if she told them she had a fellow who knew what size she wore.

Gloria Ann, a lovely colored girl with huge eyes, arrived about twenty minutes after Bible's call. She carried two huge suitcases. She was breathless and her words fell over each other as she talked.

"I got some gorgeous dresses from Bergdorf's. Still hot off the hooks."

"Open up," Bible said. "Quit gassing and start working."

"O.K., O.K., lover boy." Gloria smiled. "Keep your britches on."

Mary never knew dresses and shoes and hats could be as beautiful as the ones Gloria showed her.

"Well, gorgeous?" Bible asked.

Mary said, "Oh, Bible, I just don't know. Everything's so beautiful, I can't make up my mind."

"Have a spree," Bible said. "Take them all."

But Mary knew she couldn't take them all. She appealed to Gloria, asking her to make a selection for her. Gloria said she'd like to see her all in black. Mary thought that was stupid, but she took the dress, shoes, and hat Gloria gave her and went into a bedroom to try them on.

"Hey, don't forget these," Gloria said, throwing a pearl necklace and some long pearl earrings at her.

Standing in front of the full-length mirror in the new clothes, she understood why Gloria had chosen black for her. She couldn't believe her eyes. She looked as beautiful as any movie star. Who would ever have suspected her figure was so good? She had always thought of herself as too skinny, because she'd been scrawny before she went to the Training School, and the sacks they called dresses there had prevented her from noticing how she'd changed. As for her legs, and the black, high-heeled sandals, they were nothing less than wonderful. And the pearls and earrings accented her fairness.

She placed the small black hat on her head, whisked the half-veil over her face, and walked into the living room.

Bible didn't say anything for a minute. He didn't have to. The look in his eye was enough. Then he let out a low whistle and told Gloria:

"Take a standing order, baby. Keep my chick in black dresses that show her figure as good as this one."

If she had not known before, Mary knew she was Bible's girl now. Her only problem was escaping from her mother's clutches so she could spend all her time with him.

"I'm not usually scared of Ma," she said, "only now with me being on parole and all, I don't want to make her so mad that she'll go and tell the officer she can't do nothing with me."

Bible mocked at her fear of parole officers. He said only squares were scared of them, and besides a smart girl like Mary ought to be able to handle her old lady. Why didn't she call her on the telephone and tell her to drop dead or something? Mary didn't like his talking that way about her mother, but she didn't say anything. Instead she went to the phone.

"Hello." Ma sounded sleepy and teary.

Mary said, "Hi, Ma."

"Mary," Ma asked, "Mary, is that you? Where are you, anyway? Where you been so late? What are you always worrying me for? I got plenty to do taking care of Robert Taylor without having to eat my heart out over you."

Mary winked at Bible. "You can stop right now. You don't need to eat your heart out over me no more."

Her mother was silent at the other end of the line.

"I won't be coming home for a while, Ma."

Her mother said, "You better come home if you know what's good for you. You gone crazy or something? The parole officer'll call me tomorrow. I . . . Mary, look, come home, dear."

Mary steeled herself against her mother. She said, "You better think up a good lie to tell parole, Ma. If you don't, I got something to tell them myself. All about how Pa raped me. Then you'll never be able to keep it from the neighbors."

After she hung the receiver up, Bible took her in his arms and kissed her for a long time. She had a fleeting thought about his being colored, and then she relaxed and enjoyed his love-making.

The rest of the night was loaded with thrills. First off, Mary was introduced to Bible's Cadillac. She had not known he had it, since he had always driven a yellow Chevrolet convertible to Bertha's.

"How many cars do you have?" she asked.

He laughed and handed her into the long, sleek car. "As many as I want, baby doll."

How he drove! Fast and reckless as though red lights were never made for the likes of him. Mary thought, I'll never have another wonderful hour like this. I'll always remember this Cadillac and Bible's hand on my knee and the crazy way he drives as though there was nobody in the world but the two of us. I'll never have a better time than I'm having right now.

All the same, she had a better time at Monkey's.

Mary's first night at Monkey's was better than anything. She created such a marvelous sensation walking in on Bible's arm and believing herself as gorgeous as he said she was. She held her head high, and seemed to ignore the looks people gave her and the things they said about her.

Of course, in reality, she missed neither a word nor a look. And when she heard "hincty little ofay," as she did for the first time that night, she stored the words as compliments.

"What does 'hincty little ofay' mean?" she asked Bible later. "A man called me one."

"Snooty little white girl," Bible laughed. *"Hincty little ofay,* doll baby, means snooty little white girl. That's what you are, too, snooty with everyone but me. Right, baby?"

She nodded, while she wondered whether she really had anything to be snooty about.

Bible took her to Monkey's every night after that, and, more than anything else, she enjoyed hearing herself called "hincty little ofay."

"But, Bible, honey," she used to say, "I'm really not a snooty girl."

"Yeah, you are, baby doll," Bible would answer. "You are and you ought to be." Then after a couple of weeks had passed, he began asking why she shouldn't be snooty, a little beauty who could get a hundred dollars just for spending an hour in bed with a guy. Wasn't that something to be snooty about? He asked her many times so that she began growing used to the idea of what he wanted from her.

Still and all, she had a small minute of indecision when he brought the first hundred-dollar baby to his apartment to meet her. In spite of everything she had done before and all the plans she had made at school, she thought —but this is *really* selling myself. Then Bible let her have it right between the eyes, saying, all right, the whole thing was up to her, she was the one who would have to make the final decision. But he had thought that she would *want* to help him keep her looking beautiful. She had no idea, did she, how much it cost him to keep her in

clothes? He really wasn't angry with her, though, no matter how he sounded, just disappointed in himself for having mistaken a dumb kid for a smart woman.

It was the first criticism she had ever had from him, and
it devastated her. Here was the only man in the world
who had ever thought her worth anything, and now *he*
didn't think she was either. Why? Because she wasn't, that
was why. But she was, she was! She'd been with Bertha and
her father, and Bible, himself. Why not this hundred-dollar
baby then?

The baby was nice enough to give her a ten-dollar tip
for being a good, cooperative little girl, after everything
was over. That was something to show Bible. He would be
proud of her. He was.

THREE / No holds barred

NAME: *Margaret White (Maggie)*

AGE: *19*

MARITAL STATUS: *Single*

EDUCATION: *High School—two years*

Little Maggie White, with blue eyes and curly black hair, spews the most vulgar words she knows at potential customers in an attempt to distract them from the girlishness of her appearance. But she seldom succeeds. A delicate nineteen, she looks much younger. Only recently a fifty-year-old trick who had gone to a hotel room with her took a good look by the garish overhead light, rushed into the pants he'd removed in such a hurry and ran out of the room, calling over his shoulder that he knew he was a heel and all that, but even he wasn't bad enough to go to bed with a little girl.

"But I'm not a little girl," she said desperately. "And I know a lot. I'll do anything you want, mister. Anything. No holds barred."

That is her approach along the street. She uses it in common with the older walkers who feel they cannot meet the normal competition in the ordinary way. "Don't be misled by that brash, buxom girl, mister, come with me if you want your money's worth. I'll do anything. No holds barred." If they don't believe she would keep all the promises she makes, if they seem unconvinced of her desire to follow through on the acts she says she will perform with them, she holds her hands and arms out for them to see. The hands have ugly purple streaks running down to the knuckles. The veins looked dried up.

"See, mister, I'm a human pincushion. I'll do anything for junk. Believe me, anything, mister. Just tell me what you want. Try me out. You don't have to pay me if you aren't pleased with me. What have you got to lose? Come on, mister."

Two years ago she was an ordinary high-school student who did well in her studies, went to church on Sundays, and dreamed of being popular with boys. Nobody could have predicted what she would become, and even today the neighbor women on the quiet, refined Bronxville street, where she lived ever since she was born, shake their heads and say that if this monstrous thing could happen to little Maggie White, it could happen to any of their daughters. They become panicky when tales about her life seep back to them on occasion, and they grow strict and more exacting with their own children. They compare notes, exchanging all the information they have about Maggie and her family, in the hope that they can find out where the first slip occurred. But they never do find out. The conversation always reaches a dead end when they come to discuss her parents.

"Maggie was no slum child who grew up without love. Her mother and father are fine people who gave her everything she wanted. She was their life. If there is one girl who had no reason. . . ."

Maggie White knew that her parents lived for her. She always had known. It was so apparent she could not have missed it: in the way they competed to bring her presents, in the way they always sought her companionship instead of each other's, in a million and one ways, including the way they always wanted her to be so perfect and often criticized her because she was not. Sometimes, when she was younger, basking in their love though she did, she used to wish that they would love her less and each other more.

When she grew older she learned for a fact what she had been suspecting a long time, that her mother and father would have been divorced, but for her. Then she felt overwhelmed by a gratitude that knew no bounds and spent miserable hours trying to figure ways for paying them back. What to do? Why, what they wanted, of course. But how could she ever expect to do what both of them wanted —when mummy wanted her to be one kind of girl and daddy wanted her the opposite?

Daddy wanted her to study hard and make a brilliant school record. But mummy didn't want any daughter of hers turning into a grind. Mummy wanted her to be a good housekeeper, and daddy said he'd had enough of good housekeepers. Mummy said, "Meaning who?"

Daddy wanted her to be athletic, and mummy said, "Fine, fine. What do you want her to do, develop a muscle like Joe Louis'?"

They agreed on only one ambition for her—popularity —"with a capital P," as daddy put it. Unfortunately, she considered its achievement beyond her. She was too shy and awkward with other boys and girls. Having spent so much time in her parents' presence, she did not understand her contemporaries. Their jokes were over her head and their slang expressions were beyond her. She was frightened by their sexual aggressiveness, and she found it hard to tolerate their disrespect for grownups. She was constantly under the impression that they were laughing at her for being such a goody-goody, and half of the time they really were.

If it hurt her to have her parents disappointed by her

inability to mix, it hurt her even more to hear them talk about it as often as they did. She hated the conversations which, no matter how calmly they started, always ended with her feeling inadequate and asking herself the same old questions, "What's wrong with me?" and "Will I ever get to be a decent girl?" She hoped she would, but never for her own sake, always for her parents', because, deny it though they did, she knew that under all the tremendous love, they resented their socially inadequate daughter and desperately wished she were different.

Sometimes when they talked of the cherished popularity with a capital P, she resented them, too, and wondered, deep in her heart, whether they were not inadequate themselves and taking it out on her. Why couldn't they leave her alone if all they wanted was, as they always made a point of claiming, their "darling daughter's happiness?" She was miserable when they picked on her and happy when they didn't. She never had minded being alone for herself, but only for their sakes. "Just don't pick on me," she wanted to say, "and everything will be fine and dandy, even if I don't have all the dates you think I should."

But even while she hoped, she knew that they could not have stopped picking on her. They had given their lives up to her, and now they felt it no more than right that she relinquish her individuality in favor of their need.

"When a woman has a popular daughter, who goes places and does things," mummy had told her several times, "she begins to feel she's doing them herself. Her life lights up."

But why, Maggie would ask herself, why, if mummy wanted a different kind of life, had she allowed her own to grow so drab? She never dared to ask the question aloud, but she knew what mummy would say if she did: "I'm

living for my little girl now." Why didn't she live for herself? Maggie never asked her to live for her; indeed, she
never wanted her to.

And her father, too. Why was it so necessary for him to
have a glamorous daughter? Maybe if he had a glamorous
wife, if not mummy, then somebody else, he wouldn't need
Maggie to be so many things she was not.

She always felt mean and ungrateful, thinking such
thoughts about her parents. She sometimes thought the
only nice feature she possessed was her ability to hide her
thoughts and to listen obediently to all her parents told
her.

"I always had trouble choosing between all my dates,
dear, when I was your age," mummy said.

Looking at mummy now, the twisted mouth and the
bitter eyes, Maggie could not visualize her as Popular. But
one thing she knew, mummy never told lies. And so Maggie believed, against her better judgment, and wished that
she could be as popular as mummy had been. She particularly wished it during the hectic weeks that preceded her
first high-school prom, which was to be held a week after
her sixteenth birthday.

Mummy and daddy both helped her shop for her gown.
They took her to a fancy store and, as she might have expected, vigorously disagreed about the dress. One wanted
pink; one wanted blue.

Finally they asked her to choose between the pink and
the blue, and she couldn't make up her mind. She knew
her mother would be hurt if she chose the pink, and, if she
decided on the blue, her father would feel rejected. So she
decided to ask the sales clerk's opinion and thought envi-
ously about girls whose parents' dispositions were not influenced by their daughters' evening clothes. As usual, she

felt overwhelmed by her disloyalty. She had no right to such thoughts. She had a responsibility to do whatever mummy and daddy, who had done so much for her, required of her.

After the blue gown (the sales clerk had chosen in favor of mummy and against poor daddy) had been fitted, she found herself daydreaming about the prom. She saw herself the beloved of the sad, nervous boy Artie Ryan, who looked as though he might have more in common with her than the rough boys did. She knew Artie only casually, but she imagined him a gentleman. She visualized him picking her up on the night of the prom, exchanging courtesies with daddy, and being attentive to mummy. Actually, an ungentlemanly, pimple-faced boy named Mike Lewis, the son of a neighbor who was under obligation to Maggie's mother, had been recruited to escort her. Mummy said not to worry about Mike, dear, he was only an object to use with the ticket taker, and she could easily ditch him once the other boys, intrigued by the blue dress, began to rush her. She said, "All you have to do is act vivacious, honey."

Mummy helped her dress on the night of the prom, and made up, by her enthusiasm, for daddy's comments about blue not being her color.

Mike came with a wilted gardenia and embarrassedly pinned it on her. Mummy had tears in her eyes when she kissed her good-by with the final admonition, "Be popular, honey." Daddy said, "Good night, chicken," and held her shoulder tight.

Later, she was to be called "chicken" again, only in a different tone from daddy's. "You're chicken," Artie Ryan would say. "Yellow-belly chicken."

That's what came out of her seeking popularity by acting

vivacious. She got Mike to dance her next to Artie, and, summoning all the courage she had, winked at him. "You look handsome tonight."

Artie grinned. "Hey, how come I never realized how cute you are?"

She filed his words away for mummy's and daddy's pleasure. She thought how fortunate that she'd spent over an hour at the mirror, lipsticking on new mouths and deciding, finally, on the woman-of-the-world one she wore tonight. She hoped she could stay in tune with the mood of her mouth.

Artie asked her for the next dance, and she could hardly believe her good luck. When he danced her into a corner and kissed her, she prayed that she would be able to hold onto her new-found vivaciousness.

Artie asked her for the next dance and the one after that. She wondered when he would become bored and send her packing, thinking, I won't blame him when he does. I'm glad there's always Mike to fall back on, even if mummy did have to get his mother to make him bring me.

But Artie did not send her packing, and Mike, whether out of filial obligation or something else, remained faithful and claimed his dances between the ones she had with Artie. If this wasn't popularity, it was the closest she had ever come to it, and it was good enough for her. She only hoped against hope that her vivacity wouldn't run out before the evening was finished. It didn't. She kept on dancing, now with Artie, now with Mike, until the very end. Since the last dance was Artie's, she turned to summon Mike to take her home.

"Don't call him," Artie said. "He may have brought you to this prom, but he won't take you home except over my dead body. I'm taking you. Only we're going to a party first."

Mike didn't put up much of a fight when Artie told him, and Maggie was a little disappointed. What a triumph for mummy and daddy if two boys had come to blows over who was to bring their Maggie home. She could just see them relishing the story she could have told. But since Mike said good night very politely and even shook hands with Artie, there wasn't any story.

Artie hailed a taxicab when they left the dance. "I feel like celebrating tonight."

"Celebrating what?" she asked, knowing, but wanting to hear him say it, anyhow.

"Celebrating you." He put his arm around her and held her close.

Today Maggie often thinks back to the way she felt in Artie's embrace. It was the first time she had ever been happy to be in a boy's arms. It turned out to be the last time, too.

"When a junkie's loaded," she explains, "she's not interested in sex. When she's not junked up, she's too busy figuring ways to get the stuff she needs to think about sex or anything else. That's why I know I'll never again feel the way I did with Artie. I was so thrilled because he liked me and because I liked being so close to him." But she was afraid, too. "I thought I might say the wrong thing or that he would realize how quiet I was being. It was all right to be quiet when he had his arms around me. But what would happen afterwards? Would his friends at the party take to me? I couldn't tell jokes and I didn't know how to act when kids acted wise."

Artie seemed so solicitous that she told him how she felt. As she suspected he might, he said that he often felt insecure himself. He was better now than he had been a few years ago, but he still had some terrible times when he came among new people. Except after he'd taken a little horse. Then he wasn't scared of anybody.

Maggie had once in a while overheard kids talking about "horse." She had been intrigued by the idea of heroin thrills and wondered whether they were really as pleasing as the kids said, but she had never thought she would know anyone who was really on horse. And now, here was Artie, admittedly taking the stuff. She felt sorry for him, for she knew that people on horse had to reckon with more than thrills.

Artie laughed when she told him. "All I know is, if not for horse, I'd be one scared guy." He took an envelope out of his pocket and showed her some white powder in it. Then he got a matchbook, tore the matches out with a flourish, and placed a bit of powder where the matches had been. He held the book up to her nose. "Take a sniff."

She moved as far away from him as she could get in the taxicab. "No, Artie."

"You're chicken," he said, snithing himself. "Yellow-belly chicken. But you're the boss."

She said, "I'm sorry, Artie."

"Perfectly O.K.," he said magnanimously.

Then the cab stopped in front of a brownstone house and he paid the driver and helped her out of the cab. So, they were at the party. She felt she never should have come. How should she act? What should she do? She hoped she wouldn't behave so badly that Artie would be embarrassed to have brought her. She thought, "Mummy, how mean to make me go to the prom. You knew I didn't want to, you and daddy both. You never should have made me go." But mummy and daddy hadn't asked her to come to the party, had they? She had no right to blame anyone except herself.

Artie took her arm and steered her through a dim hallway into a barnlike room lit by two lamps. There were many girls and boys sitting around. She hardly looked at anybody, pretending to give all her attention to the record player while only half-hearing the music.

> Why don'ya do right,
> Like some other men do,
> Git outa heah
> An' git me some money too,
> Oh, ya had plenty money 1922,
> But ya let other women
> Make a fool outa you. . . .

The guests lolled in small groups on the floor and on the couch and easy chairs. Out of the corner of her eye she noticed a couple looking at her interestedly, and thought again, How am I going to be able to meet them? Suppose I lose my voice and can't even say hello? "If you've still got some horse to spare . . . ," she said. She wished she could grab a surreptitious look at the woman-of-the-world mouth she had worked so hard to make. She wondered if it was holding out better than she seemed to be.

Today, Maggie says she didn't have much sensation from her first heroin experience, but, whether because of the horse or because she believed in what Artie had said, she was able to relax and enjoy the party. At the end of the evening, he said he was proud to have brought her.

Artie came to meet Maggie's parents the day after the party and to take her to the movies. They sat in the second balcony, and he gave her more horse to sniff, holding it in the same matchbox which he had used the night before.

"I still didn't get a kick," she says, "but Artie said not to worry, I'd get one soon. I got it the third time. Well, it wasn't a kick. I just started feeling relaxed. You know, like everything's all right in the world and, even if it isn't, why should I be bothered? I wished I could go on forever feeling the way I did then.

"But after I had sniffed about eight or nine times, I found I had to have more horse than Artie was giving me. When I told him I needed more, he said I'd get to be too expensive for him if we didn't look out. He said I was getting hooked. I knew I was hooked already. I felt so heavy whenever I didn't have horse. So then Artie told me to stop sniffing and start skin-popping. That's taking the horse and shooting it right in you. I told him I didn't want to because I'd been scared of needles all my life. But he said, scared or no scared, skin-popping was the way to get the kick I needed.

"I started skin-popping. The needle hurt so when I pushed it in the first time that I had to scream. Artie laughed and called me a crybaby. He said, 'Wait'll you been popping for a while. You'll like needles all right.' He certainly knew what he was talking about. Now I look forward to the jab of the needles, because I know the pain I feel when I don't have horse will go away and the relief will come."

After several weeks Maggie found that skin-popping, like sniffing, was insufficient. Her periods of relaxation were shorter than they had been at the beginning, the effect of the horse wore off more rapidly than before, and she was left worried and tense. Artie, when she talked to him, said there was no question but that she was a gone goose now and she might just as well start main-lining.

"That's shooting the junk right in your veins. It acts

quicker when you shoot, and the feeling of being all right stays with you longer."

Once she had begun main-lining, Artie told Maggie she would have to go on her own because he couldn't afford to support her habit any longer, now that she was using ten dollars' worth of heroin every single day and doubtless would need more before long.

"But what'll I do?" Maggie asked. "How'll I ever get ten dollars a day?"

Artie shrugged his shoulders and said it wasn't his worry. He had trouble enough keeping himself in stuff.

Maggie asked him if he didn't care about her any more, and he said he cared about only one thing, and she knew what that was because it was all she cared about, too.

"I started supplying my habit by stealing from home. I took twenty dollars out of mummy's handbag. She never mentioned it, so I guess she must have thought she lost it. I also took sixty dollars out of daddy's pants pocket. That was terrible, because he accused mummy."

"If you need more money," her father told her mother, "why don't you ask for it? You don't have to steal from me. A wife stealing from her own husband!"

That night, he made his bed on the living-room couch.

"I guessed I ought to tell daddy that I was the one who had stolen his money," Maggie tells, "but how could I? I knew if he ever found out I was the one, it wouldn't be long before he knew what I needed the money for. He and mummy were suspicious, anyway. They felt there was something wrong with me, and they were always trying to find out what. They questioned me for hours about why I was so moody, and why my eyes looked funny, and how come I stayed out so late nights. So I couldn't tell about the sixty dollars. My conscience didn't bother me too

much, either. You lose your conscience when you become
a junkie. You can't afford to hold onto it."

The sixty dollars was gone all too quickly, and Maggie
knew she would have to find a quick source for more
money.

"I kept looking around the house for things that
wouldn't be missed, and finally decided on my mother's
wedding and engagement rings. She'd given up wearing
them after she and dad had their last blowup, and I knew
she'd hidden them away at the bottom of an old trunk. I
waited until she and dad were asleep before I rummaged
around for them. I kept them under my pillow till morning. Then I stashed them in my briefcase and got to school
early enough to meet Artie before class. He had a pawnshop contact and I figured he could get more money than
I could. We cut school and went to the pawnshop Artie
knew. The man gave us two hundred and fifty dollars for
both rings. They were worth a couple of thousand, but
what could I do? After we got the money, Artie called
Kingpin Jones, a Bronx peddler, and told him we'd had a
windfall. King said to stick around where we were, chew
the rag and have a cup of coffee, and he'd meet us in about
an hour."

Kingpin was a small man with a balding head. He was
impeccably dressed in brown suit, hat, and shoes, and appeared to be in his middle thirties. He smoked a handsome English pipe that did not fit in with the drummer's
personality.

"Well, Artie, old boy, long time no see. I thought maybe
you begun to walk the straight and narrow. I told myself,
'Well, well, Kingie, if Artie's a goner, who can you count
on in this crazy world?' So you got yourself a windfall, you
say. Well, well, who's the filly?"

Artie introduced Maggie as "another junkie" and suggested they stop the socializing and get down to business. He told Kingpin about the two hundred and fifty dollars in cash. Kingpin drew on his pipe, said "Well, well" again, and told them he could help them get started in their own business using the two hundred and fifty as a sort of insurance policy. With the cash they had, he said, Maggie and Artie could buy whole packages of horse from him and then divide them into capsules. Half the capsules could be sold and the other half kept for themselves. A free gift, in effect.

Maggie asked who they could sell to, and Kingpin removed his brown hat from his bald head, took his pipe out of his mouth, and asked Artie whether this kid was for real.

Maggie was daunted but persistent. "I don't know any junkies to sell to."

Kingpin smiled to show two glittering gold teeth. "Well, well. No percentage, little girl, selling junk to other junkies. What you have to do is make a couple new heads."

"Oh, no," Maggie said, and, in what she recognizes today to have been one of the last of the bursts of righteous indignation she would ever feel entitled to have, added, "What do you think I am?"

"Well, well." Kingpin placed the brown hat back on his head. "A junkie. No less, no more."

While Artie and Kingpin both mocked her with their eyes, Maggie went on reiterating that she couldn't do it, couldn't make junkies out of kids who'd never done anything to her.

Kingpin began to grow impatient. "Do whatever you want, little girl. You make your own mind up, and don't worry about taking up my time like you did this afternoon. I've got nothing to do except sit around chinning with little girls like you. I hope you like the weather we're having today, Miss Maggie! Well, well."

Artie entered the conversation then. "Don't worry, King, she'll sell for you. She just likes to bark sometimes, but she never bites. Wait'll she starts needing a shot bad enough, she'll do anything then."

Artie was right, of course.

"I took one of the few friends I'd made in school into the girls' room and gave her some horse and talked her into sniffing it. Her name was Miriam Allen. She was shy like me. I knew how to appeal to her." Maggie told her, in exquisite word pictures, how she herself, once the shyest of the shy, as Miriam well knew, now functioned socially without pain or tribulation.

"Then I lied in my teeth. I told her she had nothing to lose by sniffing. I said, 'Popping's the only thing can give you a habit.' So she tried it. Now she's hustling, too."

Being an outsider herself, Maggie knew the other misfits in her school and she could gauge and exploit their weak points.

"Poor Francine was a pushover for me. She wanted to get slim more than anything else in the world. So I had a brain storm. I gave her some horse, and I said, 'Francine, honey, sniff this and watch the pounds melt off you.' "

Maggie might have continued in her way for a longer time than she did except for a leg injury which she suffered in gym class. She had to stay home for a couple of weeks. She ran out of drugs after a few days at home, still hoping against hope that Artie, whom she had phoned several times, would rescue her before it was too late.

"The yen began around three o'clock on a Monday afternoon. I got terrible cold and hot spells and my body was one big ache. I remember banging my head against the

bedstead, trying to knock myself out, but I couldn't do it.
Mummy held me in her arms too tight. She wouldn't even
leave me to phone the doctor but just kept yelling for her
friend, Mrs. Roberts, who lived next door to us. I kept yelling too and beating mummy to make her let me go. But
the harder I beat, the closer she held me. Finally, Mrs.
Roberts came in and took charge. I tried to tell her to call
Artie, but my teeth were chattering so she couldn't understand me. She called the doctor and told him I'd had some
kind of a horrible spell, although I think now she must
surely have known what was wrong with me. He came and
gave me a shot."

That night her mother and father decided that she would
have to be sent some place for a cure.

"They argued even then. Mummy, who had talked with
the doctor, said I ought to go to Lexington. Daddy said she
was hardhearted to think of sending me there. He kept
blaming her because I'd become a junkie. Before they were
through, they were so mad at each other, they'd practically
forgotten me."

Her father won out. She did not go to Lexington.
Through the doctor's intervention, they secured her admission to a small private hospital. There she had five terrible
days, a nightmare of tossing and turning and pleading for
horse, and ten days of recuperation, and then she went
home.

"Mummy and daddy watched me like hawks," Maggie
recounted. "When they weren't watching me, they were
arguing with each other over why I was such a weak sister.
Every time they looked at me, they made me know what
a disappointment I was to them. I kept thinking about
horse and how everything was fine when I had it. One
night I called Francine up and asked if she would bring me
a shot. I thought maybe she wouldn't come because I'd

gotten her hooked. But she never was one to carry grudges, too dumb I guess. She came. I was hooked again before I knew it."

Maggie's mother attempted her next cure at home. The doctor suggested "cold turkey" this time—no tapering off. He told the mother to settle Maggie in the bedroom, making sure first that there were no sharp objects lying around. Mummy blanched at his words, but went ahead with the preparations. Maggie was put in the big, double bed, daddy brought a living-room chair in, and mummy sat watching Maggie all night.

"I started yawning after a while, and then I got so cold mummy had to cover me with all the blankets in the house. Daddy had to turn the heat up as far as it would go. Then I felt stifled. I begged mummy to open all the windows. Before she got them open, I was freezing again. I can't remember anything much I did after those first few hours. All I remember were the pains. There were needles shooting up my legs and into my stomach. My head was splitting.

"Mummy said I kept vomiting and having diarrhea so that she couldn't keep my bed clean no matter how many times she changed my sheets every day. She showed me a couple of bruises I'd given her when she tried to stop me from crawling on the floor and banging my head. She'd found some horse under the rug and thought I was foraging for that. By the time I came to myself again, she was more dead than alive."

But it became increasingly obvious after the ordeal was over that Maggie's drive was still for heroin, and, discounting some miracle, always would be. When, some three weeks after the cold turkey had been accomplished, her mother and father caught her hopped up again, they yelled at each other in a way that made it clear that now they really had, each in his own way, lost all hope for her.

"We sold our house in Bronxville, at a loss, and found an apartment on West End Avenue and 78th Street. I made some connections there and did a little peddling. I also got money from mummy and daddy once in a while. I used them against each other and they always paid me when I did. They knew what I used the money for. They just figured there wasn't anything they could do about it. But I never had enough money. And then, one day, I ran out of stuff and had no money for buying any more. I had already shaken mummy and daddy down for everything the traffic would bear just then. They'd both been threatening to have me committed and sent away if I didn't straighten up. And I was proving a flop as a peddler. So I decided to go see Kingpin at his house in the Bronx."

He lived on the top floor of an old tenement. He answered her knock himself, not debonair as he had been the first time she met him, but uncombed and unwashed. He wasn't wearing a shirt and his undershirt was filthy.

"Look who's here," he said. "I thought you must be dead and buried in all this time. Well, well."

She said, "Can I come in, Kingpin?"

He herded her into a dark kitchen that contained a wooden table on its last legs and two rickety chairs, and told her she was welcome to sit down if she wanted.

"I needed a shot by the time I got to King's house," she tells. "I felt a hot spell on me. I begged him for some stuff. He said he liked me very much but he was sorry, no money, no stuffee. My muscles began to hurt and I started to burn up. I told him I was liable to die right in his kitchen if I didn't get a jolt. Then I started to scream and curse at him. I guess he was frightened, because he gave me a jolt to quiet me. I sat on the chair and relaxed. After a while, he said, 'Well, well, you're feeling better now and I'm glad, but I hope you know you ain't on the house, girl."

When she told him she had no money, he told her girls had other media for barter.

"I know a couple of men like young kids like you. Take them on."

She said, "I've never been with a man before, Kingpin."

He scratched his bald head. "Well, well. A virgin. We'll charge the first one higher."

Kingpin called his friends who came running. Magnanimously he offered her the use of his bedroom. It was small and dank and dark. Even though it was daylight, she had to turn the overhead light on. The rough, wooden floor was almost covered with outdated racing forms and the mattress on the double bed sagged in the middle.

The customers, three fat, elderly men with halitosis, almost came to blows about who was to take her first.

"I asked Kingpin about keeping my clothes on, and he said it was O.K. with him since these customers were quickies anyhow. I felt lucky because I didn't have to take my clothes off. . . . I've come a long way since then."

NAME: *Lolita Perez*

AGE: *22*

MARITAL STATUS: *Single*

EDUCATION: *Undeterminable*

Lolita Perez is not the girl's real name. "It is better if I do not give the real name," she tells the probation officer in a sorrowful burst. "I am a big disgrace to my mama in Cuba. She does not know what I do in America. I wish her never to find out Vicente makes me go with men for money. So many men. She thinks I came here for marrying Vicente and having many fine sons. But I have no sons, not even one, because Vicente he sent an old lady with dirty hands to get my child out from my belly."

Lolita Perez was born in a small village outside Havana. She had five sisters, but she says, in all modesty, that she was the prettiest. She believes she was also the only legitimate one. Her mother often proclaimed her legitimacy in loud tones, especially around her doubting aunt, a tall, slender, unfertile woman who had never been able to bear a child of her own, but who had nonetheless managed to annex and keep a husband faithful and always scoffed at Lolita's mother.

Whenever her mother talked about her doubting aunt, she characterized her as a shrew who was eaten alive by her jealousy of fertile women.

"She is jealous of me," Lolita's mother used to tell her,

"and also of you, because she knows you take after me and will have many, many children when your time comes."

Lolita's earliest recollections of her mother are of a buxom, big-breasted woman with warmth and love to spare for her own and all the neighbors' children. Although she was an amazingly free and easy-going person who believed that children could grow best in a permissive environment of love, live and let live, she had one great obsession. For, from the time Lolita was a small baby, her mother had made up her mind that, come hell or high water, this daughter was to bear many children in respectable wedlock. There were times during Lolita's childhood when, despite a brazen continuation of her own extramarital activities, she could talk of nothing else.

It was not surprising therefore that when Vicente Rodriguez, a wealthy Cuban with a residence in New York and a shiny blue Cadillac car, came to Cuba during Lolita's sixteenth year, her mother did her best to procure him for a son-in-law. True, he was not a handsome man, with his small build and ferret face; and true, he was admittedly thirty-eight, twenty-two years Lolita's senior and looking even older, but his wealth outweighed his disadvantages. A man with a bank account could stylishly support all the in-wedlock children Lolita could manage to have. Besides, it was wise to marry a man uglier than you were. Then he would always keep you in luxury, and you, rather than some other woman, would be his complete concern.

Lolita often reflected, during the short three weeks of her courtship, about how admirably Vicente qualified as a husband who would be uglier not only than she was herself but also than almost any girl he could choose to marry. Still, when she was with him, she was sweet and charming, as her mother had instructed her to be, and when, as she had known he would do some day soon, he asked for her hand in marriage, she graciously accepted him.

Her mother, strangely, was not so gracious. She told Vicente that she was presenting him with a small jewel of a girl, and that she wanted him to promise that he would always be good to her and support her in a style that would enable her to have all the children she wanted.

"Vicente," she asked, and Lolita still remembers how bright her eyes were, "you promise me?"

"I promise you a million times over," Vicente passion ately answered.

She said, out of the great faith that had enveloped Lolita from the day of her birth, "I talk with God, Vicente. He listens when I ask something. I'll make Him curse you if you do not treat my girl right."

When Lolita heard her mother threaten to avenge any wrong Vicente might do her, she felt more comfortable about the impending marriage. She herself had always been afraid of her mother's contact with a Supreme Being. Her doubting aunt used to laugh at her mother's God, but Lolita knew deep in her heart that she could always count on Him.

Look what had happened to her mother's various lovers. Her mother loathed all of them after she had once conceived their children and prayed that her God would hurt them. One grew ill and died. Lolita's aunt tried to tell everyone that the man had been ill before her mother started praying, but Lolita and her mother knew better. A second picked up and left the little village in which he had lived his whole life. Neither the officials nor his legitimate family had any notion of why he left and where he had gone. A third, who owned a small farm, had all his crops destroyed.

Still despite the security that came from the thought of her mother's vengeful God, Lolita had periods of fear about her future life. She really did not want to get married, not just to Vicente, not to anyone. She wanted to stay home and help her mother with the housekeeping and the care of the younger children. Her aunt said that kind of unnatural desire was what came of daughters being brought up in a fatherless home and being so dependent they considered their mother everything.

She would not have talked that way if she hadn't had a faithful husband of her own to use in her jibes at Lolita's mother. Sometimes, for her mother's sake, Lolita hated this uncle of hers, although he'd always been such a nice, inoffensive little man who spoiled her when she was a baby. But since the advent of Vicente, she found she didn't need to hate him any more, because her mother didn't mind him any more, either. In fact, she thumbed her nose at him.

"Now that my little daughter is marrying a rich man," her mother used to tell all and sundry, "a very, very rich man, I have no reason to wish for the lot of any other woman, especially not a fallow creature who has not borne a single daughter able to give her the pleasure my girl gives me. A very, very rich man."

Vicente's wealth was wonderful to contemplate. Both Lolita and her mother enjoyed hearing him talk about it. He told about his tremendous New York home and all the servants who staffed it. There were a cook and six housemaids—one to comb Lolita's hair, another to scrub her back while she relaxed in a tub full of sweet-smelling bubble bath, and a third one who would be assigned the job of caring for all the expensive silk dresses her loving husband would buy her.

But, despite his wonderful wealth, it began to look for

a time as though Lolita might not marry Vicente after all and the wrathful God would have to be called upon to punish still another faithless man. For he insisted that he must be married in the United States, and Lolita's mother maintained that Lolita must be married in her home village. They battled violently, with words and with objects, while Lolita stood in silent support of her mother.

In the end, Vicente won. Mama agreed Lolita could go to New York.

Vicente said they would go by way of Mexico City. Lolita could not understand why he should want to take such a long way back. He said the reason had something to do with her getting into the United States, but she was not to worry her pretty head.

The whole village came out to see Lolita and Vicente off for New York. Everybody wore their Sunday clothes. Lolita's mother had decorated Vicente's automobile with pink and blue crepe paper on the outside and gay streamers on the inside. All the women kissed Lolita. They treated her and her mother with great respect. Lolita almost cried for joy when she saw her mother standing among the women who had husbands, with her head held as high as anybody else's.

Lolita and Vicente traveled two weeks before they arrived in Mexico City, and, true to his promise to her mother, he made no attempt to touch her. She thought his consideration boded well for their future together, but she did wish he would act more affectionately toward her. She thought that, once having arrived in Mexico and become settled, as he had told her they must do for a while, he would behave more as a fiancé ought to. But he didn't. He placed her in a grubby little room in a drab hotel, hardly more attractive than some places she had known in Cuba, and told her that he had to return to America.

She could hardly believe that he meant to leave her alone in this strange place. How would she get along? What would she do without guidance? He said she would have nothing to worry about if she followed his orders and advice. He taught her to order food through Room Service, but she was too shy. Fortunately, a maid who came to clean her room was induced to order her first meal the morning Vicente left. She asked her what she thought she wanted to eat and when she could not answer, offered to make a choice for her. The long day passed somehow and then it was evening and time to eat again. This time there was nobody to call Room Service, and she knew she would have to do it herself. She trembled as she lifted the receiver. A voice asked her what she wanted, and she answered, "Room Service." She grew confused when a woman at the other end of the line asked about her dinner choice.

At first she must have thought Lolita was trying to play games, but soon realized she was not and was, in fact, nearly desperate. The room-service woman then very kindly gave Lolita advice as to what foods to have and what ones to avoid. She even offered to come and visit with Lolita when she had some off time and to bring her a movie magazine filled with pictures of beautiful American ladies.

Thanks to the room-service lady, a kindly, motherly type, the week without Vicente went quickly, if uneventfully, and he returned, sooner than she would have had him. Notwithstanding, she threw her arms around him, pretending to be a loving fiancé, but he did not seem to need her love. He pulled himself out of her arms and went to the door and pulled it open to admit a funny, wiry-looking little man in his thirties. His name was Pedro Perez.

Vicente told Lolita that Pedro had come to Mexico in order to bring her back to the United States as his wife.

She said she did not understand, because she thought she was going to marry Vicente. Then it turned out that Pedro was already married, and everything seemed even more incomprehensible. But Vicente said she did not need to understand anything. She just had to do what he told her. He said that this Pedro Perez had in his pocket the Puerto Rican birth certificate that belonged to Lolita Marque, his present wife, and also the marriage certificate that made her Lolita Perez. He said from now on she was to forget the name her mother had given her and think of herself as Lolita, wife of Pedro Perez. She was eighteen years old, born in San Juan, a commonwealth of the United States of America, and she was entitled, therefore, to live in New York City.

Then he whispered something to Pedro Perez who kept glancing at Lolita and slapped him on the back. He told her that she was to spend the night with Pedro and do whatever he asked. She said she did not want to spend the night with any man, only with her husband, and then only after she was married to him. How else, otherwise, could it be guaranteed that her children would be born in wedlock? Vicente said Pedro would teach her how not to have any children. She said she didn't want to learn anything like that, she wanted to be a fertile woman like her mother. Vicente told her she would learn whatever he wanted her to. Then he hit her in the face with his fist and walked out of the room, leaving her alone with Pedro.

Pedro hurt her so much she cried like a baby.

The three of them started for New York by plane the next morning. Before they got to customs, she repeated Lolita Perez to herself hundreds of times and tried to convince herself that the birth certificate Pedro had given her really was hers. There was no trouble about either the name or the certificate. She was thrilled to be flying and wondered what words to use in describing her sensations to her mother, but she was also very frightened. Against her will she found herself clinging to Vicente. He let her cling and even held her hand for a while.

At last they arrived in New York. She was happy to feel the ground beneath her feet. She was interested in the airport and the people, especially the beautifully dressed women. She could hardly keep her eyes off the shoes and the hats and the furs. For this she had come to America and made peace with the idea that Vicente was to be her husband.

"Now," Vicente told her, "I must bring you to the hotel I've picked out for you to work."

"What kind of work?" she asked. "You told my mama and me we'd get married in New York."

Vicente said, "Since I already have one wife of my own, I cannot marry you."

She said, "And I, Vicente, I do not wish to be a bad girl."

"But if you wish to be a live girl," he said, without lifting his voice, "you will do as I say. Also if you wish your mama to remain a live mama."

She said, "You cannot hurt my mama in Cuba."

He smiled at her. "But I am not a man who is friendless and alone, my little one. If I tell my friends in Cuba to snuff your mama's life out, they will be glad to do it as a favor."

He removed some pictures from his pocket and flourished them in her face, tempting her to ask to see them. She could not resist the temptation, but she was sorry she had not when she saw the pictures. They were all of women, dead women. Vicente said he had killed them with his own two hands.

New York, as she first saw it from the taxi in which Vicente brought her from the airport to the hotel, and as she would always continue to think of it, was the most terrifying city a girl could come to. Worse than Mexico City. Much worse. At least they spoke Spanish in Mexico City; she could understand Mexican people and they could understand her. Look at how well she had done with Room Service there. But New York was different. Who spoke Spanish here? Whom would she understand? Nobody cared about her in New York. How did a Spanish girl get food in New York? Only through Vicente. Vicente. . . .

The hotel Vicente took her to was very tall. She had not thought a building could be so tall. She got out of the taxicab and stood gaping up at it until Vicente took her arm and led her through a revolving door that made her hold her breath in. He escorted her into the lobby and across the floor to where an elderly dark-haired woman sat in a wired-in cubicle. She looked as if she might be Spanish, but when Lolita heard Vicente address her in English, her hope died. She wondered what they were saying and why the woman kept her eyes fastened on her. She was glad when the conversation was over and Vicente steered her away from the desk and into an elevator. Here he said a few words to the young, blond operator. The boy smacked his lips at Lolita.

"I think the elevator rode us onto a very, very high floor," she says, not knowing to this day what floor she had lived on, "and Vicente brought me to my small room."

He said he had to leave for a while, but that he would be back before it was time for dinner. She lay down on the big double bed with her eyes closed, but the rest she sought eluded her. Her mind was too much of a jumble. She heard a tapping at her door, soft but insistent, and answered it against her better judgment. A tall, young man in working clothes stood and looked her up and down.

"You must have the wrong room," she said in Spanish.

He laughed, pushed into the room in front of her, and started removing his clothes. She started to scream. In Spanish, he told her to stop. She said she would never stop until he left her room, so he put his clothes back on and walked out.

Vicente came in ten minutes later, slapped her face without a word of explanation, and said for her to take her clothes off and lie on the bed naked. She thought he might make love to her and hoped she would be able to submit without saying anything. But he didn't. All he did was stand by the bed, smoking a smelly cigar. He looked down at her for what seemed a long, long time. Then he sat down on the bed and took the cigar out of his mouth and held the burning end against her stomach.

"Don't turn down any customers I send you," he said softly.

Lolita mercifully lost consciousness. When she came to, Vicente was gone and the little room was dark. She felt very hungry and, forgetting for the moment that she was in America, not Mexico, picked up the telephone to ask for Room Service. But she did not understand the voice on the other end of the wire. At first she struggled to make herself understood, but, when she knew it was hopeless, she lay back and thought that whatever happened would happen. She tried to summon the old faith she once had back in Cuba, but she needed the strong personality of her mother to make it a living thing for her. Her mother's God, always so real and close at hand before, now seemed a million miles away. She fell asleep, still vainly trying to summon Him.

She awakened to the sight of Vicente under the glaring overhead light. He was smiling, but he still appeared venomous to her, a man with a devil inside him. He sat down on the side of her bed again and brought another cigar out of his pocket. He lit it and puffed at it but made no move to use it on her.

She plucked up her courage and told him she was hungry. "I could eat grass like a goat."

If she was hungry, why in the devil didn't she go and get herself some food then, he asked.

"How can I? Who will understand me when I talk? Where can I get money for food?"

He nodded his head and asked if she was ready to follow orders now. Yes, she said, oh yes. And would she ever reject a customer he sent her again? No, never, as long as she lived. All right then, he said, she could get some clothes on and come to dinner with him.

The cafeteria he took her to was clean and bright. The sight and smell of the food made her feel better. Vicente generously permitted her to pick her own dishes. She had a hard time making choices but she enjoyed walking from counter to counter. Finally, after some haggling with herself, she pointed to a colorful salad and a slice of lemon meringue pie. Then she asked if she could have chocolate ice cream too and was gleeful at Vicente's permission.

Dinner was over before she knew it, and she was back at the hotel, with Vicente his old businesslike self again. He showed her a yellow card and told her that all the men he sent to her would bear similar cards. She was to do whatever they told her and neither ask questions nor hold any conversations with them. She was not to worry about money. The yellow cards meant the men had already paid him for her services.

"I had fifteen men the first night. I got tired. I started feeling very sick."

One man seemed sympathetic. He asked her how such a young girl had come to go into this business. His kindliness made her break down and cry. She forgot Vicente's warning and talked about what had happened to her. The man told her not to worry, that he had fallen in love with her and would take her out of Vicente's clutches. He would come and get her in a few days. She thanked him and kissed his hands.

But Vicente came in shortly after the kind man left and said he knew everything she had told him. He ought to kill her for trying to double-cross him. He would give her another chance, however, just one more, and if he ever caught her talking to customers again, he'd cut her tongue out and slice it up as a present for her mother in Cuba.

For six weeks Lolita worked in the hotel, taking on from fifteen to twenty men a night. Although she cannot be sure, she thinks each man paid Vicente from five to twenty-five dollars. She, herself, never saw a dime of the money she earned. Vicente paid her hotel bill and bought her meals. Occasionally he took her to the movies on a day after she had had an exceptionally full night.

"And one time he gets so very nice. He takes me out and buys me a pretty red dress for seven dollars. Also new sandals with high heels. I look all dressed up fine. Then he says I am through with the hotel business. I will start going with the yellow men in this place called Chinatown. I tell him I don't know how to go with yellow men, but he says I got no worry, Esther will show me everything I need to know, Esther Rodriguez."

She and Vicente met Esther, a tall, dark, flabby woman in her forties, in a Chinese restaurant on Pell Street. She was sitting at a table with a couple of yellow men who got up when Vicente and Lolita came in. Vicente greeted Esther effusively. He seemed to like her. He laughed and joked with her, and he asked her opinion about a couple of matters Lolita did not understand. She talked to him as though she felt his equal. Once she yelled at him. Vicente listened politely and made no move to hit her. Lolita could hardly believe her eyes.

"I do not know why he is as good with Esther till he tells me she is the best girl he got. 'The little boss lady,' he says. 'You don't listen to Esther, Lolita! It's nearly as bad as if you don't listen to me. You understand?' I say, 'Sure.' He turns to Esther and says, 'I am going now. Tell the little one everything. I leave her in your hands, my Esther.' "

Esther told Lolita that Vicente had nine girls working in Chinatown. Other Cuban men and a few Puerto Ricans also had girls there. Most of the Cubans, like Lolita herself, had Puerto Rican birth certificates, either forged through a contact in Puerto Rico or purchased. All the men, Cuban and Puerto Rican, had only the friendliest feelings for one another, and so it behooved the girls to act friendly to one another, too. This did not mean, however, that Lolita could become too friendly with any girl, no matter how much she liked her, unless Esther gave her permission. Perhaps, as a matter of fact, she would do better, while she was new, to steer clear, except for exchanging ordinary amenities, of any girls except Vicente's. One never really *knew* the girls from other contingents and if, by chance, one of them were to attempt to lead Lolita onto bad paths, or maybe tempt her into doing Vicente wrong, and if she yielded, as a young innocent conceivably might, why what a worthless thing her life would be then.

After the lecture Esther showed Lolita all over China-town. She took her up one winding street and down an-

other. She led her up and down the stairs of old law tenement buildings and walked her up and down long corridors. These were furnished-room houses, she explained,
where the yellow men lived alone without wives or children. Each door she saw signified a room that housed a
single Chinaman who might be in need of a girl. Lolita's
job was to knock on the door and solicit the man in the
room. It was really very simple. Esther, herself, did the
head work and assigned the houses she was to work. All
Lolita had to do was walk along halls, knock at doors and
call, "Me-me."

"You can say *me-me?*" she asked.

Lolita nodded.

Esther said, "Say it."

"Me-me."

But Esther said her voice was so low the yellow men
would never hear her. She'd have to learn to speak up for
herself.

She said "Me-me" more loudly.

Esther said she was learning. She said that as soon as a
yellow man opened a door to her, if he didn't ask her in
immediately, she was to place her foot in the door so he
couldn't close it if he wasn't pleased with his first look at
her. She was to set her price at twenty dollars to begin with
and allow herself to be bargained down to five if necessary.

"How can I ask any price?" she asked, confused at this
new independence. "Do these yellow men speak Spanish
then?"

Esther called her a dumb little chicken and showed her
how to use her hands for setting price: ten fingers held up
twice meant twenty dollars, held up once they meant ten,
and so on.

Lolita didn't know whether yellow men understood
such signals, but Esther said they had had so much contact

with other Spanish girls they were bound to. Then she walked her through a couple of other hallways and pointed out something she had missed on her first tour—the Spanish signs on the Chinamen's doors written in various shades of lipstick. Orange. Flaming Scarlet. Camellia Pink. These were the signs left by girls who had experienced the inmates' attentions, and pointed up the customers' bargaining habits. Men who could be expected to accept a girl's top price were written down as "good." Then there were the "cheap" men and the "don't bother with him" ones.

Esther told her she'd better pay attention to the signs because if she got involved with too many cheap or don't-bother men she wouldn't be able to earn her daily quota. That, by the way, was one hundred dollars. One hundred American dollars, she asked, and every single day? Esther said, exactly. What happened if she did not make her quota one day, she asked, and Esther answered that Vicente didn't understand about any such days, and she knew one girl he almost killed last week because all she brought him was seventy dollars.

On that note, she ordered her to solicit her first customer and promised to hang around and watch so she could tell her if she did anything wrong.

Lolita knocked at a door which bore a "good" sign. For a minute there was no answer. "Maybe nobody's home," she said, relieved to leave that door, even if only to go on to another one. But Esther told her to hold on and in a little while an old yellow man in a kimono came out. She got ready to stick her foot in the door but there was no necessity. The yellow man had no idea of shutting the door in her face. He bowed politely and summoned her into his room.

It was a small room containing a dresser, chair, and double bed. He indicated that she was to sit on the bed.

She wondered if his smile was perpetual. It changed to a giggle when she held her twenty-dollar hands up. So she changed to her ten-dollar hands. He stopped giggling and nodded so vigorously she thought his head would fall off. Then he stopped nodding and bowed to her. He bowed after he finished undressing. It was really a funny sight. He bowed again when he ushered her out into the hall. She hoped Esther saw him.

She tried five more rooms on the same corridor under Esther's watchful eye. Only one indicated that he had no need of a me-me girl. Each of the other four gave her ten dollars.

The job became harder after Esther left. She knocked at many doors and said "me-me" many, many times, but she knocked and talked too softly. Whether nobody heard her or whether the yellow men behind the marked doors had no need of me-mes that night, she was able to solicit only one other customer before 3 A.M. She grew frantic when she realized she had only two hours left before 5 A.M. when Vicente would come to collect, and with forty dollars still to earn. So she knocked harder and said "me-me" louder and was so successful that she gave Vicente one hundred and ten dollars that morning. He patted her on the head and told her that as long as she continued to do so well, so long would she have nothing to fear from him.

"So far," she says, "I make my quota every night since I come to Chinatown. Still, I am afraid. Suppose tonight I don't. What will Vicente do to me then? What will he do?"

FIVE / The Blonde Hippo

NAME: *Lee Balish*

AGE: *29*

MARITAL STATUS: *Single*

EDUCATION: *Ungraded (feeble-minded)*

"The Blonde Hippo," as Lee Balish has come to be known, is huge-hipped and big-bosomed, with blue eyes, round and wondering as a baby's, and long hair, light and stiff and straight as straw. She is a money-maker, and Big Bill Bloom, the pimp, is more pleased with her than he is with either of her wives-in-law, skinny little twin redheads who call themselves Brenda and Frenchy Love.

All four of them, Brenda and Frenchy, the Blonde Hippo, and Big Bill himself, live in a two-bedroom apartment on 28th Street. Brenda and Frenchy have the big bedroom and the Blonde Hippo, a come-lately, has the tiny hall bedroom containing nothing but an oversized double bed. Big Bill divides his nights, turn and turn about, between Frenchy and Brenda, who share him, and the Blonde Hippo.

Big Bill and the Blonde Hippo play games on the nights they spend together, all kinds of games with hands and feet and faces. First off, they get in bed and see who can look wickeder. Big Bill, tall and stout, with a large-pored pasty face and squinting blue eyes, would seem to have the natural advantage, but the Blonde Hippo can bring into the combat all her long years of practice, years when she used to stand at the mirror and makes faces at herself for hours on end.

She began making the faces when she was a little girl. Sometimes they'd be droll and convivial, so that she would have to laugh with pleasure at the sight of them. They were, however, abhorrent more often than nice. Her moods determined the kinds of faces she made at herself, and they were always influenced by whether on one day or another her family showed her the love and affection she craved. Oh, the jolly, jolly faces she could devise on the days Ma, Pa, and Lila Mae seemed to love her. If only they had been able to love her more. If only they had been able to keep her from knowing how she saddened and shamed them.

Lee was a comely infant and she grew into a healthy, strapping child. It was not until she was three years old, and still not talking like other children, that her parents, both schoolteachers, began to grow anxious about her. Why wasn't she talking? What was wrong with her? They asked each other, but did not answer, with the truth both of them suspected deep in their hearts. Different children, they assured each other, developed differently.

"Why," the father said, "you know my cousin Netta and how she talks, talks, talks. Well, she didn't begin until she was five. There you are, my dear, and that's only a single example. I could give you dozens."

The mother nodded. "Yes, I know, darling."

"Do you?" the father asked her. "Do you really know? Or are you just trying to make me feel good?"

"No," she said. "I'm not trying to make you feel good. Honestly, I'm telling you what I believe for myself." And she really did believe what she was saying for one warm, wonderful moment.

"She's just slow, that's all. But, don't worry. I'll work hard to teach her. She'll catch up to the other children."

Well, Lee did not catch up. She was four years old, then five, when she began to talk a little, but only a little. And she was not up to playing with the neighbors' children, and some of them began to call the child "looney" and "dopey."

Finally the mother, wounded beyond endurance, sat down with the father and told him the plain facts.

"We've got to be honest," she said, "at least with each other. Oh, darling. . . ."

And he, imperturbable and distant, a blond giant she felt she had never really known, said, "Very strange. Here all these years, I've been operating under the delusion that we have been honest with each other."

"No," she said, "no. We've been scared, you and I. And we've got to be brave. We owe it to the child. If she's a moron. . . ."

"You're the moron," he said shortly. "You, not Lee."

She said, "Oh, my God."

He said, "Please, I'm sorry," but was impelled to add, "Damn it, my family's healthy on both sides."

She drew herself up. "My family, too."

"Yes, yes," he said, "I know. I didn't say it wasn't."

She said, "I can take a hint. You don't have to say things in so many words. I happen not to *be* a moron, even though my husband thinks I'm one. You consider my family. . . ."

"Look," he said, "I don't think anything except what I've told you. If the shoe fits, wear it—you and your family."

And then he came back and begged her pardon over

and over again. She told him she forgave him but she remained bitter toward him, not alone for what he had said, but also because she blamed him for the child. Deep in her heart she felt, your fault, your fault. In the future, the mother and father would quarrel from reversed vantage points. He would be the one to face reality and she would run and hide from it. He would talk about mental deficiency, struggling to break through the barriers she set up, and she would laugh in his face and say, "Don't be silly, dear. The child's just slow and needs a little help."

She devoted her whole life to giving Lee the help she thought she needed, working with her from morning till night, and in the process repudiating her home and her husband. She spent hours teaching Lee to say words and to dress herself. The little girl, anxious for affection and eager to please, tried to do right. She tried with everything in her, trying, trying until she became hot and perspired so that her mother, watching, had, perforce, to pity and bid her stop. Once in a while, Lee experienced a small victory, learning, for instance, to put her shoes and socks on frontwards instead of backwards, but most of the time, for all her fine intentions, she could not master the simplest tasks.

Then it was, during the lame times, the impotent times, that the mother saw her child as her cross. Then it was that the mother, despite all the love she had in her, despite never-ending patience, had to look at Lee without joy and without pride. Strangely, the child knew the meaning of her mother's look. Or, if she did not know it, she felt it. And since there is more to a person than intellect, and since Lee was and still is today good and kind inside, she went on trying for her mother's sake to overcome the insuperable obstacles.

But it seemed that the older Lee grew, the harder it

became to please her mother. Naturally, the mother, spending all her time with the child and having no other life of her own, had to keep on rationalizing Lee's handicaps. After a while she succeeded in persuading herself that the child was uncooperative, not unintelligent. And so she treated her failings with severity. She often slapped her for her mistakes. Of course she was sorry afterward. Lee forgave her each time, just as today she forgives Big Bill Bloom when he slaps her around. As she does with Big Bill now, so she did with her mother then—waited until the spleen had spent itself and then came round with smiles and pats and kisses.

Some of her mother's friends tried to make her understand what her demands were doing to the child. But she turned away and would not listen to them. Nor could she tolerate their pity. So, gradually, she separated herself from them. She began to grow apart from her husband, too. She no longer tried to please him as she had been used to doing. Now when he came home he was as like as not to find her in a filthy house dress and with her hair uncombed. Actually, none of her clothes fitted her any more, for, having begun to give Lee pieces of candy as rewards, she also began eating the sweets herself. The two of them, mother and daughter, grew very fat. And the father caviled and carped at them both and began spending less and less time at home.

There was no telling what would have happened between the mother and father and to Lee herself, for that matter, if Lila Mae had not been born during the year Lee had her sixth birthday. She was a pretty little baby, Lila Mae was, and the parents, adoring her, began to forget their enmity toward each other. More than that, the mother, having a new baby to care for now, began to spend less time with Lee, so the child felt some of the pressure removed from her. She might have been happy for the first time in her short life had it not been for the fact that, like it or not, she had to go to school.

Obviously, she could not learn like the other first-graders. Nor could she be interested in the class program. She became very restless during school hours and she was always crying. When asked what the trouble was, she could not say. She never followed orders, either. Told not to squirm in her seat, she would promise not to and the next moment would do it again. Then, if she felt like it, she would get up and go for a walk in the hall without requesting permission. She was pained when the teacher became angry with her, truly grieved to have offended, and yet half an hour later, she would be repeating the misconduct.

So, finally, not knowing what to do, the principal sent for the mother. She came, distraught, hostile, and defensive. She said Lee was a fine, intelligent child and blamed the teacher for all her difficulties. But one thing she did agree to do after the principal had spent a couple of hours urging her—she agreed to have Lee examined. Not that she doubted her child's mentality, she hastened to assure the principal: it was merely that she wanted, once and for all, to justify Lee in the eyes of the world.

Then began the heartbreaking trek that parents of feeble-minded children know all too well. There were trips to medical doctors, gland specialists, psychiatrists, and psychologists. There were tests and treatments, with the mother praying to God and hoping against hope. Of course, there was no hope, but she believed the quacks who told her there was. The father knew better, but she rejected him along with the honest doctors.

One of the honest ones told her right out, "You're not a rich woman. You can't go on this way."

And she said, "Oh, can't I? Doctor, you don't know a mother's heart."

"Lady," he said, "your child's hopeless. That's all there is to it. Why can't you understand? *Hopeless.*"

"Sir," she said calmly, "doctors have been known to be wrong."

And she went on her way for a year, two years, still looking for a comforting word, pouncing on anything the so-called experts suggested to her: glandular treatments, X ray, heat therapy, cold therapy, anything. At the end somehow, she knew the facts! When she told her husband she knew, he talked about sending Lee to a school for the mentally handicapped.

"Better for her and better for us," he said.

She was shocked and unbelieving. "Who's us?"

"You and me," he said. "And Lila Mae."

But how could she have sent Lee to one of those schools? Now that she faced what her child was, now that she knew beyond a question or a doubt—now, of all times, she had no choice but to stand by her.

"I'll never send Lee away," she told her husband.

And so Lee's childhood went by. She grew to be eight and nine and ten years old, and one day her father left home and her mother said he wasn't coming back any more, but not to worry because he'd send money enough to take care of them all. As though Lee worried about money or even knew what it was for! She missed her father because, now that he was gone, she forgot his bad temper and remembered the times he'd laughed with her.

Home was different with Pa gone and school was different, too. When she was eight years old and still in the first grade, the principal, acting over the mother's objections, had her removed to the special class called "Ungraded." Some of the children, protected by their innocence, had no idea what "ungraded" meant. But Lee knew. The kids told her when they met her in the hall. "Dummy, dummy, got a fat old tummy. You're in Ungraded. You're in the dummy class. Dummy. Dummy. Got a fat old tummy." A few didn't taunt her, but looked at her with coldly curious eyes and tried to discover what she and the others did all day.

"Hey, dummy, what do you do in the dummy class?"

Flattered by their interest and wanting to please, Lee tried to find words describing the ash trays made out of shells and the baskets woven of raw raffia. But she never could find the words and the kids always left, laughing, before she could finish telling them.

All the same, it didn't matter because for all the bad at school, there was the good at home—little Lila Mae, Lee's joy and her delight, her sweet and her beloved. When Lila Mae was a baby, the mother allowed Lee to help bathe and feed her and the days seemed to fly by. First it was spring. Then came summer, fall, and winter. Then another spring. And another summer. And Lila Mae was toddling around, following Lee like a little shadow. Then, before you knew it, she was five years old, and six, and seven.

Those were the happy years for both the sisters. Such wonderful games as they used to have—"Wash the Baby's Face," for instance. That was really a very simple game with Lee providing the zest and the power and Lila Mae contributing the patience to be washed over and over again. Sometimes, Lila Mae's face looked a bit red and sore after the game, but you'd never catch her complaining. And when the mother tried to get her to tell what had happened to her face, she was true blue and wouldn't tell tales on her sister.

The two girls had wonderful secrets together, too. The

mother often tried to find out what they were talking
about on the days they'd sit shaking with laughter, but
she couldn't understand when they told her.

"Hinky, dinky, parlay vous," they'd say, wanting to let
her onto the team, "hinky, dinky, parlay vous."

But the mother never got the joke and always looked
at her girls with a grave and stony face. Lee felt sorry not
to be able to share jokes with her and wished with all
her heart that her mother would understand.

And then, one miserable day during Lee's fifteenth
year and her sister's ninth, everything changed and Lila
Mae became as blind and undiscerning as Mama had ever
been. Suddenly, for no good reason, she stuck her nose up
in the air and would not play any more. She said Lee only
knew baby games.

A short while after Lila Mae's desertion, Mama also
abandoned Lee. She seemed to love her less than she used
to. Doubtless she could not help herself. Here was Lee, a
girl going on sixteen and still needing you to love her as
you would a baby. How could you treat her the way you
would a small child? No matter that you could envision
her need and know it to be like a baby's, still you could
not help yourself. When she climbed onto your lap, she
who was taller and larger than you yourself, you began
to feel as though you had an elephant sitting on you.
Even though you had always been a loving mother, now
that you were faced with this big, demanding creature,
you could not help flinching at her infantile fawning.
Besides, now that she was sixteen, you *had* to know the
truth about her, and despite yourself, to see it straight.
Was it any wonder, then, that the hardness came out as
never before, and that you wanted suddenly to shield yourself instead of this strange daughter?

Of course, you would still go on doing all the things

you used to do for her, supervising her washing and her dressing, as though she were indeed a baby. But the doting and the tenderness her childlike soul requires, this you could no longer give—especially not in the face of the realization that having lost your husband and all your friends on her account, you were now about to lose your normal daughter, the one who might be the comfort you'd be needing in your old age. The new hostility Lila Mae had conceived for Lee had to be reckoned with. It could easily poison her feeling toward her mother.

And so it was that at one and the same time, Lee Balish, through no fault of her own, came to lose both her mother and her baby sister. Still, she was not completely abandoned, for she made friends with a neighbor girl of seven, Maryann Jones. The two of them became inseparable, playing the same kinds of games and sharing the same sorts of secrets as she and Lila Mae once had. Until one day Maryann's mother, Mrs. Jones, intervened and broke their friendship.

Now all Lee had were her dreams—someday, miraculously and unaccountably, Maryann would belong to her, Lee, instead of to that mean Mrs. Jones. Then, what a life they would make together: washing faces only when they wanted to or as often as they felt moved to, sixteen times a day if it suited them; eating what and when they pleased, strawberry popsicles that melted while you ate and went swish-swishing down your dirty little chin. Tootsie Rolls and frozen Milky Ways. And, oh, Bubble Gum. They'd go around and blow it all over the neighborhood. People would smile as they watched their mouths move so fast and wouldn't even bother to say, "Look at the dummy blowing."

It was a beautiful dream she had for many long years. Sometimes she still dreams it today. She still thinks about

Maryann's mother, too. That mean old Mrs. Jones. If Lee
could be said to hate anybody in the world, Mrs. Jones
would be that person.

Now in her pimp's apartment, she goes through the
magazines the Love girls collect, desperately seeking pictures of ugly women. When she finds one she brings it to
her wives-in-law, Frenchy and Brenda.

"Hey," she asks, "who does this remind you of, anyway?"

If the girls are in a good mood, they say, "Who? Why,
old beat-up Mrs. Jones, that's who." But if they are feeling bad, they sing a different tune. "You, you," they
taunt. "Old, ugly, dopey you."

Then Lee asks Big Bill Bloom to intervene for her.
Occasionally he does, and then she knows he loves her best
of all his women, and her happiness knows no bounds.

"Bill," she says at such times, feeling impelled to make
him know how much he means to her, "if I had a little
baby, I'd give it all to you."

Once she did have a baby, a sweet little doll of a girl,
and sometimes, especially on the nights Bill is with her
wives-in-law, she wakes with a rankling need to hold it
in her arms. Her own little baby. And yet her mother had
come while she was still sick in bed and taken it away
some place. God alone knew where.

After Lee had started feeling better she went all over
trying to find her baby. But it was no use. Mothers ordered
her away from their carriages. Her own mother, crying
and wringing her hands, threatened to have her locked up
if she didn't stop looking at strange babies. People were
complaining about her, she said. She also forbade her to
go with boys or men any more.

But Lee was twenty-four years old by this time and she
needed to go with men and boys. She liked having them
make love to her and they treated her nicely when they

were with her. Some of them brought her presents, dime-store jewelry, bottles of toilet water, and the varicolored ribbons in which she still delighted. After a while she began to ask for gifts from all who wanted her, and she hoarded what she got so that her room was turned into a veritable treasure trove. Of course, her family, knowing nothing about how she came to accumulate it, ridiculed the treasure trove. Mama called it a "pile of junk," and stuck-up Lila said, "Hey, Lee, what'll you charge to haunt a garbage pail?"

Oh, that stuck-up Lila Mae. If she only knew what Lee knew—that her dear boy friend, Hal Burton, had made numerous contributions to Lee's treasure trove. True, he spent his evenings with Lila Mae, sitting in the living room and singing sentimental songs while Lila played them on the piano. But there were plenty of afternoons when he met Lee and went with her either in the alley which she had come to call hers or in somebody's hallway. He told her not to tell Lila Mae about their afternoons. He said he would stop liking her if she did. She couldn't have borne Hal's dislike, not Hal's or anyone's, and so she kept the secret.

She never told about the other boys either. It felt so good to have them like her so much. Sometimes she'd go with one boy and the others would stand around waiting their turns. And once in a while, a man would fondle her. That always made her feel fine. Then, too, men would whistle when Lee passed them in the street. She was flattered, but Mama, who heard them once in a while, became angry and walked along muttering: "Like an animal. Like an animal." Lucky for Lee, the mother was busy with private students these days or she would have spent all her time supervising her daughter. Doubtless she would not even have permitted Lee to take lone walks if she had been able to help herself. But because the father was no longer sending money home and it was up to her to support the family, she had to spend all her free time working and had to let Lee go more or less her own way.

So Lee went her way, seeing the men and the boys who wanted her, and happy because she could oblige them. But there was a great hurt mixed in with the happiness, a great hurt and a great melancholy. For out of all the men and boys she went with, there was not one she could call her friend, not one who would take her to a dance or to a movie, not one who would come and sit at home with her, as Hal Burton came and sat with Lila Mae.

Then one day she met Big Bill Bloom and everything changed. She was first attracted by his squinting blue eyes and his hair that was as straight and blond as hers. Somehow the hair and eyes seemed a bond between them. She could not cease pointing out the resemblance. Over and over she said, "Your hair's like mine. Your eyes are like mine."

He laughed each time she told him and when she stopped, he told her, "Your hair's like mine. Your eyes are like mine." And when it came time for the two of them to go together and she offered him a choice between the alley and a hallway, he said he didn't want to go to either one and took her home to his apartment instead. What a fine time they had, too, drinking whisky, playing records, playing games, and then getting into bed together. It was a wondrous evening in spite of the two girls, Frenchy and Brenda Love, who lived with Big Bill and seemed to hate the sight of her. She didn't know why they should hate her, but Big Bill said not to mind. He said they'd grow to like her after they got to know her better.

Lee went home at midnight. Big Bill took her and on

the way he asked her for a movie date. Naturally, Lila Mae and the mother could not believe in the date when she told them about it the next morning. Lila mocked and the mother looked pitying and told her not to be too disappointed if Mr. Bloom didn't show up. But Lee knew he just had to come. He couldn't let her down.

Well, Lee, all washed, dressed, and inspected for the cleanliness of neck, ears, and fingernails, sat waiting for the bell to ring. But it didn't ring. And now it was eight o'clock. Lila Mae announced the time.

"Eight o'clock, Lee."

Eight o'clock and no Bill Bloom. He had promised to come at eight. He had promised faithfully.

"Eight-o-five, Lee," Lila Mae said.

Where was Bill Bloom? Where was he? And now it was eight-fifteen. And eight-thirty. Still no Bill. At a quarter to nine Lee's eyes were full of tears. Then the door-bell rang and the mother, some of the old-time tenderness back in her voice, said, "Honey baby, it may be somebody else. But God, how I hope it's Bill."

And, of course, it was Big Bill. True to his promise. And with an orchid for Lee. The mother pinned it on her while Lila Mae watched with shocked, unbelieving eyes.

Lee had many dates with Big Bill after that. They went to the movies and to dances and always ended up going to bed at his apartment. One night he told her he loved her and she asked what about Frenchy and Brenda. Then he said he didn't love them as much as he did her, but they worked for him and so he was loyal to them. He also told her that if she would work for him, she would always be his favorite. So she began to go to his apartment every day and to sleep with the men he brought for her. Sometimes there were only a few, but sometimes there

were so many that they had to sit around waiting for her,
taking turns the way they used to do. Each man, when
he finished with her, paid Big Bill ten dollars. It made
her very happy to be helping him out this way and he
always told her how much he loved her for doing it.

A little more than a year after Lee and Big Bill had
met, Lee's mother died of a heart attack. Lila Mae, Hal
Burton, Big Bill, and Lee were the only ones who went
to her funeral. Lee cried and cried and only stopped when
Big Bill told her that, from now on, she could come and
live with him and the two Love girls. She has been there
for four years now and when you ask her how it is, she
looks at you with her baby-blue eyes and tells you that
it's wonderful when she makes lots of money, because
then Big Bill loves and cherishes her. And as you must
know, she lives for his love and affection and will die if
he ever withdraws it.

SIX / Harlem, New York

NAME: *Melissa Jane Washington*

AGE: *37*

MARITAL STATUS: *Single*

EDUCATION: *Eighth grade*

Melissa Jane looks a gentle, humble, hymn-singing type.
All the same she is solitary and morose, a woman who
will not mingle. Every night, without holiday or letup,
she walks the streets of Harlem and prays to find a Negro
customer or two. But colored men do not seem to like
her, and so she goes with white tricks against her will
and instinct.

"Someday," she says, "a big white horse'll be a-kickin'
in my stall an' he'll turn aroun' an' say I done him wrong.
Me, I'll tell him, 'Excuse me for livin', white man.' But
he won'. All he'll do is whup me good. I'll be shoutin' to
him to stop for Jesus' sake. But he won' stop nohow. White
man gets goin' an' nothin'll stop him.

"I know this black an' evil day's comin' soon. I'm
prophesyin' it's comin' soon. I'm just sittin' aroun' an'
a-waitin' for it to come."

And whenever she undresses before a white trick, as she
does on occasion, her black skin appears a badge of shame
to her. And when her white trick touches her, she feels
doomed at his touch.

All her life as a little girl she was terrified by the

thought of white people. Both her parents had taught her to be.

"Stay out'n white folks' way," Ma had said.

And Pa had echoed Ma, "Stay out'n white folks' way."

And this was the only matter on which the two of them agreed. Otherwise they were a million miles apart. Her ma was one of the precious ones who had forgotten everything but Jesus, and her pa was a gambling man, a whoring man, a sinning man. Her ma was a square box of a woman with a skin so dark brown that malicious folk were always calling her "black face." Ma knew how to answer them though. She always spoke humbly. "Black face don' matter a cent or a gee, so long's the heart's pure inside of me." But Pa, well, Melissa Jane didn't know how he was in his heart, but he was wonderful on the outside. A tall, copper-toned man with a proud Indian walk, always pluming himself and riding the high horse, chockfull of swank and pomposity that would have been offensive in a fellow who wasn't so handsome.

Poor Melissa Jane was a mixture of both her parents. Born with her mother's looks, she aspired to her father's self-esteem. Naturally, her parents, as well as her nine sisters and brothers, all older and better-looking, ridiculed her for being, at one and the same time, ostentatious and unprepossessing. Still they loved her very much. And she loved them too.

Today she says that the love all the family had for her and one another is the outstanding recollection of her early life.

"Ma 'n' Pa'd fight about things, Pa's whores an' Ma's churchgoin', since Pa thought she'd ought to stay home more, but them fights didn't mean a thing. They wasn't bad fights a-tall. An' they always ended up with Ma and Pa gettin' in bed together. Us kids used to listen at 'em

gruntin' an' groanin'. We knew what they was doin'. Poor
Ma. Sometimes she'd start cryin' about it. 'I'm ruinin'
my po' little innocent chillun,' she'd say. An' Pa, he'd
say, 'Well, what can I do? When I go around to other
womins you don' like that. An' yet when I lay hands on
you, you don' wan' that neither. Woman, make up your
min'. I'm a healthy man's got to have a gal. Well, what
do you say?' Then Ma, she'd say, 'Yeah, sure. I'm a
healthy woman, too. I got to have my husbin' when he
lays hands on me.' An' listenin' to her, I'd know she
wanted Pa so bad. I wish I could want some man thataway
now. My ma, she jus' died for pa when he laid hands on
her, an' she couldn' say no, even though she was so shamed
to have us chillun hear. So she'd say, 'God, forgive me.'
An' then she'd go with Pa. An' I'd hear her gruntin' an'
groanin'. The place we lived in only had two rooms and
when you was in one room you could hear 'xactly what was
goin' on in the other."

The shack in which Melissa Jane spent her early childhood was on a cotton plantation in Georgia. It was built
of boards set up on rocks, and it was bare and dreary,
inside and out. It had no glass, only board windows. In
the winter the family lived without air and got light from
a kerosene lamp or the open fireplace where Ma did the
cooking. All the children had colds from winter's beginning to its end.

But the warm months were the good months, because
then the board windows could be opened and the sun
would sneak in sometimes. Not only that. During those
months Melissa Jane could plant and harvest her garden,
peas and beans and cabbage greens and onions. She could
can them or eat them fresh, and she could give them
away as presents.

"Here," she could say to her poor, half-blind Gramma

Bess, who had been a slave in this very territory, "here, I brung you a little somethin'."

And Grandma, who loved Melissa Jane best of all her grandchildren, would be sure to make a fuss. "If you ain't the smartest an' the goodest-hearted little child I ever done see. Takin' care of your garden so good an' bringin' me the *pro*duce out'n it. I think I'm goin' to get down on my ol' knees this minute an' thank God for makin' you so nice."

Yes, those were the good days for Melissa Jane. And there were other good days, too. There were the Saturday afternoons when Pa's lodge had their biggest doings: barbecues and sings and children's parties. And there were the parades through the fields and along the road, with Pa always in the lead, always in front—and him, with his proud Indian walk, and his bright green uniform, and the gold helmet on his head. Indeed, he was a gorgeous sight to behold.

And there were the church feasts where her black-faced mother shone for her piety and devotion, and the big meetings and revivals, always certain to feature the mother's testimony. She would rise with her square face shining and offer inspiration to transform the most evil of the congregation.

"I done cut myself loose from sin, an' anybody can do what I done. Oh, my darlin's, I just took a sharp knife an' I just cut myself loose. I got converted an' stopped my tarryin'. I got th' blessin'. I met Jesus an' he was the one led me to the water. He done led me. Oh, my honeys, oh, my babies. I seen a angel with a sword. He was the one baptized me an' said all my sins been washed away. Then I said, 'Oh, thank God, I'm free from sin. The Holy Ghost struck an' I jumped like as good as if I been sittin'

on th' burnin' bush. Oh, my honeys, oh, my babies. Amen.
Glory to God. Follow me, darlin's. He'll help you over
everythin'. He'll help you if you're poor or sick. Hal-
lelujah!"

And there were other good times. Sometimes a couple of
the other children took Melissa Jane hunting and fishing
with them. And once in a while she and her whole family
would dress up and get into their wagon and make the
beat-up old mare giddap and go to where their relatives
lived.

But as Ma used to tell her all the time, colored children
had to expect more bad than good in their earthly lives.

"Honey," she'd say, "for them of our complexion, livin'
on earth's one long sufferin'. But it'll be better when we
get to Heaven. So keep God in front of you an' when livin'
gets hard, remember dyin's easy an' Heaven's above."

Ma's talk infuriated Pa. He'd say, "Woman, if your religion ain't gone an' made a white folks' nigger out'n
you. Why does God want brown folks sufferin' on this
earth any more'n he wants white ones doin' it?" Then
he'd turn to Melissa Jane and say, "This is one time your
ma don' know the truth of what she's sayin', baby girl."

But Melissa Jane knew her mother really did know the
truth. There was much more bad than good in the life of
a Negro child. When you and your whole family worked
in the cotton fields and still went hungry most of the time,
that was bad. And when your father, your smart, handsome
father, was gallingly afraid of the white man whose field
he was sharecropping, that was bad. And when you saw
the school bus filled with white children pass your door,
while you had to walk five miles to school no matter what
the weather, that was bad. And when your big brother
Mack James cried because he wanted to go to high school

and couldn't, that was bad. And when your ma had to leave your home and go working in white folks' kitchens, just so she could tote some leftovers home to you, that was bad. And when your ma and pa couldn't buy you shoes to wear in the wintertime and you had to stop going to school because it was too cold to walk barefoot, that was bad. And when the white boys and girls you sometimes met on the road called you names and you knew you dared not taunt them back, that was bad.

Sometimes, Melissa Jane cried when she thought of all the bad in her life.

But Pa said, "Don' cry, Melissa Jane. Don' cry, lil' baby gal. An' don' think you need to wait 'til you get to Heaven to be delivered, neither. Your pa's goin' to be your God. He's goin' to take you right out of this mean ol' Southlan' and bring you straight into the promised lan'—Harlem, New York."

There was nothing Melissa Jane enjoyed so much as sitting around the fire with Ma, Pa, and the other children, and talking about Harlem, New York. It was Harlem, New York this, and Harlem, New York that, and, oh, just wait till you get to Harlem, New York.

"Once we make it to Harlem, New York," Pa used to say over and over again, "you'll all fill your bellies up an' never go hungry no more. I'll buy y'all a couple pairs of golden slippers and you'll never go barefoot no more, oncet we get to Harlem, New York. All we got to do is save th' money's goin' to get us there."

So the whole family worked and scrimped for years and saved money on food and on firewood. They never minded the hunger and the cold.

"Ain't nothin' you can't step over," Melissa Jane explains today, "if you jus' got a lil' dream to help you do it.

Me 'n' my family had the dream. Oh, lawdy, Lord, it was
sweet to have an' hard to lose.''

She tells today how the dream was not just a dream of
comfort and lazy living; it was born out of her father's
passion for freedom and hunger for dignity.

"My pa used to say, 'Baby gal, I ain't goin' to be a slave
no more, oncet we get to Harlem, New York. I'm a-goin'
to be a man like other men.' I said, 'Pa you're a better
man than anyone.' An' I was rememberin' all the times
he walked in th' parades and acted a little bit stuck on
himself. So then he told me the parades an' th' uniforms
don' mean nothin', and I cain't know what he means till
we get to Harlem. He said, 'Wait'll you see me, baby gal.
Jus' wait'll you see me in Harlem, New York.' "

They left Georgia in September of 1933, a couple of
months after Melissa Jane's fourteenth birthday. The
aunts and cousins and the old grandmother gathered to see
them off. They all contributed as much money as they
could get together and had a love feast that included three
kinds of meats and six kinds of vegetables. There was also
plenty of liquor for those who wanted it. Ma forgot she
was a precious one and had a few drinks. She began to
look very gay. The old grandmother drank, too, but the
liquor made her sad. Melissa Jane put her arms around her.

"Grandma," she said, "I'm a-goin' to miss you like
anythin'. How'm I goin' to get along without seein' you?"

"I'm the one should be sore troubled," Grandma said.
"I'm th' one's old an' lived most of my life away, an'
might be dead before I see you again."

"No," Melissa Jane said, "no, Grandma, no."

But the old grandmother shook her head and said, "Nex'
time y'all come home from Harlem, New York, it'll be
jus' so's you can put th' ol' granny in her coffin."

And Melissa Jane thought she might be right and felt sick at the thought of leaving her. She began to feel better only after the trip had begun. And, strangely, once they arrived in Harlem, New York, she felt depressed again, not only at the thought of the half-blind grandmother, but also because she was disappointed at her first sight of the promised land. It terrified her. The big buildings, and the concrete sidewalks, and the people who walked along and looked like foreigners, even though they were dark-skinned.

The family began to look for a place to live the morning after they arrived. All of them except Melissa Jane had high hopes. The father and the mother and the older children chattered about the luxuries they thought they would find. They talked about indoor bathrooms, and real plumbing, and enough space for the girls and boys to have separate sleeping quarters and not be herded into one bedroom together. They talked about light and air and being warm no matter what the season. Melissa Jane grew almost joyous as she listened to them. But her optimism did not last beyond the first two tenements they looked at.

Finally they found a place for twenty-five dollars a month, and had to use most of their savings to cover the first month's rent. It was little better than the Georgia shack had been, just one room where the whole family had to sleep, hanging blankets as partitions, and a kitchenette. The longed-for indoor toilet was in the hall, used by five families. And the vaunted plumbing leaked so that water was always seeping through from the apartment above. There were rats in the building and in the apartment, and because they were hunger-driven they sometimes came out in full view of the family. The boys soon grew accustomed to the sight of them, but the girls, and especially Melissa Jane, were terrified and remained so as long as they lived in Harlem.

Then it was winter and the living was harder than it had been when they first arrived. Now the plumbing froze and sometimes stayed frozen for days. They could complain to the landlord, but they knew it would not do any good. They knew what he had already told the other neighbors: "You can move if you don't like conditions in my house." The year before, 1932, had witnessed the greatest Negro migrations north, and Melissa Jane and her family knew they were lucky to have found any place at all in Harlem, for there were dozens of families waiting to move into their room as soon as they moved out. So they took what came and told themselves the winter would be over soon.

But it was a long, long winter and seemed to last forever. Oh, it was snowing and it was cold. There were gaping holes in the skylight of the building so that the winter air swept down the staircase and into the apartment. There was no coal, and no money to buy it with. And Ma, the precious one, the devout and consecrated one, had to scour the neighborhood in the hope that she could pick up some coal. Melissa Jane knew that Ma understood her foraging was really stealing. Melissa Jane knew Ma faced it in her heart. And Pa, his golden helmet forgotten now, also roamed the streets in search of coal.

Pa could not get a regular job anywhere in New York. He tried for weeks and months. He went all over, to stores and shops and factories. But he had no skill, and besides, every place was laying off that year. Melissa's big brothers also tried to get jobs and could not. Sometimes Pa or one of the boys got an odd job that would last a day or a week. Ma and the two older girls did better than Pa and the boys, that is, they worked more regularly. They did domestic work, and each earned up to two dollars a day when they worked.

Melissa Jane was the only one who went to school. She would rather have worked, but Pa and Ma wouldn't hear of it. She hated school. Half the time she didn't understand what the teacher was talking about. Neither did the other kids who had come from the South. But the teacher had no time to explain or even to find out what they didn't know. With sixty-three in her class, she had all she could do just keeping order.

"Sometimes sittin' in that ol' class given me a terrible headache," Melissa Jane explains today. "Some child was allus yellin' or bustin' another one's face in. They was awful tough little chillun. They wasn' scared of nothin' or nobody. My mama used to say, 'Godamighty, honey, them young boys an' girls is older'n Adam an' Eve. I guess it's 'cause they never had no one to baby them up th' way I used to baby you.'"

But these days Ma wasn't around to baby Melissa Jane. As the months wore on she spent less and less time at home. She'd have to leave for work at seven o'clock in the morning and she wouldn't be finished until eight or nine that night. And then she'd go off to some church meeting the precious ones were holding. Oh yes, she found her church almost as soon as she came to Harlem, and she began to live for her nights there. Melissa Jane, although she would have liked to have her at home, considered her fortunate to have found an outlet from the sordidness of the Harlem life.

Pa found an outlet, too. He began drinking more heavily than he had in Georgia and he continued his gambling and his whoring. Ma said God only knew where he got the money, but Melissa Jane's oldest sister said that his whores paid him to go to bed with them. Ma used to cry and tell her to keep her evil mouth shut.

So Pa had his drinking and his whoring and his gambling. And Ma had her holiness. And Melissa Jane felt as though she had nothing but sorrow and sadness.

Sometimes, lying awake and freezing in the night, she thought of Georgia's sunny days and warm nights, and the whole family sitting at home together, and of half-blind Grandma Bess who loved her best of all the children. And she thought about the green fields and the vegetable garden she used to grow. And she thought about all the relatives who were around whenever they needed a helping hand. Sure it was true they'd been hungry in Georgia. But now they were hungry even though they had picked up their roots and come all the way to Harlem, New York. Why did Pa think Harlem was better than Georgia? It wasn't better. All it was was lonelier.

She met the boy, Zachariah Smith, when she was fourteen and a half and still dying of lonesomeness. He was seventeen and dicty-looking with his good hair and light complexion, and she couldn't understand why he would want to have anything to do with such an ugly little dark-skinned girl. He'd come to see her when nobody was home a couple of days a week and she'd let him make love to her. After a while he grew tired of her and didn't come to the house any more, but by that time she was pregnant.

Pa noticed it first and she admitted everything when he questioned her. He grew very angry and wanted to hit her, but then he started feeling sorry for her and tried to blame the boy. She said that she was just as responsible as the boy was, and then her father began to act like a crazy man. He banged his fist on the table and shouted that the white men were the ones who were really to blame.

"Makin' it so a man cain't get a job an' take care of his family. Makin' it so he got to live on a black evil street. The gals all go bad aroun' here, carryin' babies instead o' books. Baby gal, my heart's a-bleedin' for you. Still an' all, I cain't help you out. I cain't help you nohow, baby gal. Th' white men's got me so I cain't make a move."

He told her he would bring her to an old lady who would take the baby out of her, but Ma heard about it and wouldn't let him.

"A baby killer," she screamed. "You cain't murder my daughter's baby. I ain't a-goin' to let you."

Pa screamed back, "An' I ain't agoin' to let you give my baby gal such a load to carry."

In the end, they did not go to the old woman. Melissa Jane had her baby at home. Her mother and Mrs. Johnson, another holiness woman, delivered her.

"I suffered somethin' awful," she says today. "I screamed so loud an' all the neighbors came runnin'. My ma said I was shamin' her by bein' such a baby. She didn' mean it an' only said it to take my min' off th' bad pains I was havin'. But I felt low-down to be shamin' her after everythin' she done for me. An' then Mis' Johnson, she tol' my ma, 'Well, Lawdamighty, lady, why shouldn' she act like a baby, seein' she is one?' An' ma said, 'No, Mis' Johnson, she ain't a baby no mo'. Now that she got a baby of 'er own, she got to stop bein' a baby gal 'erself.' "

Melissa Jane named her baby Jack. He had good hair and a light complexion like his father, and Melissa loved him the moment her mother put him in her arms. Nor did she feel disgraced because she'd had him.

"Plenty young girls was havin' babies without marryin'," she says now. "All of th' families took 'em in an' kept 'em jus' like my own done. Th' families was glad to have th' little things, although nobody could afford to feed 'em

good. I quit goin' to school after my little Jack come an'
I tried to get me some work to do. I hearn a big bunch o'
talk about how they had truan' officers in Harlem, New
York, was goin' to come after me an' make me go to school,
but none of them came. I figure they're for white chillun
only, an' don' care if colored ones goes to school or not.
Anyways, I went out lookin' for work an' lef' lil' Jack with
Mis' Johnson.''

After trying all the employment agencies and being
eased out by the more experienced girls, she landed in
the Bronx slave market. Here she came and stood with the
other women who sought work, trying always to underbid
them. She and the others stood and held penciled signs
that showed how cheaply they would work. They would
get there at six or seven o'clock in the morning in order
to grab the most conspicuous spots and try to attract the
attention of the white housewives who came to look them
over. White men came, too, and sometimes women who
had come to apply for housework went off with them
instead.

Melissa Jane began to resent her father during the
months she hung around the slave market. She began
to condemn him for having brought her to this. Georgia
was bad. It was terrible. But Harlem, New York was worse.
Where was all the good her father had promised? He and
his fine talk and his whoring and sinning and gambling!
And her mother, she and her holiness. Ma was no better
than Pa. Everything was her parents' fault. If not for them
she wouldn't be here, standing and exhibiting her muscles
to the white ladies who came to look her over.

And because she was a young girl and had good muscles
that belied her smallness, she was often chosen over the
older women. Then some of them cursed her and a few
shook their fists at her. One old toothless one maligned her

every day for her youth and vitality and for the way she undersold the others with her cheap prices.

The jobs, when she got them, were dirty and demanding. Sometimes she had to wash windows high up and she was frightened of falling—but not so frightened as she was of the women she worked for. Actually, as she recollects it now, some of her madams were good women who treated her kindly and urged hot lunches on her. But some of them denied the hot lunches, even though they were supposed to be part of the bargain. And what could she do? With jobs so few and far between, she had to hold onto what she got. And, of course, the lunch was not everything. Some madams were courteous and polite and behaved as though Melissa Jane were a white girl. Others treated her like dirt. But, knowing her own circumstances and thinking of little Jack, she'd bite her tongue and keep quiet.

Little Jack worried her too. He was growing up cute as a button and crawling around and learning to talk. But he had a bad cough that hung on, and he didn't seem to be as energetic as other babies of his age. A couple of the neighbors thought he had the lung sickness. But Ma said that was silly. He wasn't coughing any blood, was he? Then, one night he started coughing blood. And he kept coughing and couldn't stop. Melissa Jane didn't know what to do with him.

"Ma said, 'Wrap him up good an' bring him to th' Harlem Hospital.' I said, 'Ma, I cain't do it. I cain't take him there. It's a butcher shop.' An' it was, too. I been in there one time visitin' a frien' of mine. I seen how it was. Sick folks was a-sleepin' on the benches an' they was a-sleepin' on the floor. I seen a lady th' doctor was jus' done operatin' on a-sleepin' on some chairs. I couldn' of brung my baby there. I'd of died before I done it. Poor lil' Jackie. Leastways he died with his ma's arms aroun' him an' not in no beat-up ol' hospital."

Melissa Jane, all of eighteen, felt as though her life had ended after the death of her son. She continued to go to the Bronx slave market every day, but she didn't care any more whether she got jobs or whether she didn't. And one day while she stood waiting for housework, a man approached her and told her he'd give her a dollar and a quarter if she'd come with him. She indignantly told him no, but his offer tempted her all the same.

Afterward, she thought day and night of all the money she could make, three or four dollars a day, maybe five. And she began to grieve because she hadn't begun to prostitute sooner. Little Jackie might never have died if she had, for then she could have supplied him with the meat and eggs and milk babies needed. She began to watch the whoring girls in the neighborhood. They didn't look raggedy, and they spoke as though they always had plenty to eat.

One day she asked one of the whoring girls how it felt to go to bed with strange men.

"I feel low," the girl answered, "but no lower'n when I was houseworkin' an' some madam acted like I was wantin' to steal from her an' went through my bag before I went out of her house. I never stole nothin' from nobody an' why did she have to do that for? Honey, I don' feel so low now as I did in them days."

But Melissa Jane persisted. "Are you 'fraid of th' ones you go with?"

The whoring girl said she wasn't afraid of most of her men. Men only tried to hurt you once in a while. Usually it was the white men who did.

"If you're goin' into th' business," she told her, "look out for the white men. They're th' ones'll do you wrong."

But once she started streetwalking for her living, Melissa Jane found that white men were the only ones who wanted her.

"I go with them," she says today. "I cain't get nothin' else. But I'm ascared. I don' know what they're wantin' with a colo'd gal. One time I asked a white man an' he tol' me, 'Gal, there's two places where niggers is as good as white folks—the bedroom an' th' graveyard.'"

SEVEN / Sweet Daddy Low

NAME: *Jean Lee Simmons*

AGE: *24*

MARITAL STATUS: *Separated*

EDUCATION: *College graduate*

Other prostitutes who know her dislike Jean Lee Simmons.
Strangely, although she is a strikingly beautiful woman,
they are contemptuous rather than jealous of her.

"Me jealous of Jean Lee?" Nance O'Brien, a pudgy,
red-faced old-timer, laughs at the notion. "Why should I
be? She's a human garbage pail. I know she looks like she
belongs at the Ritz with that gorgeous body and those
big, baby-blue innocent eyes. But so what? Innocent!
Ha-ha, as the old saying goes. I got only one thing to say
if you ask me if I'm jealous or not. My tricks come back
to me once in a while. Jean Lee's tricks never come back."

Jean Lee admits that Nance is right. She has never, in
the four years she has been a prostitute, had a customer
come back after he's been with her once. Having studied
psychology in college, she is inclined to be analytical about
the reasons why. Analytical, and, in the way of some intellectually lonely people, driven to reveal her deepest
self.

"I want too much from my tricks. Do you know what
that means? Can you possibly imagine the incongruity?
I'm a prostitute. These men are buying me, and yet I want
too much from *them*. I'm one girl who needs my customers

105

worse than any of them have ever needed me. And they
know it. I try not to let them know but they always find
out. I loathe them and still, after they're finished with
me, all ready to go back to the hearth and home and their
pure little wives, I'm not ready to let them go. I keep
pulling at them. I couldn't stand to have one around me
too long, and still I keep pulling at them, wanting something. God knows they have nothing to give me. So they
get mad. I'm rotten for their egos. Other girls can con
them along. 'Oh, sweet daddy, you're such a great lover,
honey.' But any line I attempt sounds hollow. How can I
say, 'Sweet daddy, you're a great lover,' and at the same
time be clutching out for something the poor things don't
have to give? I try not to clutch. But I always do, anyhow.
And so, in the long run, my customers are bound to know
that money's the least of everything with me. They know
I'd go with them for free. You'd think they'd like me for
that. *Like* me! They hate my guts.

"A woman like me, who's got to keep clutching and
demanding more from them, is a waste of money to them.
A woman like me tells them, in effect, 'You're not big
shots, pals. You're not the great lovers those other little
whores make you think you are. You've done nothing for
me.' How can they like me or think about coming back?
They've got troubles of their own. They don't have to be
burdened with me and my odd sex needs."

Jean Lee cannot remember exactly when her sex consciousness began. She recollects reading books dealing with
sex with some other girls from her school, the Packer
School on East 82nd Street, and being vitally stirred by
them during her earliest adolescent days. She recalls sexual
dreams and lascivious imaginings when she was fourteen
and fifteen years old.

"I never talked much about my feelings," she explains.

"I certainly never told anybody at home. Both mother and dad were such proper people, I'm sure they wouldn't have known what hit them, if I'd said anything to them or acted like I sometimes felt impelled to."

But at school she gave way to her impulses. She was provocative with the boys and sometimes with the men teachers.

"But I never slept with the boys I led on until Billy Sachs," she says. "We were both sixteen. I'd known him almost all my life. He was handsome and brilliant. He had a sense of humor. I guess I thought he was the most wonderful boy in the world."

All the girls had their eyes on Billy, but nobody was surprised when Jean Lee won him. After all, the handsomest boy ought to go to the prettiest girl.

"I was flattered to have Billy like me best. I was so proud of him. We planned to get married when we were eighteen. We thought we would quit school then and take jobs, or our parents would see us through college after we were married, if they wanted to. We used to talk about the home and children we would have. We both wanted a large family. We really were happy together until... well, one night Billy and I were the only ones home, and I sat on the couch with him as close as we could get and he started to kiss me. All of a sudden, the closeness and the kissing didn't seem to be enough for me. I began feeling far away from him. I felt lost and I thought I could find myself if Billy could only hold me close enough. So I begged him to hold me closer. He did. I said, 'That's not enough, Billy.' He said, 'I can't get you any closer.' I said, 'You can. You can.' I began talking to him in the language I had read in those books. The words that spouted out of my mouth! I couldn't believe I was talking the way I was. I wanted to say, 'Darling, I love you.' That's all. Just

'Darling, I love you.' But I wanted to say those other words from the books too. The more dreadful they were, the more I seemed to want to say them. They excited me so. They excited Billy too. Awful! Nauseating!

"Billy made love to me after a while and that was awful too. I guess it was as terrible for him as it was for me. He looked as though he loathed the ground I walked on after everything was over. I started to cry. I remember he didn't try to comfort me. He just said, 'I've got to go now.' I said, 'Yes, sure.' He said, 'See you around sometime.' I said, 'See you around sometime,' too. That was that."

Jean began going with other boys after her breakup with Billy. She got a reputation. The boys who had had her made jokes. She knew, and still she went on going with them, even soliciting them.

"Believe me, I felt low—like an animal, but a trapped animal. I say trapped, because I honestly couldn't help what I was doing. My mind was occupied with sex day and night. I was tortured by my visions. I was only relieved when I went with a boy and then the relief didn't last. It turned into disgust at myself after everything was over. What kind of dirty slut was I, anyhow? Why was I so different from the other girls I knew? What was the matter with me?

"During my better times I tried to talk myself into believing I was in love with all the boys I went with. I even tried romanticizing myself and, since I'd always read a good deal, identifying myself with some of the more enigmatic literary heroines. Once in a while I'd think of myself in terms of the poem from Faust. You know:

> Two souls are dwelling in my breast,
> And each is fain to leave its brother,
> The one fast clinging, to the world adheres,
> With clutching organs, in love's sturdy lust,

The other strongly lifts itself from dust,
To yonder high, ancestral spheres.

"But in the long run, I knew I was dirty, not romantic.
If I hadn't known myself, my friends would have informed
me. Friends! The things they said about me! The boys
were worse than the girls."

Jean Lee married when she was twenty. She married
a man she met on a blind date which a friend of her
mother had arranged for her. Naturally, he knew nothing
of her sordid reputation. He was a young lawyer who had
heard her mother's friend talk about how pretty and accomplished she was. At first Jean Lee hadn't wanted anything to do with a blind date—particularly one emanat-
ing from so respectable a source.

"I have plenty of boy friends," she told her mother's
friend.

"But Barney's different," the friend said. "He's my idea
of a perfect man."

Jean Lee wanted to tell her to keep him for herself
if she thought he was so perfect, but she said, "If he's
all the things you say he is, why does he need a blind
date?"

Her mother's friend smiled. "He doesn't need a blind
date, honey. He just needs you."

Jean Lee doubted it. "Thanks for thinking of me, but
I'm not going on a blind date with anyone."

Nor would she have gone if her mother had not begged
her. "For me, Jeanie. Do it for me. I don't ask you for
favors very often, do I?"

Later, after she met Barney and had several dates with
him, horseback riding in the country, sailing at the shore,
the theater, the opera, all the museums, she blessed her
mother's insistence.

"He was the most marvelous man I ever met," she says.

"I was transformed by being with him. I thought, if only I can keep him happy all our lives—I say keep him, because during those early days he seemed as happy with me as I was with him. And he said he'd never been happy before. God knows, I never had. I'd never known what it meant to be absorbed in another person and to feel that you could have no life without him but that with him you were fine and wonderful.

"In a way, it was as though all the complications of my life had suddenly unraveled. I don't mean that they disappeared completely. On the contrary. I found that I still had to keep seeing men. Sometimes I'd take three or four a night. How I always hated myself afterward. But there was nothing else for me. I was wise enough to know that I dared not go to bed with Barney. Nobody can know how I wanted to, though. He was my great hope. I kept telling myself, 'There's nothing wrong with you that Barney can't cure.' Sometimes I'd laugh out loud at the thought. 'The only trouble has been that I've never been in love before, and now I am in love, and Barney'll do what nobody else did for me. He really loves me. The others never did. That's why I was so frantic with them. I'll be relaxed and satisfied with Barney.'"

Barney began seriously courting Jean Lee almost from the day he met her. He gave her a beautiful engagement ring on their tenth date. When he put it on her finger, she thought she had never been so happy before. He said he wanted her to continue at college throughout their engagement, but that they would be together every moment she could spare from her classes and he could take off from his office.

They began buying furniture two weeks after they announced their engagement. Jean Lee enjoyed shopping with Barney. His taste in furniture was different from hers; he liked traditional and she liked modern, but their small conflicts were challenging rather than irritating.

"I loved to have Barney interested in furniture. He was different from my friends' fiancés, who told them to just go ahead and get anything they wanted. He said he was as much concerned as I was with the pieces that went into our home."

Finally the shopping was accomplished. Jean Lee had lit on a brilliant compromise to assure its success. She would choose the basic pieces, and he would pick the accessories. After their furniture was bought, they had to shop for an apartment. They were fortunate to find exactly what they'd been looking for, a huge living room with a fireplace, a small bedroom, a good-sized den, and, strangely, in the middle of New York, a real country kitchen.

Jean Lee fell in love with the kitchen. She had never been domestically inclined before, but now she fantasied herself in a cute apron, the original, delectable dishes she would create, and Barney bringing his office associates home, and all of them envying him and calling him "a lucky dog."

"Barney, old boy," they said in her dream, "what did you do to deserve this?" Then they turned to their wives, fearful of having hurt their feelings, and patted them on their plump shoulders—all the wives had plump shoulders in her dreams—and assured them that they were good cooks, too.

Finally, when Jean Lee was twenty and graduated from college, the wedding day arrived and the long waiting time was over.

"My wedding was lovely," she says. "Mother and

Dad spared no expense. Over two hundred guests came
to the reception at the Park Sheraton. I wore a low-cut Hattie Carnegie gown with a huge train. Everybody said I
looked beautiful. I know I felt beautiful inside and out.
I told myself, 'I'm going to forget all the dirt. I'm starting
a new life with Barney now and it's going to be clean and
good.' "

But there was a nagging fear inside her all the same.

"I told myself everything would be all right because it
had to be. But what assurance did I have it would be? Look
at all the men I'd had before and how farcical we were
together. Could love really make the difference? I tried to
tell myself of course love would—of course—of course.
I kept repeating those two words 'of course' as if they were
the only words I knew, or as if they were a prayer or something. But then, while I was thinking 'of course,' a terrible
thing happened. I felt the same old sexual imaginings. I
can't describe them. They were vulgar and weird, and
that's all I can tell you about them. I thought, Barney or
no Barney, I'll never find myself. I'm crazy and I might as
well face it. If I were a decent woman, I'd leave right now,
walk out on Barney and the wedding and everything."

She didn't, though. Somehow she managed to say "I do,"
and to kiss the bridegroom, and to comfort her weeping
mother and mother-in-law. "My two mothers," she said
sweetly, "and I love them both very much." Somehow she
managed to dance with Barney and with all the other men
who wanted to dance with her and to accept her friends'
congratulations with fitting graciousness.

"Then it was time. After a million years or two seconds
I was in the bedroom of the Pullman car to California that
Barney had reserved for our honeymoon. He began to
make love to me, gentle love, and I thought, you fool, if

you only knew. And then I thought, Oh, Barney, be good
for me, be right, you're my only hope, darling, my last
and only hope."

But Barney was no better for her than all the other men
had been and she hated him. No! She loved him. She loved
him desperately. He was her Barney. Her only love. But
she hated him, too. She wanted to bite at him and slap
him and hurt him as much as he was hurting her. How was
he hurting her? He was so sweet and thoughtful. "As
though I'm made of glass," she thought, "but I'm not made
of glass. Oh, Barney, please, I'm not made of glass."

Afterward, while Barney slept, she struggled with her
feelings.

"I lay in bed, miserable, telling myself I loved Barney
and all the time feeling impelled to go out and find myself another man. Maybe then my tension would go away.
I thought, Jean Lee, don't you dare get out of this bed!
It's the end of your marriage if you do. Then I thought,
it's the end of my life if I don't. The visions coming at me,
the nauseating pictures driving me crazy. And I thought,
Barney, my beloved last hope, I'm finished now. But there
was nothing for me to do except go out and get a man. I
started to put my clothes on. Barney woke up. He said,
'Baby, what's the matter?' I said, 'I'm just nervous, I guess.
I was going out to get a little air.' He said, 'Wait. I'll go
with you.' I said, 'No, please.' But he insisted. We stood
on the train platform for about an hour and all the time
I kept disciplining myself. I said, 'Don't let Barney know
what you are. No matter what happens, don't let him
know.'

"But I did let him know. I kept clutching at him in
bed, wanting more and more from him. He tried. He tried
so hard to satisfy me. Poor lamb. No man could have tried

harder. But it was no good. It was just no good, and so I knew nothing would ever be any good for me any more.

"My honeymoon was a nightmare—for Barney as well as for me. I watched myself night after night, taking his strength away from him. I wanted to stop, but I couldn't. I was driven. And all the time something in me blamed Barney and wanted to hurt him the way I was being hurt. I'd tell him he was inadequate. Then I'd cry and tell him, no, I was the one. All he said was that maybe he could do better once we got home."

Jean Lee pretended to believe him.

"I'll never forget our first night at home. Finally, after he couldn't stand my demands another moment, Barney told me, 'Please, baby, let me go to sleep.' I looked at him. I said, 'All right then, *go* to sleep.' Then I said, 'Isn't it awful how two people start and how you end up when everything's over? You become utter strangers. No closeness after everything's over, is there, Barney?'

"But Barney was asleep before I finished talking. I stayed awake, hating him because he was asleep and I wasn't. Then a dog began to bark. I thought it must be a black dog, and I have never heard a dog before bark in such a terrifying way. I told myself I can't lie here and just listen. So I got up and put my clothes on and went down to Eddie Pastor's bar. I picked up a man and went to the Earle Hotel with him."

The man's name was Mort something or other. He was a traveling salesman chock-full of smutty stories he insisted on telling. He told them all the time he was undressing. He was a strange-looking man, small and fat and red— not just red-faced, but red all over his body. He was near-sighted and he kept blinking his eyes.

Afterward, he looked sick and disgusted with her. He

put his clothes on fast, as though she would stop him if
he didn't hurry. He left the room before she did.

"Well, 'bye now," he said, "and thanks a million."

She said, "You're welcome, I'm sure." Then she smiled
to herself and thought that breeding showed no matter
what, didn't it?

"At that moment," she says, "I wanted to die more than
I ever have in my life. Depending on your point of view,
it was fortunate or unfortunate that I had no instrument
with which to kill myself."

Jean Lee arrived home at six o'clock. Barney was frantic.
He told her he'd been wanting to call the police but had
been afraid to. He didn't ask her where she'd been. He
said he knew she was miserable and he was to blame. He
said he loved her and she said she loved him, too.

"More than anything else in the world?" he asked.

"More than anything else in the world," she said.

He put his arm around her and led her back to bed.
They lay and cried in each other's arms. And then it was
seven-thirty and he had to get up for the office. He begged
her to stay in bed and not bother with his breakfast. She
said, "What? Me stay in bed and miss breakfast with you,
when I know darn well I won't be seeing you all day? What
do you think I am, crazy or something?" Then they laughed
like two lunatics, and he said, "Well, I could call you up
some time during the day if you asked like a nice girl."
And she said, "Call me up. Big deal." And he said, "Well,
if you don't want me to...." And she said, "Oh, but I do,
I do." Then he said, "Darling," and the nightmare night
was over for a minute.

But only for a minute. Because after Barney had kissed
her good-by and she had admired the wholesome look of
him walking out—nobody would suspect, would they, what

she'd put him through that night—she thought, "If I were a decent woman, I'd leave him. I'd find some way to make him free of me." But she couldn't leave Barney. What good would her life be if she did? He was her only hope for salvation.

She began to clean the house, scrubbing floors that had been scrubbed by her cleaning woman, making dirty work for herself. Nothing helped. She gave up and went out to get some men. She took one to a fleabag hotel on 46th Street and the other to one on 48th Street. Then she called Barney and asked whether he couldn't please come home to lunch. She said she knew he was busy but she had to see him. "I guess I'm shameless," she said. And he said, "I'll sock you one if I ever hear you talk that way about yourself again. Remember, you're talking about the woman I love." She said, "Yes, I remember. Oh, darling, I remember."

She practically dragged him into the bedroom when he came home and he left without eating any lunch. That was when she vowed she'd save him from herself, no matter what, and went to Eddie Pastor's again and picked up three men in quick succession. Then she went home and tried to read. But it wasn't any good so she went back to Eddie Pastor's. A young man in a lumberjacket and tight-fitting pants was drinking Scotch at the bar. He was clean-cut and she liked the looks of him. She sat down beside him and ordered a Scotch for herself.

"You're the prettiest thing's been around here in a long time," he said.

She smiled back. "You're not so bad yourself." She downed her Scotch in a couple of gulps.

"Next one on me, baby?"

"Sure," she said, "and the one after that."

He put his hand on her knee. She let it stay. She hoped

he would say something, that he would ask her, so she wouldn't have to do the asking. Maybe I can play hard to get, she told herself, smiling at the thought.

At last he said it. "How about having a good time, baby?"

She got off the bar stool. "Come on."

"Where?"

"Just come on," she said.

She led him to the apartment. She had never taken a man there before. "At least that was clean for Barney and me," she thought. "Now it won't be clean any more. Now I'm dirtying my home up, too."

She couldn't wait. She began talking those words to him and he grew excited.

Afterward, after he had made it clear there was no use clutching any more, she looked at him lying on Barney's side of the bed, fully clothed. God, she thought, he might at least have taken his clothes off, and grew nauseous.

"Please excuse me," she said.

He said, "You're excused, baby. And how!"

When she came out of the bathroom, she said, "Go home, now."

He smiled. "I'm accustomed to paying for my good times, honey. How much did you say this one costs?"

She said, "Go home now. That's all."

He said, "I must be a greater guy than I think I am, to have a girl like you work for love instead of money."

She thought if he didn't leave soon, if he didn't stop taunting her, she'd be unable to control herself. "Please," she said, "go home."

He said, "Will fifty dollars cover the charge, baby?"

"Yes," she said, "fifty dollars will cover the charge."

He pulled two twenties and a ten out of his wallet and put them on Barney's bedside table. Then he opened his jacket and showed her the badge pinned on the inside. "I'm an officer," he said. "And I'm taking you in."

"What kind of an officer?" she asked.

"Why, honey baby," he said, "you weren't born yesterday. An officer of the law. You know, police, cop, policia."

He walked to the door, opened it, and whistled out. Another good-looking young man in a lumberjacket came in.

"Well, Mike," the man who had been with her told the other one, "this one's a fifty-dollar babe."

The man named Mike eyed her speculatively. "You could do better, dear," he said in a gentle voice. "You could get a hundred, two hundred. The girls who do have nothing on you. Tell me, you ever been arrested before, honey?"

"No," she said, "never. And I don't know why you're arresting me now."

The man who'd gone with her said, "Poor kid. Poor little innocent babe," in a sing-song voice. "Don't know what she did that was wrong at all, at all."

"I didn't do anything you didn't do," she said.

Both men laughed and told her to can the stuff and get her coat, because they didn't have all day to waste on the arrest of one prostitute.

She had often seen the police station they took her to from the outside but never dreamed she would be seeing it from the inside. It didn't look like a police station at first glance, except for the lieutenant and two other uniformed officers who were sitting at a narrow desk. It was painted green and the walls were beginning to peel. Aside from the officers' desk, there was a large table and a couple of straight chairs.

The man called Mike pulled a chair out for her. "Sit down, dearie. I'm sorry we don't have better accommoda-

tions for you ladies. But what can we do? The City of
New York considers this good enough. Too bad, isn't it?
But then we aren't often honored by the presence of elegant
ladies like you."

She thought she could bear anything that happened
from now on, if he'd only keep his mouth shut.

The man she had been with pulled out a card and began asking her a lot of personal questions. What was her
name and was the name she was using her real name? How
old was she? Did she have any children? Was she married?
Living with her husband? Did she have a job?

After she had answered all their questions, they told her
she would be arraigned the next morning in Women's
Court, and that, in the meantime, she was to make herself
as comfortable as she could on the wooden bench. She
thought she would not sleep a wink, but she must have,
because they had to waken her when the man came to
take her to court.

Court seemed such a strange place. She was herded,
along with ten or eleven other women, into a small caged
area that led into the courtroom, and was told to sit quietly
until her turn came. She spent her time examining the
other women.

She was amazed at the look of them. They were so different from all her notions of what prostitutes looked like.
There was a midget among them, and a short woman who
looked to weigh every bit of 200 pounds.

Jean Lee could not believe that any man would pay
good money to be with the likes of these. Yet if you listened to their talk, they would all seem to have as many
customers as they could handle.

"If you cruise one trick and he says no," the 200-pounder
said pompously, "there's always another one. If nine of
them don't happen to like your style, the tenth one may.

I go up to a trick and if he looks like I'm feeding him arsenic, I say, 'What's the matter with you? You like them skinny instead of fat? Drop dead, then. I'll find one likes them fat!' "

"Amen," the midget said feelingly.

The fat girl turned to Jean Lee. "You must be a new one," she said. "I can tell what you're thinking from the look on your puss. You don't believe there are guys could like me and Midge here better than a girl with a shape like yours."

Jean Lee said, "Yes, I do believe it." Although, of course, she didn't—then.

The girl called Midge smiled at her. "All kinds of wacks in a bag of tricks."

There was one nice Negro girl in her late twenties. She was tall and dignified, and she looked as if she took some pride in her appearance. She smiled at Jean Lee, and Jean Lee smiled back and asked her name.

"Lorraine Smith," she said in a warm voice. "Tell me, honey, you been in before?"

Jean Lee shook her head no.

"This is my eighth bust. But I only been in the clink four times. Say, you scared?"

"Yes," Jean Lee said.

Lorraine took her hand. "Don't worry. This is a good judge sitting today. He likes to hear himself talk, so he bawls us out a lot, but the old coot's heart's in the right place. He's liable to call you a tramp, but if he can, he'll let you walk. He's no six-months baby like some other judges I could name you. They'd slap six months on you soon's they'd look you in the eye. They talk nice and polite and make you feel like they're sorry for you. Nice little gentlemen they are. Then, when push comes to shove, they say 'Six months in the workhouse. Oh, I hate to do this to you. It hurts me worse than it does you.' It hurts them, yeah, yeah, they should live so long. How come you got caught, honey? Did you cruise a bull or something?"

"What do you mean?" Jean Lee asked.

Lorraine laughed. "You *are* new in the racket. You're still wet behind the ears if you don't know the lingo. Let me help you out. Cruise! To pick up. Bull! Cop. Cruise a bull. Pick up a cop."

"I didn't know he was a bull when I cruised him." For some unaccountable reason Jean Lee savored the unfamiliar words.

Suppose I were a prostitute, she thought, moved by the warmth and interest the girl Lorraine seemed to have for her. What would it be like? I'd have friends then, people I could talk my business over with, because that's what it would be if I were a prostitute, just a plain business. People could understand me the way these girls understand each other. But to be a prostitute. How awful. How awful? Any worse than what I am doing now? "I didn't know he was a bull when I cruised him," she repeated.

"Nobody does, baby," Lorraine said.

Her voice was so kind, Jean Lee felt impelled to tell her her true story. She told about her life before her marriage, and about her life with Barney, and about how, despite her love for him, she had to go out and pick men up.

"And you never made a dime out of it," Lorraine said regretfully. "Kid, kid, how dumb can you get. I can see right now I'll have to take you under my wing."

I have a friend now, Jean Lee thought, and no need for pretense with her. She knows me and still wants to be my friend.

Lorraine advised Jean Lee not to tell the judge that the officer had made love to her. "He'll never believe you, anyway. Even if he did, he couldn't admit it. How would it make New York's Finest look if the judge said, 'I guess these cops are human!' You cruise a trick and a bull picks you up, the judge is all set to listen to your argument. After all, it's only you against the trick then. But you cruise a cop and the whole thing's different. It's you against New York's Finest. You don't have a chance. You'll only cut your throat with the judge if you try to cut New York's Finest down. I know, honey; I learned the hard way and I'm not jiving you. All you got to do is say, 'Guilty, your honor,' and keep a real sweet smile on your puss and you'll walk, you being a first-timer and all. Take my advice."

Jean Lee took Lorraine's advice. It was hard to adhere to when she saw the man with whom she'd been the day before raise his right hand and swear to a complaint alleging that she had picked him up, taken him home with her, and asked him for fifty dollars.

But, trusting Lorraine, she pleaded guilty. The judge gave her a long speech and remanded her to the House of Detention pending sentence.

When she got to the prison, she called Barney's office. His secretary told her that he had not come in nor called in his whereabouts. Then she called home. Barney answered on the first ring.

She said, "Hi, darling."

He said, "Oh, thank God! I had visions of your being dead or something. Are you all right?"

"I'm fine," she said. "I guess."

"Well," she could tell he was hesitant about putting the question, "where are you?"

Now, she thought, this is the time. I can tell him the truth and make him free of me once and for all. It's the only right thing. Right for whom? Not for me. How could I live without Barney?

"Jeanie, where are you?" he asked again.

"I'm in jail," she said.

He said, "What did you say?"

"Sit down if you're standing up," she said. "They are accusing me of being a prostitute, sweetheart."

Barney was quiet.

She said, "Did you hear what I said?"

"Yes," he said, "I heard. You must be crazy, Jeanie."

She said, "Not me. You're the crazy one—to have married me."

He said, "Jeanie, I'm coming right down."

She said, "Forget it. I'll tell them I don't want to see you. If you really want to help me, don't come. Please, Barney. I'm begging you."

He started to say something else but she never heard what. She hung up on him.

Three days after her arraignment, appearing in court for sentence, the judge, true to Lorraine's prediction, suspended her sentence and let her walk. Since Lorraine walked too, they left the courthouse together.

"Boy," Lorraine told her, "am I glad I beat that rap I don't mind the workhouse so much. What's sixty days anyhow? Life's long and I been in worse places. Only thing that worried me was my sweet daddy and one of my wife-in-laws taking over and getting to be head chick while I'm in the clink. That I would not care for."

"I'm sorry," Jean Lee said. "I know I sound ignorant. But I don't know what you're talking about."

"I'll buy you a drink to celebrate us both being on the outside and tell you all about it," Lorraine said.

They went to Tony's, a joint across from the courthouse, and guzzled Martinis. Jean Lee had four to Lorraine's seven, and Lorraine talked about the life of a prostitute. She talked with the idea of convincing Jean Lee.

"I'll take you up to Harlem and introduce you to my

Bob's pal, Sugar Joe. Next to Bob, he's the smartest sweet man around, and I got a feeling he'd blow his top over you. If you want to try him out, I can call up right now to make a date. What do you say?"

Jean Lee said, "Well, I'd like a chance to think things over and. . . ."

Lorraine couldn't wait to hear her out. "If you think you're nicer when you give it away for free. . . . Look, honey, you got the wherewithal. Now all you need's the guts. Of course, as I told you, if you think you're nicer. . . ."

"I don't think I'm nicer. It isn't that." She looked up from her drink and saw a car like Barney's parked in front of the courthouse. "Look, I've got to get out of here right now. That car looks like my husband's. I know it isn't, but. . . ." She felt herself getting hysterical. She pulled a ten-dollar bill out of her purse and left it on the table. "I couldn't face him. I've got to go this minute."

"Well, alreet." Lorraine took her arm. "What are you waiting for then? Let's go."

They rode up to Harlem together. Jean Lee was grateful for Lorraine's constant conversation. She reopened the subjects she'd begun in the court—her wives-in-law and her sweet daddy.

"My sweet daddy's my man. I love him like crazy. My wife-in-laws are the other girls he's got hustling for him."

"Why do they hustle for him?" Jean Lee asked.

Lorraine said, simply, as though no other explanation could be required, "Why, because he's a sweet daddy."

"But isn't he your sweet daddy?" Jean Lee asked.

"You're not just beating your lip," Lorraine said. "Doggone right."

"Then why do the others hustle for him?"

Lorraine smiled. "You wouldn't believe those girls could be that dumb. They think he's their sweet daddy, too."

"Doesn't that make you jealous?" Jean Lee asked.

"No," Lorraine said. "Why should it make me jealous? He's just jiving the others along so's he can get some money together, and then we're getting out of the business. He and I intend opening up a fancy joint on Lenox Avenue." And added, "What good'd it do me if I was jealous? What good would it do me, anyway?"

In the months and years to come, Jean Lee Simmons was to learn a great deal about the relationships that exist between prostitutes and their pimps, and learn to accept those relationships emotionally—in fact, to live with them. But intellectually, she would understand them no better than she did now.

Lorraine went on describing her sweet man, and Jean Lee reflected that she must love him as much as she herself loved Barney. Maybe more. For could she visualize herself working and giving Barney every dime she earned, and Barney taking it from her, and not just letting her prostitute herself but even urging her on because there would be more in it for him? And Lorraine could convince herself that such a one loved her? And love him in return? But, Lorraine said, of course she could love him, wait till Jean Lee met him and saw for herself.

Three hours later she met Lorraine's sweet man, Bob, and Sugar Joe, his buddy, at the Baby Grand Bar on 125th Street. The two men looked amazingly alike, both tall, slim, coffee-colored, somewhere in their forties. They both smelled piny and their hair was flattened down and shining with pomade. They both smiled when Lorraine introduced Jean Lee to them and looked at her as though she were a horse they were evaluating.

Sugar asked Lorraine, "Your little friend in the game, honey?"

Lorraine said, "Not yet. But she wants to be."

He said, "Copesetic."

Jean Lee got very drunk before the night was out and went home with Sugar Joe. He had a nice apartment on 58th Street in a house she didn't think would rent to Negroes. She didn't get much chance to look around, because they headed directly for the red, velvet-canopied bed.

"It was good being in bed with Sugar," she says, "not satisfying, but good in a way it never had been with Barney. I could be as low as I needed with him. I said the terrible words to him and he said worse ones back. Nothing I did shocked him. I had to clutch at him, too; he couldn't satisfy me any more than any other man could; but he wasn't horrified to think I'd have to go out and look for other men after I got through taking what he had to give. All he wanted to do was insure I'd be well paid. I don't have the words to explain what a relief his casualness was to me. I joined his stable in the morning. Naturally."

He was a temperamental man who always looked for slights where none were intended. He was particularly sensitive to Jean Lee, because she had been to college and he had never finished elementary school. He often cuffed her for using a word or a phrase he did not understand, and she learned to take his abuse and to be abjectly apologetic as soon as she knew she had displeased him in any way. But he did get her plenty of customers, all she could take care of, and then, on the nights when he was not occupied with his other girls, he took her to bed himself.

"I got to where I'd do anything for those nights with him, give anything." She gave and still gives five to six hundred dollars a week. "Nobody can understand how I feel, but, during my more lucid moments, I know what he means to me. Here is a man who knows me, really knows me as I am, and he can stand me. He can come to bed with me, knowing that I've had ten men before him, and not want to beat my brains out. I know he looks at me and sees dollar signs, and that makes me feel good. It makes me know he's as low as I am, even lower in some ways. Sweet Daddy Low, I call him. I don't have to worry about hurting him, the way I always had to worry about Barney. It's comforting not to wake up in the morning and look at a man and think you're ruining him. This boy's already ruined, so nobody can touch him. He's rotten and he's cruel. I hate him so much I could kill him sometimes, but even when I hate him most, I know I need him—and always will."

EIGHT / Cadillacs and handmade shoes

Almost every prostitute, no matter how high or low, has her pimp. When she can she keeps him well, even luxuriously, certainly better than she ever dreams of keeping herself. So many pimps drive Cadillacs and Lincoln Premiers that they have become known as a badge of the profession, and a girl whose pimp cannot afford one feels that she is letting him down. Most pimps wear hand-stitched suits, handmade shoes, and hand-painted ties.

A few prostitutes, the high-priced money-makers, may share their pimps' luxuries, or at least provide themselves with a few, especially if their work requires that they have them. The call-girls who need good wardrobes and good addresses, for instance, feel that they must have money enough for both before their pimps can claim what they consider their share. But it is a fact that the majority of girls, the streetwalkers and lower type of bar girls, live in hovels and have no more than two or three dresses at a time.

Why should prostitutes spend their hard-earned money on men who seemingly give them so little in return? Nobody outside the prostitutes' own world can begin to understand the reasons, and the girls themselves honestly do not know. They shrug their shoulders when you ask them and tell you that that's "the life."

Carlotta Ferenzi, an old-timer who worked in many of the better houses in San Francisco as long as thirty years ago, shakes her head and says, "What do you expect a girl to do, anyways, live by herself? She's got to have a man of her own."

Carlotta, a philosopher and historian of sorts, recollects, from her earliest days in the business, "A girl without a man might's well be without an arm or a leg. Nobody'd have anything to do with her. She'd be called an *outlaw* in the houses I used to work. No madam would hire her. Why should she? After all, a free girl couldn't be so dependable. Money wasn't so important to her, and she didn't have to put herself out if she didn't want to. Why should a madam take a chance on her when there was always a girl who *had* to have money for her man? Any madam'd have to be a damn fool to take an outlaw over a girl with a man. Believe me, outlaw girls certainly had a hard time. It wasn't only the madams. The other girls treated them rough, too. They wouldn't be seen talking to them because their men wouldn't like it."

Today the free girls are still outlaws, and other prostitutes who value their relationships with their pimps still will not be seen talking with them. Such are the social pressures that make for conformity here.

But most prostitutes are driven to seek out pimps by their own inner needs rather than by social pressures. They are not so unlike other women that they do not need to know that somebody belongs to them. Where else can they look for love and tenderness? Surely not from their customers.

The recent testimony of the hundred-dollar baby in a well-publicized case against a young call-girl and her madam is illuminating in this respect. The hundred-dollar baby, testifying under the anonymous name of Edward Johnson, unblushingly admitted that he and the girl had been in bed naked; but when asked whether he had ever taken her to dinner or the theater, he sprang up as though he had been shot and hotly denied that he "would do such a thing."

Most of Mr. Johnson's cohorts would share his point of view; taking a girl to bed is one thing, but being seen with her is something altogether else again. Enjoying her sexually is one thing, but being companionable with her is not part of the deal. Prostitutes, for their part, would be the last to admit that they need companionship from men. Most of them say they wouldn't take it on a silver platter from any men except their pimps, a finer breed than other men.

"I couldn't stand to be with a square guy for one month," Carlotta Ferenzi says. "He could offer me diamonds and furs and everything fine and I'd just tell him, 'Keep it yourself, Joe, because you're too much of a square guy for me.'"

By a *square guy* Carlotta means anyone not in the racket, in other words, any man not accustomed to living off prostitutes' earnings.

"I had a friend one time," she says seriously, "who married a square guy. Now, this gal was like me, a racket broad from the word go. So I knew she could never be happy. He was very nice to her, the way square guys usually are to their broads, gave her money, bought her things, opened up a bank account for her. That really was something, because us girls don't go in for bank accounts.

"So when she came to my apartment to see me one time, drove up in her own car and all, I said to her, just chewing the rag, 'Tell me, Mame, are you happy with that square?'

She didn't answer my question right away. After a while she said, 'Happy—who knows what's happy? All I know is that now I don't have any more trouble with the po-lice!' I said, 'Mame, I know you. Tell the truth, hon. Are you happy or just contented?' She said, 'Well, I tell you, Carlotta. Now I never get taken to jail any more.' I told her, 'Every girl to her own dish and I'm not going to tell you how to live your life. But, me, I'd rather go to jail than live with a square.' "

The suggestion that selling one's body to keep some man in luxury might be a square kind of procedure would bring only a laugh from Carlotta, who would say that squares couldn't be expected to understand the motivations of racket broads like her.

"Well look, you take a square guy and his broad. All right. Every morning he goes out to work. Maybe he likes his job, maybe not, but he figures he's got to get money for his broad. Right? He'd be ashamed if he couldn't take care of her. Well, racket guys and broads are just a little turned around. Girls like me know they've got to get out and hustle to get their man some money. If a girl can't, she's ashamed of herself. I been in the life thirty years and had one pimp or another every single day of it. Old as I am right now, I got a pimp. He's on the stuff and he needs me bad. When I get pulled in, he lays up on his bed and hollers for me. I feel good to know I can afford a pimp at my age. I'd be ashamed if I couldn't."

She admits that her previous pimps, not having been on narcotics, and able, therefore, to have fuller stables, didn't always give her the feeling of being needed that this one does, but they satisfied her all the same.

"When I was working in those Frisco houses I had men who'd come in to see me for a little while, maybe take me to bed, collect the money I'd made that week, and then go on to some other whore. But still, I knew he was there if I needed him. He might go my bail if I got arrested. Things like that, what I mean, he was my man, see?"

She says that racket broads scoff at "square broads' ideas of love and hearts and flowers." All the racket broads want is the assurance that their men speak their language, think the same thoughts they do, and do not condemn them.

This seems little to ask, but prostitutes do not believe they are in a position to ask much of anybody, especially not their pimps. Here, in this most important relationship, their lack of regard for themselves is nakedly apparent. They can talk all they want about how they would not take square men on silver platters, and maybe a few of them really mean what they say. But the vast majority admit they consider themselves unworthy of being loved as fully as square men seem to love their square broads. It is a rare prostitute who does not feel deep down that the simplest housewife is better off than she is. But she will not admit it if she can help it. She will go on pretending to the best of her ability that everything her pimp "dishes out" is all right with her.

"Look," young Anna Lands says, "if a man does the best he can for you, what else do you expect from him?"

Anna's pimp, Brad, is a small fellow in his thirties, with a bald head, a blond mustache, and a sunken chest. The best he can do is to give her thirty dollars a month for rent, forty dollars for food, and an occasional small amount for new shoes and a hat, out of the three hundred dollars she brings him every week.

"If I could make more money," she says, "I could get more out of Brad. That's why I wish I had more looks or something."

Anna is twenty-two, going on twenty-three, an ordinary-

looking girl, too skinny, and with colorless hair and eyes.
Nor is she very personable. Her voice is shrill and her walk
heavy for such a slender person. But her youth helps when
she solicits men. Of course, she could never earn three
hundred dollars a week, or anything near it, if she weren't
a prostitute, and so she guesses she won't be able to afford
to leave the life for a long time. But some day. . . .

"Brad's got all kinds of expenses right now. He's got to
pay a hundred and fifty a month on his new car. Then,
there's the apartment. It costs like crazy. And he don't
like to wear anything that's not the best. Can't say I blame
him. I just wish I had more looks, that's all."

She never used to worry about her looks before. She had
always known she was no beauty, but she never minded
as long as Brad hadn't seemed to.

"He'd tell me I was a cute kid every once in a while, and
I'd be glad he thought so, even if I didn't myself."

Lately, he's stopped telling her. He's got a new girl, a
second wife-in-law for Anna, and he seems to be spending
all his energies on her.

"She's no beauty either, but you ought to hear Brad
dearing and dolling her all over the place. I could die. I
keep wondering what's she got. Blue eyes. So what? Her
hair's bleached. It's just like straw. She's too fat. Audie says
fat is sexy. Audie's my other wife-in-law. My favorite. My
roommate. She and I live together and we get along swell.
I get along fine with everybody, all but that new horse of
Brad's, but Audie's my favorite friend. I really like that
girl.

"Sometimes Brad comes to see us and all three of us
sleep together. I don't think I'd like it with any other girl,
and, if he ever tried to sleep with me and that new horse
at the same time, I'd tear her straw hair out. But Audie's

O.K. Us three can have a lot of fun. Brad used to say he liked us a lot because we know how to share and share alike. If I got two tricks, I'd give Audie one. She'd do the same for me. But not for that new horse. I wouldn't give her one of my tricks if she stood on her head. I guess Brad'd want to sock me one if he heard me talk this way. I guess he'd think I got no right to keep a trick from any wife-in-law, since all the money goes in the same pocket. But I don't care what he thinks. I'd never give that horse one of my tricks no matter what Brad said."

Nobody can know the price that contemplating this small revolt costs Anna Lands. She feels as though she has no right to such evil thoughts. Her only comfort is Audie, her pal, who eased Anna's guilt by admitting once that, given a choice, neither would she steer tricks to the sexy one, wife-in-law or no.

"Audie said she'd take every trick herself instead of giving any to that one, and she didn't care how tired she'd get. She'd take her men any place and do everything, but she'd tell them before they began anything that they'd have to be quick like bunnies. Zip. Zam. Thank you, ma'am. She's smart, Audie. I'm glad I got her, now that Brad's spending most of his time with that one. We have fun together. Sort of crazy, I guess. We go to Coney Island. The rides are good. That roller coaster! Wow! I think it's scary, but Audie, she just loves it. She could ride all night if her money just held out. I like the merry-go-round. I know it's corny, but I like to try for the brass ring. I got it one time. You're supposed to give it back to the merry-go-round man; it's stealing if you don't. But I didn't. I took it home to show Brad I really had won it. He told me I shouldn't have wasted my money, and Audie stood right up and told him he shouldn't act that way and ought to be glad I could have a little fun without him.

"She's a real friend. Sometimes, after we're through working, her and I walk along the street eating peanuts and spitting the shells in the gutter. One time we took a horse and buggy and rode all around Central Park. We held hands, and I don't know about Audie, but me, I made believe she was Brad. I sure like Audie."

At the same time Anna is contemptuous of Audie, for Audie is a fool to believe, as she does, that Brad loves her. He likes her, of course, but Anna is his real, his only love. She knows, even if nobody else does. Sometimes he may act as though he cares for the others, that new horse for one, but Anna knows he's only acting. No other way to keep cows satisfied, so they'll continue to work and give their money to him and, in effect, to her.

Audie and that new horse are both working for her, if they but knew, for Brad is taking all the money his cows bring in and saving every cent he doesn't need for living expenses. Then, as soon as he saves enough, he and she, Anna Lands, are going to leave New York and go to a small town to live. They'll open a grocery, or a hardware store, or some other business a man needs no special training for. Training. That's Brad's trouble. If he'd had training for anything, he'd have left the pimping business a long time ago. And taken her out with him.

It would be impossible to shake Anna's belief, for it is her whole reason for living. And Audie, of course, believes in Brad as implicitly as Anna does. Only she knows that Anna is the deluded little pussy cat, and, come the happy day of prosperity and independence, she, Audie, is the girl he will take out of the life and ensconce in the small-town store.

It is a curious and alien world these people live in. A lawyer who has, for more years than he cares to remember, been an intimate confidant of prostitutes, remembers the day a prostitute known as Frenchie came to consult him. After their professional business was concluded, he asked about her pimp, Louie.

"How many girls does Louie have?"

She counted them off on her fingers. "Five, including me. I got four wife-in-laws."

"And how do you all get along together?"

"Oh, fine, fine. But," she said, "we didn't always used to get along so good. We used to have terrible fights. All Louie's fault, because he used to sleep with the girl who brought him the most money that day. Well, you know how that'd make the rest of us feel about the girl he stayed with. We hated her like poison, till we got wisened up and got together and decided we were going to tell him a thing or two or three. 'Listen, pal, no more of this going with the girls who get the most money, see? Since when's that fair? All of us is in your stable, right? And we all try to do our best for you. So you got to go with all of us, and it don't matter who brings the most money in.' We drew straws to see which was going to be the one to tell him. Just my rotten luck it turned out to be me. Boy, was I scared! Louie never liked nobody telling him how to run his business. Supposing he decided to sock me."

"Why should he sock you?" the lawyer asked.

"Why shouldn't he sock me? I was butting in his business, wasn't I?" She smiled. "He didn't. Instead, he was real sweet and said he always liked to do what his girls wanted. So now he stays Monday with Mary, Tuesday with Ida, Wednesday with Tillie, Thursday with Lorraine, and Friday's my night with him."

"He must be quite a fellow," the lawyer said. "And what does he do with his Saturday and Sunday nights?"

"That's just it." Her face flushed up. "We know the

bum's double-crossing us on weekends with a good girl."

How do the pimps do it? How do they manage to keep their stables? Nobody knows the answers: not judges, or police officials, or psychiatrists, or social workers. The mistake they make is to think they know. They talk to a minority of prostitutes who have become so disillusioned with their pimps that they are ready to talk to the authorities, and they accept the stories as the whole of the pimp-prostitute picture, when, in reality, it is the merest part.

The result is that official sources tell us that pimps hold their girls through physical force and intimidation. Police and court personnel have many records of pimps and prostitutes basically similar to the following two given them by girls who had taken as much as they could from their men.

Mary Jones, 19, tells about her pimp, Forzell Huston

"He used to beat me up bad all the time. I loved him at first but I got to hate him after a while. One day I decided I didn't want to work for him no more. When I told him, he got his knife and began slashing me all over my arms and face. He cut one of my wife-in-laws in the eye and made her blind. I told her to tell a bull but she was ascared to."

Jean Rivers, 37, tells about her pimp, Billy Boy

"I told him I was through and he said the hell I was. So then he started cutting me up and saying if I wasn't going to work for him, I wouldn't work for nobody. He cut me all over, especially around the face, so it would show and men wouldn't want to sleep with me. So I decided, O.K. Billy Boy, now I had it, this is the last time you'll ever cut me up. I went out on the street and cruised a trick I thought might be a bull. I pegged him right and was I glad when he brought me in. Jail's safe these days when Billy Boy makes my house so hot."

Many pimps have vicious tempers. The number of recorded knifings of prostitutes, large though it is, is infinitesimal compared to the number of beatings. Almost every girl can tell you, if she will, about the time when "my man blew his top and really laid me out till I was black and blue." And that includes the loving, loyal girls as well as the disgusted ones. But the fact is that the vast majority take the beatings in their stride: as much a part of the life as everything else. "Sure my man gets mad sometimes. Why wouldn't he? Yeah, he beats me up when he gets mad. So?"

Most prostitutes are as horrified at the interpretations the outside world puts on their men's actions, as that world is by their men. Take Anna Land's reaction after police and probation workers, seeing her with a black eye and a hurt jaw and presuming, logically enough, that her beloved Brad had given them to her, questioned her.

"They tried to get me to say Brad beat me up, but I wouldn't tell them nothing. I don't want them to put my man in jail. They got no right. If my man and me have a fight, what's it their business for? Then, when I don't want to tell them, they say it's because Brad's got me scared and might kill me if I talked. Boy, what those people don't know about Brad and me could fill a book. I wouldn't tell them about my own man. None of my friends would neither."

She is right. Most prostitutes would not open up about their pimps if they were tortured. Indeed, police and court personnel know numbers of girls who would and do go to jail in preference to ratting on the men they live with. They do this not so much because they are afraid of what the men will do but rather out of loyalty and love. It may be true that they live in virtual bondage to their men, but the condition is a voluntary one, and its roots must be sought in the prostitute's background as well as in that of the man she keeps.

There is only one principal exception to the rule of voluntary bondage of prostitutes, and it is neither native New York nor native American. Cuban girls are the only prostitutes who feel threatened by their pimps, and are, many of them, working as virtual slaves.

The Immigration and Naturalization Service, which deports foreign pimps and prostitutes to their native lands when possible, has record after record concerning Cuban girls, and each is more shocking than the other. The cigar burns on the naked stomach suffered by Lolita Perez are by no means unusual. The burning cigar is a favorite method among Cuban pimps for keeping girls in line. So is "the squealer's mark," a cut from the forehead to the lower lip. Many Cuban girls, eager to talk to Immigration, are afraid, because they all know girls whose relatives in Cuba have been injured or killed because they opened up at the wrong time.

The Cuban pimp differs from his American counterpart. He is dangerous and hardened, for the good reason that he is a racketeer rather than merely a man who lives off women, and that he generally has little or no personal interest in his girls. Aside from an early pretense in Cuba, when he may offer marriage, as Lolita Perez's man did, or a good job in the United States, once he has solicited his girl and brought her over here, he makes it clear that his interest is all business and no romance. It is almost impossible to find a Cuban prostitute who believes that her man intends to marry her some day or that he feels any affection toward her. She *knows* she is nothing more than a business proposition to him, and if she values her life, she will be good business.

Cuban pimps are better businessmen than most of their American brothers. Many of them run their activities on an international scale, utilizing contacts back in Cuba and also in Mexico and Puerto Rico. There have been times when the Immigration and Naturalization Service has unearthed information about officials in Mexico and Puerto Rico who have been on the pay rolls of Cuban pimps. In Puerto Rico, they have sold birth certificates, either forged or not, to pimps who have had no other way of bringing their girls into this country. In Mexico, they have served as transporters for Cuban girls smuggled in to await Puerto Rican birth certificates which would permit them to enter the United States as citizens of this country.

Most Cuban prostitutes are assigned by their pimps to the green pastures of Chinatown. The assignment has proved enormously profitable, making Cuban pimps easily the wealthiest men in their fraternity. They keep their girls working on a quota and under the most stringent supervision. Most of them require a minimum of one hundred dollars a night from each prostitute.

Chinatown offers excellent opportunities for any pimp, and the fact that it is Cuban-dominated reveals that American pimps would not easily pit themselves against the organization, acumen, and strength of the Cubans.

Louie De Lord, an old-time pimp with a substantial stable of his own, says, "Hell, I'd have my girls beating Chinatown in a minute if I was in a mood to tangle with them spicks and maybe gamble my life away. Everybody

knows it's the juiciest part of town. The Chinks are pushovers."

They are pushovers because most of them are here alone,
and have been for years, and because our immigration law,
with its Oriental exclusion policy, precludes their ever being able to bring their women here. They are also pushovers because they are inclined to be gentlemanly toward
the girls they go with in a way that few American tricks are.
They are, in other words, "lousy witnesses," who refuse to
give testimony against the women they sleep with. And
because their refusals are sometimes sly rather than direct,
any pressure the officers or the court might exert on more
obviously uncooperative witnesses must come to nought
with them.

Like Wong Lo, who was in Women's Court some months
ago, most Chinese tricks smile engagingly at judge, officer,
and prosecuting attorney, and could not ever be accused of
being hostile to the American way of treating prostitutes.
They say, most of them, as Wong Lo said through the
Chinese interpreter, yes, the vice-squadder had found him,
as he claimed, in a room with a girl. With *a* girl or this particular one? Why, *a* girl, of course. But was the girl this girl,
who was presently being pointed out to him? Few Chinese
witnesses ever manage to remember.

Wong Lo peered carefully at the girl, Dolores Moreno,
with whom the vice-squadder claimed to have found him
in bed, and then looked at her again. He took off his
glasses and requested the court's permission to examine
her closely since, when he'd been in bed with her, he'd
seen her at close range and without the aid of the spec-
tacles. He stood, a slender, dapper, perturbed young man,
and opened and closed his eyes in a tremendous attempt
to be accommodating but had, despite his best efforts, to
give up finally.

"Well," the prosecutor asked, "was this the girl?"

He ignored the attorney and stared, still minus his glasses, at the judge. "I am sorry I cannot answer that question. You see, Your Honor, all white women look alike to me."

So the Cuban pimps function freely in Chinatown. Their girls are seldom arrested since convictions are so difficult, and money pours into their pockets.

"Nobody can imagine the money these Cuban pimps make," a special agent for the Immigration and Naturalization Service said recently. "Why, only last month we had a procurer who made more than $180,000 a year out of this business and a couple of little side affairs, like dope-smuggling. He was always ready to throw the money around in graft. All the Cuban pimps are. They make so much, a little bit going out can't bother them. I remember what happened to me when I first started with the Cubans in Chinatown. We went to a shabby, little room to get this poor dirty-looking fellow. He figured who we were before we explained ourselves. He didn't say anything. He just went to a closet and took out a plain cardboard box and gave it to me and my partner. There was a couple of thousand dollars in it. He went to another closet and got two more boxes out. They all contained folding money. Seven thousand altogether. And that little fellow didn't even know how much he was giving us. He couldn't count. We turned it all over to the Bureau of Internal Revenue and they're still trying to find out how much he owes in taxes.

"Then there was this pimp, Sari. He was about forty, very handsome, and a smooth operator. We got a tip that he was holding three kids about fifteen years old in a house in East Harlem. When we went to pick him up, he came right along with us, got in the car without having to be pushed or anything. After we started driving, he said,

'Look, if you let me out at the next traffic light, I'll leave four thousand dollars to be split between you.' "

Sari's audacity was not surprising. He had entered this country a few years before on a visitor's visa and had then purchased his Puerto Rican birth certificate. But he had considered the identification incomplete and somewhat dangerous and so had maneuvered himself a faked Coast Guard certificate.

"He signed himself on a merchant ship going from New York to Boston," the special agent says, "and applied for his seaman's papers there. He secured them as a U.S. citizen. They were more than identification. They also enabled him to show a means of support. Pretty smart operation, eh? It takes guts to get messed up with the Coast Guard. Actually, Sari is not the only one. I could name quite a number who did it. Then there are a bunch of them who manage to get themselves put on the pay rolls of ship-cleaning companies. Not that they'd ever dirty their hands. They just have some contacts who put them on the pay roll, so if they need to they'll be able to show a legit means of support. Good contacts. Boy, these Cuban pimps got them all over.

"One pimp we put away not too long ago had his contacts in Mexico and in New Jersey. He'd have his girls brought to Mexico by his Cuban contact and kept there until one of his American contacts, an ex-army-air-force pilot, flew over and brought them back to this private airfield in Jersey. There, another of his American contacts, a local police captain, picked them up and brought them to the madams who were lined up to receive them. Boy, what a bunch those guys are!"

But what—and who—are Cuban pimps? It depends on who answers the question. Immigration men say they are vicious and depraved, and despite their exploits, cowardly.

The prostitutes who work for them regard them as semi-devils, but their favorite girls think of them as friendly types who stick close to one another.

But one fact everybody agrees on—almost all Cuban pimps were by their own standards and most certainly by ours deprived and underprivileged in their early lives.

"I always was poor boy," Juan Ricardo says at the height of his career at age forty. "This way I become rich. I was hungry. No more. Money, she talk, and I am big man now."

He does not see anything condemnatory about what he does to earn his money. Since money talks and he has it, he feels himself an able, admirable fellow. He lives, as most people do, by the standards and mores of the world which made him. Human life was always cheap in that world; love was a luxury only the rich could afford; and sex was everybody's outlet. You spent all week grubbing for your food and shelter and looked for sex in between the grubbing.

Juan never spent a single day in school. He cannot read or write either Spanish or English. He has no reason for considering his activities antisocial. He never did believe pimping to be wrong, not from his earliest youth, when a well-dressed American from Chicago first solicited him and a few other Havana urchins to serve as runners for the peep shows he conducted for the boatloads of foreign visitors.

"I was seven years," he said, "when I learn to bring people to the show."

That much English he picked up when he was seven—enough to laud the virtues of his show more expansively than any other youngster lauded his. He waited for the boats to come in and then walked up to likely looking American gentlemen and ladies ("Plenty American ladies, she come to my shows," he still boasts today) and told them how, if they came along with him, they would see some real sights. Not just men and women doing the ordinary and extraordinary, but women and young boys and men and virgin girls and, for those who preferred different thrills, women with women and men with men.

The American gentleman he worked for encouraged him to peep through the holes himself, so he would know what he was talking about. He did so well that by the time he was eleven, being a nice-looking youngster as well as a knowing one, his boss promoted him from runner to actual show participant. He played the part of a virgin boy who tried desperately to exhibit the male virility his girl partners, eighteen or nineteen usually, demanded from him. After a while, he learned to clown his part and became the butt of some ill-at-ease jokes from an aroused audience which tipped him high for the laughs he provided.

"I make more money than my papa, who is proud of how I do."

His papa died recently, still proud of this successful son who has hacked his own way out of the jungle he was born to. Before he died, however, he issued a warning to his boy. He said the world is for strong men to conquer and Juan has proved himself strong. But he must remember to use his strength well, and to conserve part of what he gets with it, because, as every old man knows too well, strength is, at best, a transitory thing. When a man passes the fine middle years and grows older, it is as though he were getting younger all the time until, finally, he becomes as a little child again. And look you, his father told him from his deathbed, you were only a runner when you were a small fellow, and unless you use your strength well now, and make sure that you are provided for in your old age, you may, during the latter years when pimping becomes too much or too hard, find yourself being a runner again and what a comedown it would be.

This is what makes fiery Juan run and keep taking risks and flying in the face of dangers: his fear of the future and his basic insecurity.

American pimps are similarly driven by fear and insecurity. Curiously, a good 90 per cent of them are colored men and most of them have at least a white girl or two in their stables. Some of the white girls hail from the South, and they do not always come from the lowest economic groups either.

Black Cat is thirty-five years old. He is a slender, satin-haired man, one of numerous pimps whose entire stable consists of Southern white girls, four of them at this particular time. He has had seven to eight during other years. He is a hard taskmaster, one of the hardest around, and, still, he usually has a choice of girls.

Black Cat's nickname is based on the fact that he is known to be an unlucky kind of fellow, not ever for himself, but always for the cows in his stable. His girls are not only attractive but experienced: the kind of girls who, before coming to Black Cat, managed to avoid cops and complications, but who now are always running in and out of bad troubles. Most of them had been call-girls before joining him and had worked subtly enough to avoid the officers' notice; but Black Cat makes it impossible for them to afford the luxury of subtle solicitation these days. The kind of money he wants from them requires girls who are not afraid of taking chances.

Not that he mistreats them when they don't get enough money. He is one pimp who has never put a hand on any of his girls. All he does when they present him with their earnings is to count the money, somewhat sardonically, and say, "Thanks a lot." But he never kisses or puts an arm around a girl who doesn't bring in what he thinks she should.

"He's got a way of making you feel like a dog when you don't do what he wants," Patricia Reardon explains. "He gets that certain look in his eye so you wish you didn't have to face him."

Patricia is one of Black Cat's top girls. She is in her early thirties with blue eyes and black hair. Before she became a prostitute, she was a strip-tease artist, called an *exotic dancer.*

Patricia was born and brought up in Asheville, North Carolina, by a widowed mother who was and still is a Fundamentalist preacher. Patricia and her younger brother, Tommy, killed in Korea, were raised on the Bible.

"When other kids were hearing stories out of children's books," she says, "I was being read to from the Bible. I memorized whole passages before I was six, and by the time I was twelve I knew the Good Book cover to cover. Sometimes I read it because my mother made me, and sometimes I just read it because I was so doggone lonely. I had no friends when I was little, but my mother used to say, never mind mortal kids as long as I could walk with God and Jesus."

Walking with God never was enough for Patricia though, and she did mind about the mortal kids who used to tease her, never accepting her mother's daughter just as they could never accept her mother, the crazy preacher-lady, who, by some fluke or other, always managed to attract the raggledy-taggledy the minute they hit town.

"I was always alone when I wasn't with my brother. I used to go to school by myself. I wanted to make believe the other girls' company didn't mean anything to me, so I'd sing hymns as I walked along the road. I'd sing out loud so I wouldn't have to hear the kids talking to one another. I stopped after a while because I found out they were calling me 'Hymn-book Hannah' behind my back."

Her loneliness was not alleviated until she got to be about fifteen and discovered she had a figure.

"I forgot all about God and the Bible then. I couldn't think about anything but myself. I got to be crazy about my hair and face, and especially my body. I'd get in the nude and admire myself in the mirror."

The boys around school, who had joined the girls in making fun of her, began to be attentive that year. They clustered around and asked her for dates. She was very flattered, until she realized that the lonely petting parties they wanted to take her on were never preludes to more legitimate invitations. Boys liked to neck with her but they still did not ask her to their parties and dances. Lush figure or no, she was as much her strange mother's queer daughter now as she had been when she was little.

At sixteen she married a twenty-one-year-old boy new in town. He was effeminate and she could not kid herself into thinking she was in love with him; but she decided to take a chance because, at the very least, she would be getting away from home. Her mother, though she voiced the proper token objections, welcomed the marriage because "in her heart she thought I might do worse."

But Patricia was miserable. She wanted warmth from her husband and he had none to give. Their sex life was unsatisfying from the first night. During the early days he tried to have relations with her, but he stopped trying after a while. He also began encouraging her to show her body off to his boy friends who were never averse to "the peep show."

They were divorced two years after they were married. She was eighteen years old.

"I had a baby right afterwards. Janine. A friend of my husband's was her father. He said he wasn't, and I didn't argue with him. I figured to hell with him. Since my mother said she'd take the baby anyhow, there was nothing I wanted from him. Janine was an adorable baby. She's still a darling girl. Fourteen years old now, and been living with my mother since she was born. Well, that's the best way. For her, I mean. But, sometimes, I get so sorry for the poor kid.

"Like a couple of weeks ago she wrote me a letter saying she liked a pair of shorts I sent her, but I could've saved my money since I should have known her grandmother would never let her show her knees. All the girls in the neighborhood wear shorts, but Janine's got to wear old-fashioned gym bloomers. Poor little kid. Home used to be the same way for me. I think it wasn't as hard on my brother. I used to wish I was a boy instead, and now I wish Janine had been a boy. Boys have an easier life."

Patricia is always talking about how boys have easier lives and her conversation is revealing. It is one clue as to why she might have turned to prostitution. Her life is full of clues. Her second husband is one. He was an alcoholic and he beat her black and blue sometimes. Her mother, who always walked her own way so securely, thought she ought to grin and bear the beatings. She said a twice-divorced woman was not a pleasant creature in God's sight.

So Patricia, knowing that she would seek a divorce, felt cast out by God, man, and her mother.

But Patricia, unlike her mother, could not walk her own way. She needed other people and was always hurt because they did not need her. Still, she never revealed herself by a word or an act and always carried herself proudly, as though she, like her mother, felt herself above the crowd. She became a prostitute soon after she became aware of the vicious fact that her body was all she had to sell.

The recognition came after she had left Asheville and become an exotic dancer in the big cities and vacation resorts—Miami Beach, Chicago, Philadelphia, and, at long last, New York. Men drooled when she stripped. She made friends with the other performers and began considering herself one of the gang. When a girl friend who had star billing in a 52nd Street club solicited her for a hundred-dollar baby and openly admitted that he'd be paying her a twenty-five dollar commission in addition to the hundred for Patricia, she took him on as much to oblige her friend as for any other reason.

But none of the clues as to why Patricia Reardon became a prostitute begin to explain why a Southern white girl of religious upbringing seeks her love, such as it is, from a selfish, uneducated, irreligious colored man. How can a Southern white girl do all that this one does for a black man?

Like Black Cat's other girls, Patricia started as a call-girl. Her tricks, when she functioned as an independent instead of a cow, had been hundred-dollar babies who came highly recommended. Now, in line with the activities of her wives-in-law, she solicits in bars on the nights she has no other calls. She, who would once have collapsed at the idea of going to jail, has gone four times since Black Cat first came into her life. Each time she could have saved herself by revealing Black Cat as a pimp who lived off her proceeds. She was happy to go to jail instead. And each time she was there she lived for the mornings when she could look out of the barred cell window and see Black Cat out on the street. For this much he did to earn her gratitude, every time she went to jail for him. He came, rain or shine, in his sleek black Cadillac, and stood and looked up at her for a long moment. Just so she knew he was keeping faith with her. Not much, to be sure, but for her enough, and more than she ever knew about anyone else in her life.

He stands, this Black Cat, every morning of every day she spends in jail, and waves up at her before he steps back into the Cadillac she helped buy for him; and nobody can know the meaning his beckoning hand holds for her. It is stronger than all the judges, cops, and jailers put together. As long as he keeps coming and waving at her every morning, as long as she can point him out to her girl friends, "That's my sweet man beating the sidewalk there," she will stay in jail to protect him, and never ask out for fear of casting a smidgin of dishonor in his direction. If need be, she will go to jail again and again for him, until she gets to be so old he will discard her, the way pimps always do discard their old women. But she doesn't believe that now. Other pimps, maybe. She'll go farther during her worst moments. Other pimps, yes. But Black Cat is different. He loves her and would never kick her out. She can always count on him—she hopes. So why worry about the future, when you can take satisfaction from all your present blessings?

Patricia Reardon was brought up in all the tradition

of North Carolina. Indeed her mother hated Negroes
more than any of her neighbors did. She found them
physically revolting. The sight of their brown faces nauseated her. A woman alone and unable to afford white
male help, she still would not have a colored man to help
around her house. She would rather do men's work herself, finding it distinctly the lesser of two evils. She said
all Negro men were thieves and murderers and feared
that, living in a manless house, if she let any of them in,
they might take it into their heads to murder her and
her children. She always preached about Negroes to the
white unwashed who composed her regular congregations.
Today she still preaches about colored people, the same
sermons as before, only delivered with a shriller voice and
a greater heart.

"She's worse than she used to be for two reasons,"
Patricia says, "first, because of what's happened and second
because of Janine and all that school business down South.
She wrote in a letter the other week that she'd rather see
Janine dead than going to school with colored kids—be-
cause then she might travel the same road I did."

But Patricia never went to school with Negro children.
She used to share all her mother's prejudices, and she remembers too well how, when she regarded herself as the
lowest of the low, she was saved from touching bottom
by the comforting concept that, bad as she might be in
God's, her mother's, and everybody else's eyes, she was still
better than Negroes were. She remembers how she used
to yell "nigger," not just along with the other white children, but louder than any of them. She used to think of
worse taunts than the others, in the vain hope that this
might make them accept her. Maybe, if they had accepted
her, she might have gone on calling "nigger" all her life,

if just calling "nigger" made her pleasing to whites, even though there were times when she would have felt guilty over it.

"I used to play with this little colored girl. Kids do play together when they are young in my town. I liked her. She was a sweet kid. But then I stopped playing with her. My mother saw us together and prayed over me and bawled me out. I felt ashamed to think I ever liked her, and every time I passed her after we stopped playing together, I called her a dirty little nigger. My mother said I had no white friends on account of her."

But the white friends did not come trooping to her door after she gave the colored child up. She really had not expected them to. She had just hoped against hope that they might, and she was glad for the loss of the colored friend even though they did not come. In a way, that is. What really made her glad was that now she could feel at one with her mother over something.

"I often took on my mother's feelings," she says. "Sometimes I do it today. The story of that little girl reminds me of something happened after Black Cat and I first got together. I was arrested and held in Women's Court. The social worker there wrote my mother for some information and Ma came to New York. Black Cat waited outside of court for me, and when Ma and I came out, she caught onto who he was, just seeing us together. She's no dope, you know. She looked in his face and I heard her say to him, 'All my life I hated alley cats worse than anything in the world except niggers. God, but I hate niggers.'

"Listening to her I wanted to throw up. To think I'd been sleeping with a nigger! I hated Black Cat's guts and never stopped till Ma went home. Thinking of her this minute, I hate him even though I love him."

Again then, how can a Southern girl with vestiges, if

not more, of the Southern prejudices, become so involved with a Negro man? That question cannot be answered except in the light of all her life and all her experiences. It can never be generalized. Patricia's "how" is far different from that of all her wives-in-law. One of them, Jo-Ann Smith, is a good example.

Jo-Ann is in her middle thirties, a once-pretty blonde who has begun to fade. She was brought up on a farm in Georgia. She was seduced, literally, and carried off by the stock traveling salesman, and she started to prostitute after he left her. Despite her shame, she wrote home informing her parents of her activities. Their letter disowning her had not been unexpected, but still, she tried to commit suicide when she received it. She is known as a flagellant to her wives-in-law. One who knows her early background through a sister who came to New York says that she must always have wallowed in orgies of self-condemnation. She is still wallowing.

"I'd like to take all the money I make," she says, "and throw it in Black Cat's face."

Of course, she never will. Black Cat serves much too important a function for Jo-Ann. He is the best medium she has discovered yet for punishing herself. "Prostitutes are low enough, but me, I'm even lower, and I got a nigger lover to prove it."

Patricia's "how" is at the opposite end of the pole compared to Jo-Ann's. One important reason she hangs onto Black Cat is that he makes her feel high instead of low. He makes her feel warm and wanted in a way that nobody else has ever done, black or white.

"He calls me honey-baby. You ought to hear his voice."

In the long run Patricia's need to be loved is stronger than her need to conform to the culture of her native South. How could it be otherwise? If there is one generalization that can be made about all the Southern white girls who have taken Negro lovers, despite the barriers their cultures imposed, it is that they were never really part of their cultures anyhow. Secure Southern girls do not overcome taboos and take colored lovers; nor do they become prostitutes. To discover why they reject their cultures, one must first ask why their cultures rejected them and sickened them to the point where they were willing to go out and sell their bodies. Denied fulfillment, they come to feel as Patricia does: that Black Cat is more important than the culture which helped produce her and whose taboos would deny her the satisfactions he provides.

"He wants more than my body," she says. "He cares about me. Of course I love to spend my nights with him, but, after all the tricks I take on, it's not sex I look for from him. I want that too, sure, because that's a way I can be sure he cares about me. But what I really want is to feel his arms around me. I want to go out with him and know that he doesn't mind being seen with me, to feel I belong to him and that he worries about what happens to me."

All the girls say that sex is the least of their relationships with their pimps. They have, by the time they have been prostituting a while, disciplined themselves to the point where the physical act seems unimportant. They cannot afford to respond to sex with their customers even if they were equipped to do so. They can only respond to the men they think belong to them—their pimps. And so, to a prostitute, sex with her pimp is more than sex. And going out with him is more than going out. It is a sign to her starved soul that she is as human as any other woman.

When Black Cat takes Patricia to the Harlem bottle club they frequent, he treats her like a girl friend, not a whore. He is a friend and companion there in a public place, and he remains her friend and companion in their private relationships. When he comes to see her, when he calls her on the telephone, he acts interested in what she wears and eats and how she takes care of her health. It does not matter that he is only concerned for business reasons. Her life has made her into a past master at idealizing nothings. In some ways, she begins to think of herself as his wife.

A series of telephone conversations between them, as intercepted by the police recently, point up the relationship Patricia has developed with Black Cat. The last conversation of four which had been recorded was presented by the police as evidence that Black Cat was living off the proceeds of Patricia's earnings and that she was a prostitute. In it, he told her he needed money and she agreed to get some for him. The three conversations leading up to the fourth were not concerned with money at all but rather with the things that any two people who were fond of one another might discuss on the telephone. All four conversations, recorded and transcribed, were presented during one of Patricia's trials for prostitution. She was called "Defendant's Voice" and Black Cat was called "Incoming Male Voice."

Conversation on 3/11/55

INCOMING MALE VOICE: Hello.

DEFENDANT'S VOICE: Hello.

INCOMING MALE VOICE: What are you doing, baby?

DEFENDANT: Just sitting here and thinking about you.

INCOMING MALE: I got worried about you. Gee whiz.

DEFENDANT: What did you get worried about?

INCOMING MALE: I tried to get you for three-quarters of an hour and your line was busy, busy, busy.

DEFENDANT: Honey, those were business calls.

INCOMING MALE: Well, gee whiz, I was worried.

DEFENDANT: I'm sorry, baby.

But her voice revealed she was glad to have him worry about her.

Conversation on 3/13/55

INCOMING MALE: Hello, honey.

DEFENDANT: I'm sick.

INCOMING MALE: Why, baby, what's the matter with you?

DEFENDANT: I started bleeding again.

INCOMING MALE: Oh gee, baby. . . .

DEFENDANT: It's not heavy or anything. Just a little bit.

INCOMING MALE: Listen, baby, didn't I tell you not to take a bath? Will you please listen to me next time and not take a bath when I tell you not to? Gee whiz, honey, you ought to listen. (His advice may not be in line with the most informed medical opinion, but at least he cares when she bleeds. Nobody else does—not even the best and most ardent of her customers.)

Conversation on 3/17/55

INCOMING MALE: How's tricks, honey?

DEFENDANT: Oh, hello. I went to the Bronx and got those things, the hat and pocketbook.

INCOMING MALE: A big hat?

DEFENDANT: No, little. Sporty, to go with a suit.

INCOMING MALE: Oh, sporty. Well, I like a big hat.

DEFENDANT: A big hat wouldn't do.

INCOMING MALE: Really?

DEFENDANT: It wouldn't be nice.

INCOMING MALE: Well, if you say so.

DEFENDANT: I saw some green shoes to go with my bag. Green.

INCOMING MALE: French heels?

DEFENDANT: You dope, I couldn't wear French heels with a suit. A suit needs medium heels.

INCOMING MALE: Well, I like French, but if you say they wouldn't go. . . . I saw a pair of green shoes with French heels I wanted to buy.

DEFENDANT: No. Don't. They wouldn't look right with my suit.

INCOMING MALE: Well, O.K. I want them to look right.

Knowing Patricia's life story, one can understand why she would be willing to pay high for the attentions, such as they are, that Black Cat renders her. But that still does not answer the question of why a *Negro* pimp. Why not a relationship like the one with Black Cat, only with a white pimp instead of a colored one? The reason is simple: white pimps are few and hard to meet. Statistically, Patricia's chances of establishing contact with a white pimp are about one in ten. Pimping, like domestic service and other jobs lowly enough that white men do not want them, is predominantly a colored man's occupation. Pimps, like prostitutes, are not born to their occupations. They are fitted into them.

Black Cat's story could fit any one of many with only minor changes. He was born the third of seven children in Tennessee. His father, an occasional sharecropper, left the home when he was ten: just grew tired of a nagging wife and too many children with never enough money to feed them, and picked himself up one morning without saying good-by to anyone, even leaving his only suit behind. His mother's first lover inherited it.

Black Cat's mother did not mind the father's leaving. In fact, she was glad he was gone. All he had been was another mouth to feed, anyway. He just couldn't seem to find a job he liked. The only jobs open to him were dirty and demanding and didn't pay enough. Black Cat's mother, standing, dark-brown arms akimbo, sturdy, muscular legs placed wide apart, used to ask what enough was, anyhow. "Anything's better than nothing," she used to say, tossing the few dollars she made onto the table but keeping the solace bottle of rye whisky close to her chunky body, a protective hand over the nozzle, another hand poised ready to strike in case the old man had any idea of sharing the solace with her. She used to let him share in former years, even though he'd not been able to get or hold a job in those years either. But he'd been a good lover then, a sweet lover who could make her forget in the nighttimes the miseries of all her daytimes.

Now she was hunting another sweet lover like Black Cat's father had been in his younger years. She had different men on different Saturday nights, playing generous, kindly sweet mama with those whose loving pleased her and discarding the others "like old, brown banana peelin's."

"Wasn't nobody's business what she done with her daddy-o's," Black Cat says today. "That old lady was deserving of a good time one night a week. The way she worked like a dog all the time. Wasn't nobody's business."

Actually, in the small, unprivate shack, it turned out to be the whole family's business. All the children heard the sounds of the mother's contentment, and of her dissatisfaction when she screamed at her lover of the moment and told him to get out of her bed that very instant, but not before he gave her back every dime of the hard-earned money she'd spent keeping him in cigarettes and rye whisky all week long.

"You waitin' on me, boy, just laying aroun' all week waitin' for my handout. Just jivin' me and jivin' me along, and can't even fix me up fine. Ain't got it in you, boy, to fix a lady up. Go on home now, before I shoot your kinky head off."

She told him how she had taken food out of the mouths of her babes to bribe him. Only now she said she was through. Her children would always be first with her from now on. She could be grateful to that lousy lover for one thing. He'd taught her a lesson she was sore in need of learning.

If, on the other hand, the Saturday-night lover had done his work well, she talked differently about the mouths of her babes: so big they were and always open and damned expensive to feed. She told all that she would do for her daddy-o if only she didn't have to do for the kids. She would buy him a gold watch and a chain to hang it from and suits like her madam's (Black Cat laughs today at what he used to conceive a madam to be in those far-off innocent days of his childhood) husband used to wear to the plant he owned.

But Black Cat, listening to her talk to her light-o'-love, did not resent her for a moment.

"I lain on the floor with my younger brother—him and me put quilts down for sleeping there—and I was happy, happy Ma was getting such good lovin'."

He was happy because he often felt sorry for her on the days and nights that weren't Saturday. He knew too well how she worked and all the reward she got or could expect for the long hours. She left home at six o'clock in order to reach the madam's by seven, so that she could have a hot breakfast ready for the madam's husband by quarter of eight. The madam herself ate at a quarter of ten, off a tray in her bedroom. Then there were the two children, the little boy and girl to be dressed and combed and fed and fetched for. There was all the laundry to be done. The madam liked sheets changed three times a week, and the big house, ten rooms and three bathrooms to be kept, as the madam always put it, "spanking clean" and "in apple-pie order."

Black Cat's mother used to come home at nine, full of good ambitions about cleaning her own shack, but ending up with a lick and a promise, because her feet hurt so bad she wanted to soak them in hot water. Sometimes the soaking didn't help. She would spend hours with her feet in the boiling water which he and his brothers took turns heating. She would cry with pain, but still never take her feet out of the pan, because she was a persistent woman who wouldn't give up her belief that the hot water would stop her miseries one bright day.

"Poor Ma," Black Cat says softly with painful recollection. "A woman'd need a powerful lot of lovin' to make up for them achin' feet."

Her aching head, too. She got terrible, blinding headaches, but could never give in to them at work, because, now that she was growing older and no longer as desirable a worker as she had been in her younger years, she did her best to give her madam the illusion that she was as healthy as a horse.

Her whole work life was a lie, although to Black Cat it seemed more a puzzle than a lie. Every time she and her own children found themselves together in the madam's house, it was only the madam's children who got all her love. The way she picked those blond tykes up in her arms and made over them, calling them funny little love names, and every time she passed them by, every single time, giving them affectionate love pats.

"Who is it you're liking better, Ma," he used to ask, trying to keep the betraying quiver out of his voice, "me

or them white kids?" standing up straight and awaiting
her answer, just as though he didn't care at all and his
whole world wouldn't crumble if she answered wrong.

"Why, you, my honey-baby. Sugar doll."

Right as her words used to be, he could never quite
believe in them—or in her. He'd seen her tell too many
lies, play too many false roles—if they were lies and false
roles. Sometimes, he didn't know which was lie and which
was truth, which was good loving Ma and which was vicious
liar.

Once when he was eight and had accompanied his
mother to the madam's house for some reason he can't
remember now, he fell and skinned his knee. It hurt. So
he cried, not knowing in those days that some white
madams considered tears the God-given privilege of good
white children. His mother, passing, picked him up to
cuddle him a little, and the madam, passing also, looked
disapprovingly at the two of them and said that perhaps
she would do well to fire his mother and hire a childless
woman who could give proper love and affection to the
children she was hired to care for.

He stood right there, eight years old, and heard his
mother uncle-tomming that white madam all over the
place, heard with his own ears how she said that, although
he, Black Cat, was her own son, she had to admit that
he was a little black devil all the same. God have mercy
on her soul, hard as she tried, she couldn't seem to love
this son of hers, while the madam's children were golden-
haired angels, and such smart little ones, too. How they
played the piano. What a sturdy child the madam's boy
was. How well he could swim for such a small fellow.
The little girl was a dancing doll—nothing more nor less.
She was so proud of her two children, not that black devil
but the two lovely golden-haired ones, and she had no

greater satisfaction than keeping them looking beautiful and clean.

Black Cat wanted to say that he might have been a good swimmer and piano player if he had had the opportunity, but the words stuck in his throat.

Back home that night his mother soaked her feet and called him to her. "Come on over here and love me up a bit, boy." That meant she wanted him to kiss her and caress her face with his hands. He didn't want to go over and love her up and only went because he feared she might cuff him if he didn't. But with all the not wanting to go to her, he loved her terribly and wished he could be like her—strong, self-willed, not weak and vacillating, as his father had been. No question about it, no matter how much humble pie she ate in her madam's home, Black Cat's mother ruled her own roost and always had, even when his father had been there.

And why shouldn't she? Who got up for work before the sun rose, and had bunions on her feet, and a head that never stopped aching? Who supported the family anyhow? Not Black Cat's father. Why, then, shouldn't his mother be the one to rule? There was an old saying she had, and he remembers now that it went something like this:

> When you pay, sonny,
> You say, sonny.
> You don't pay, sonny,
> Better not say, sonny.

Sometimes, quoting this saying as often as she did, she seemed mean and inconsiderate. He wondered how it would be if he'd suddenly get a windfall of money and bring it all to her, but not before he'd take her old saying and throw it back in her teeth. "Listen to this one, Ma. Just listen to this:

> When you pay, ma,
> You say, ma.
> You don't pay, ma,
> Better not say, ma.

That would show her what was what and who was who,
she and all that preaching she was always doing about how
all her menfolk took advantage of her. "Like father, like
son," she used to snarl at him and his brothers, meaning
that the bunch of them were too lazy to get jobs. She was
wrong, though. He and his brothers were not lazy. They
were just too proud to do the jobs that were open to them.
They would have taken store clerks' jobs, if anyone had
been willing to hire them, but they didn't want to take
on the jobs of sweeping up the clerks' droppings.

And yet, in spite of all the conflict he had with her, he
loved his mother very much and knew, deep inside, that
she loved him too. It didn't matter that she acted bitter,
because she was so tired all the time. He knew how she felt.

Sometimes, on the rare nights she came home without her
solace bottle and feeling less tired than usual, they would
talk about his future. Her madam's boy was slated to be a
lawyer, and she said she wanted Black Cat to be one too.
He would fight the colored men's battles, she said, and set
his people free; but they both knew that he would be
nothing of the kind. The one-room colored school, hous-
ing grades one through eight, did not turn out lawyer
material. Indeed, only a few of its graduates went on to
high school.

No, Black Cat knew very well he would never be a
lawyer. He always knew it. He wasn't fated that way.
Aside from everything else, he wasn't very smart at reading
and writing and such. He sometimes thought that, if only
someone had helped him learn, things might have been
different. There was no one around to help him. Miss

Wilson, the teacher, was always busy tending to the little kids, and his mother couldn't read and write, herself.

But, in the long run, reading and writing proved to be unimportant in his life, anyway. A man didn't need those skills to be a good lover.

After his mother, tired of the South and wanting a fling at something else, brought the family up to Harlem, he got himself a "skinny old mama stringbean" instead of a job, and devoted himself, for a short while, to keeping her happy. He was not yet seventeen and she showed him how—not that he ever required much showing. His sweet mama stringbean said he was "a natural born from the word go," and she lived for her Saturday nights with him.

She wanted to give up her sleep-in job so she could spend all her nights with him, but he stopped her by making it clear, without actually telling her in so many words, that she'd never be able to support him in proper style off the proceeds of days' work, which could not be counted steady. So she kept her sleep-in job and saved most of her week's salary for him. She had a small savings account when he first met her, and she dipped into that for him too.

But it seemed as if the more she gave him the more he needed. Besides, he developed an eye for the younger, prettier chicks after he'd been with her for a while. It wasn't long before he discovered that, if a good-looking boy played his game right, a mama stringbean was nothing more than a steppingstone to slicker chicks and better things.

Could Black Cat logically have taken any other direction than he did? Perhaps, but where could it have led him? Nowhere but the same dead end from which his father, children or no, had finally to seek escape. Negro pimps, drawn almost entirely from the lower economic classes, must, if we are to have any chance of discovering their motivations, be viewed by the light of the lives of other men in their groups. What happens to the men who are not pimps? Are they good family men? Are they any happier than the men who become pimps?

In so far as it is possible to generalize, the answers to both questions are the same. No, the majority of them are not—not good family men and no happier than the men who become pimps.

Robert Jenkins is a case in point. He is a handy man in his early forties, who has never in his life been able to stick either to a job or to a woman. He has had four wives, a number of sweethearts, and so many different jobs that he has been unable to keep track of them all. As for the jobs, he says that one was more impossible than the other, dirtier, more poorly paid. As for the women, this is what he says: "All my womins were nothings, thought they were somethings. Bosses. Always bossing, bossing. How come? Because there's plenty good jobs for womins. But none for mens."

Bill Miller, unemployed but expecting to get a good job tomorrow, for the past thirteen years has been supported by his wife and daughter. He has this to say about them both: "Mean. One of them's meaner than what the other one is. One of these days I'll up and get me a job and walk out so fast those two ain't going to see me for dust."

Bill Miller and Robert Jenkins are victims of their world, more sinned against than sinning, and so is Black Cat.

The roots of oppression grow deep in lower-class Negro America, and there is no way of knowing whether they will produce a Black Cat or a Bill Miller, neither of them calculated to bring comfort to white America. Black Cat may be smoldering more openly, but Bill Miller is smoldering, too. He does not like the role white America has assigned him any more than Black Cat does. The only difference is that Black Cat has found a sort of escape for himself from the indignity that the lower-class Negro man has always been heir to—the indignity of having to sacrifice his male prerogatives to the women in his life.

In lower-class Negro America, the women, not the men, control the purse strings. Domestic jobs for women are always available, always have been, and always will be. Jobs for men are dirtier, less desirable, and less available. So that even men who are fortunate enough to have been raised with their hearts in the right place and a yen for a wife and children of their own soon find the realities of their economic situations overwhelming. It is not just the dirty work and the low pay alone; these they might be able to tolerate. It is the superiority of the women who can do so much better than they that is so constantly galling. In a sense, the able women become unfeminine and domineering, and the men, resenting the domination, keep trying to prove in the only ways open to them that, although they may be down, they are not out. They do it by playing the numbers, and getting drunk on whisky, and making up to enough women to look as though they count for something after all.

In effect, pimps go the other men of their class one better. They take advantage of the reversal of the male-female role instead of sitting around and lamenting their lot. They say to the women, "All right, be the breadwinners, then. We've got to let you since we have no other choice, but pay us off, as we would be paying you if we were in your positions. We will be sexual objects for you since we haven't training or capacity for anything else. All we ask is that you pay us for being what we are."

TEN / John is for John Doe

The most important links between our world and the strange world prostitutes inhabit are the customers, the tricks who make the profession profitable. Court attachés call them "Johns," as short for "John Does."

As the word *Johns* would imply, prostitutes' customers were historically anonymous men in the court drama. Now they are used as witnesses to testify against the women.

"I hate most of my tricks," says Peggy Collins, fat, red-haired old-timer. "They come panting at you like dogs. Then, when push comes to shove, the rats get up on the witness stand and sing like birds. Now, do you call them men? Take the law in this city, too. It's a wacky law'll let a man go with a girl and then get up and tell all about her and get her put in jail, while he goes off like it was a one-way act he didn't have anything to do with himself. Listen, if a girl's guilty why ain't the man who goes with her just as guilty?"

Peggy's question is echoed, in one form or other, by many who are concerned with the control of prostitution. In New York, as elsewhere, the law which regards the prostitute as a criminal and at the same time recognizes her partner as a routine witness to prove her criminality has

excited the widest controversy. Some people call the law
"schizophrenic." Why, they ask, should our society be so
double-faceted? Why should a man be permitted, even encouraged, to have his good time and then to walk away free
while the woman who has provided it for him is punished?
Others say that punishment is not the answer for prostitutes' tricks any more than it is for prostitutes themselves.

Who *are* prostitutes' tricks and what drives them? We
have never made a real attempt to find out. Why? Perhaps
because we are afraid. There is a natural human reluctance
to discuss sexual morality openly. It is even more difficult
for us to approach men and women who are sexual deviants with any degree of objectivity.

Actually the answers to the questions of who and what
are prostitutes' customers are challenging and shocking.
For prostitutes have all kinds of customers. Certainly they
cater to the perverse men who require strange titillations,
but they also cater to "respectable" men, good husbands,
good fathers, salt-of-the-earth types who are recognized as
the pillars of their communities.

Prostitutes have customers of late middle age and over
and have made a specialty of analyzing their needs and
catering to them. Some of them understand better than
most people the problems older men can experience in
their sex lives.

"Poor things," vibrant twenty-seven-year-old Anna Gray
says. "They come to us because they're afraid they aren't
men any more and their own women wouldn't want them.
They figure with us they can try, and if they don't succeed,
well, so what? We won't make fun of them the way their
own women might. And we know what to say to make the

old codgers feel good. 'Honey, you're the greatest,' we say, or, 'I don't know any young man who's as good a lover as you are, doll.' I wonder why their wives don't tell them those little white lies themselves. The way I figure it, most of them don't come to us for variety, or because they want young girls, or anything like that. They only come because they're afraid they aren't good enough for other women. They're the saddest fellows in the world."

Anna Gray is right. Sit around Women's Court for a day or two, and you will be overwhelmed by the pathos of many of the older witnesses. They are often bewildered by their own roles, humiliated and embarrassed by their presence in court. Many of them sit in court and hate themselves for their associations with the women with whom they have gone, and they tell themselves they will never be caught dead again with the likes of prostitutes; but, still and all, deep in their hearts they know they will, because they are driven by the need to overcome a feeling of sexual insecurity now, and the drive is almost stronger than they are.

"What good am I in the world, if I can't be a man any more?" sixty-two-year-old Martin Lanna asked, after he had shamefacedly finished testifying against the twenty-year-old prostitute with whom he had gone. "And why is it that a prostitute can make me feel like a man, while my own wife can't? Sometimes after I go with a woman, I look at myself and say, 'Martin, are you really the man your family thinks is so great? You're not great. You're disgusting.' And yet those girls make me feel good while I am with them. I forget everything else. It's like a dream. I guess all old men have sex dreams. Or maybe not. But I can't help myself. I go to the movies. I watch television, and I see myself being a wonderful lover to a beautiful young girl.

So I go out and pick up a prostitute. A fine end to my beautiful dream. I never met any prostitute yet who was the kind of girl men dream about. But they do give me the illusion I'm young again—for a little while."

Why does this tall, dignified man need the illusion? Outwardly he appears satisfied. He is an engineer, and, although he is not rich, he is comfortably fixed. He has a home in Connecticut, which he and his wife built when they were first married forty years ago. His wife is lovely and charming. He has a son whom he considers "a good friend," and three grandchildren whom he adores and who love him very much too. He has many good friends both in New York and Westport.

"Still I'm ready to risk everything for an hour or so with some prostitute who'll make me feel like the young man I really know I'm not. Sometimes I think I must be crazy.

"I look at my wife and she's not growing any younger either. But she doesn't seem to mind. Why can't I be like her? I take pleasure, just as she does, in the comforts of old age, our children, and their children. But still, even when I'm with them, I start wondering if I'm played out as a man, and before I know it, I've left my home and gone hunting for a young chippy who'll reassure me. I manage to forget while I'm with her that I am paying a high price for the compliments she pays me.

"Oh, how terrible when I remember, though. There are times when I can't bear to look into my wife's face. She has such a good, kind face. Then there are my grandchildren. I can't stand to hold them on my lap. I feel as if I could sully them with my dirt. And sometimes I look at my daughter-in-law. My son's wife is a lovely girl and really precious to me—and I think, 'Patricia, darling, what would you say if you knew your old father-in-law was with a girl last night who's ten years younger than you are? Could you still respect me? Or would you want to turn your back on me? Would you look at me and wonder if my vulgar seed was in my son? Could you ever grow to hate him on my account?'

"Sometimes after I've been with prostitutes I come home and start to cry. All my life I've been a man who couldn't cry. So my wife becomes frightened. She puts her arms around me and holds me close, and I know how much I mean to her. One time, when she asked me what was wrong, I almost told her. But I bit my tongue and kept my mouth shut. Sometimes I wake crying in the middle of the night because I've dreamt that my wife has left me. Then I feel out for her and I am comforted to know she is in the bed beside me. So I tell myself, 'Darling, darling, I'll never go to prostitutes any more.' But still I go. I could suffer an eternity for one single hour of the illusion of youth. Why are men so stupid?"

But not all older men suffer for their illusions. Prostitutes all know men who take unqualified pride in what they characterize as their achievements with them. These are the ones who have learned to deal with their unholy secret urges and even to be proud of them. They are like children with new toys, less inhibited now in their old age than they were when they were young. They boast about their "conquests" and quote the prostitutes on their "virility." They never stop vaunting their exploits, not even when they find themselves sitting in courtrooms.

Angelo D'Annunzio is such an old man. He is seventy-six years old, a small man with white hair, sparkling dark eyes, and the courtly manners of an Italian gentleman of the old school. Recently he was a witness to the prostitutional activities of a buxom, thirty-year-old woman who had been found by two vice squadmen in a hotel room with him. He sat as though the witness bench from which he testified was a throne and talked kindly but condescendingly to the judge and the two attorneys who questioned him. Asked to describe his activities with the woman, he said, "I was promenading on Seventh Avenue when I eye on her and she eye right back on me. I got near to her and I say 'hello' and then we two begin to promenade till we came to a place, a hotel it was, but I don't remember the name."

"Did you and she have any talk before you got to the hotel?" the prosecutor asked him.

He nodded.

"What kind of talk was it?"

"Talk of friendliness." He smiled at the judge and held the smile until he elicited one in return.

The prosecutor asked, "What do you mean by friendliness?"

He stopped smiling. "You really ought to know that yourself."

"But I don't know myself."

"Then I tell you. Having a good time between her and me."

"Did you offer to give her any money?"

He hesitated before he answered. "No money. Only a present. Seven dollars."

"What happened after you got to the hotel?"

"We take a room. What else?"

"What did you do in the room?"

"What did I do in the room? What did I do in the room? Why, I done the same as you yourself would do." He grew coy. "Or maybe you wouldn't. Maybe *you* wouldn't."

"Did you remove your clothes and did she remove hers?"

"No," he said, "no, we didn't. I was starting to get undressed, but two policemen came in and make me stop. We could not have good time because the two policemen came to the room. Why they do that, anyways? Why is their business what a man and a woman do together between them? She likes me and I like her. So why the policemen care if we want go together? I got the satisfaction, she got the satisfaction, only the policemen says no. They stop us. Why?"

Later, after the woman he had been with had been adjudged a prostitute and sent to the Women's House of Detention, he expressed his resentment over the judge's decision to his son who had accompanied him to the court. The son, a burly man in his late forties or early fifties, was embarrassed in the presence of the court personnel who were standing around and listening to his father, but the old man didn't care.

"What for they send that girl away? Just because she gives me a good time? Why they want to stop citizens from having a little fun?"

His son, speaking more for the court personnel than he was for his father, said, "Dad, prostitutes are bad women."

"Bad!" He looked ashamed to have borne such a son. "How you know that, Mr. Smarty? Believe me, street woman is very good woman. A man in my years, where else I get a young woman like I need, except she is in the street?"

He turned philosophical. "I tell you, my son, a country should be proud when it got old men can still keep young women happy, like me. They all tell me the same—I'm better than young men. You should be proud, my son."

His son continued to look embarrassed.

He said, "You ought respect your father. You don't respect me, I tell you what I do with them young women. You want I tell you?"

"No, Dad," his son said. "Please."

"You should be proud. I tell you. . . ."

His son grabbed his arm and started walking him out of the courtroom. "All right, I'm proud. O.K.?"

"Yeah, O.K." He withdrew his arm and walked jauntily out in front of his son.

Prostitutes approve of customers of Mr. D'Annunzio's quality. They particularly approve of them in contrast to the ones they get from the other end of the age pole—the teen-age boys who come to them at about the same rate numerically speaking as the older men do. Between them, oldsters and teen-agers comprise, according to many street-walkers' most accurate figures, somewhat less than one-third of their would-be clienteles.

"I say would-be," fat, fortyish Margie Gannon says, "because no girl in her right mind would take those little punks on if she could help it. Most of them are plain mean."

Prostitutes all say that the teen-agers, in striking contrast to their elderly customers, are coarse and offensive. They are exhibitionists, inclined to come in groups and perform for each other's benefit. Many of them request aberrant acts, not because they like them, but because they enjoy regarding themselves as sophisticates. Naturally the women resent the motivations almost as much as the requests.

"I hate those punk kids like poison," Margie Gannon says, "because I know most of them need us girls like holes in the head. But if you listened to them talk, you'd think they were big men burning up for a woman. Funny, but they all seem to like my type. I'm sorry to say I can't return the compliment. Would you believe it, a funny-looking fourteen-year-old punk once told me he'd never have come to me if I wasn't as old as I am. And as fat. Yes sir, that

little thing who wasn't shaving yet had the gall to tell me
he liked his women fat. How do you like that pot of apples?
Fourteen years old, *he* likes his women fat! He was just
one of a whole slew of kids I had last year. They came out
of a private high school. They were rich kids and *spoiled*.
Wow, they weren't afraid of anybody, especially their parents. Why, I know punks whose parents know all about
their coming to me but are too scared to stop them."

Many of the younger customers who land in Women's
Court could serve as prime examples for Margie's theories.

Young Jim Credon, sixteen years old, says his parents
know all about his activities. "Every once in a while, they
try to talk to me but I don't let them get to first base. After
all, they never have told me what to do before. Why should
they think they can start now?"

Seventeen-year-old William Arnold says, "My folks
would hate to have me think they're old-fashioned. Mother
always tells me, 'Billy, darling, you have a modern mother
and there isn't anything you can't tell her.' I always like
to tease her because she's so doggone teasable, so once I
said, 'Oh, there's one thing, mother.' She said, 'No, there
isn't, Billy.' I said, 'How'd you like to hear about my
whores then, ma?' She said, 'Don't be silly,' and made believe she thought I was kidding her. I don't think she really
did. I'm pretty sure she knew I wasn't."

But many parents, who are not timid with their sons
and who do their best to control their comings and goings,
find themselves no match for the social pressures the boys
are exposed to outside their homes. They are defeated before they start trying to influence their sons by the prevalent concept in young America today that sex, not sex and
love, but sex alone, the mere completion of the sexual act,
is a verification of male prowess. Sex and lots of it is one
of the important means for attaining status in young Amer-

ica, and nowhere is that more evident than among prostitutes' youthful patrons.

"What do you mean, what do I want with prostitutes? What do you think I am, a pansy or something? I'm a fellow's got to have my girls."

Of course there *are* some boys and young men who are driven to prostitutes more by their own physical needs than by social pressures. They are not nearly so prevalent as the others, however, and are regarded with greater sympathy by the prostitutes themselves.

Nineteen-year-old Charles Roberts is typical of many teen-age tricks. He tells his own story:

"I'm in my junior year at college. I'm premed. I have a year of college and four years of medical school ahead of me. I also have years of interning ahead before I can expect to earn a living. This means I can't begin thinking about marriage for at least seven years. Naturally sex is going to be a problem for me. What do I mean, *going to be?* It already is. The girls I go with don't have the same needs I do. They want to go out on dates and to have me kiss them and neck with them. But they really don't want to go to bed with me or any man. Maybe I shouldn't say 'want.' I really mean 'need.' I guess girls' feelings aren't as strong as boys', and so they can resist them better. Sometimes I feel so tensed up after a date, particularly with a girl I like, that I don't know what to do. I mean, I'm physically ill with wanting a woman."

He is a good-looking boy and knows plenty of girls he could have affairs with, but affairs with girls who are not prostitutes involve obligations he does not feel ready to shoulder.

"If you have an affair with a girl you like," he said, "you might find yourself getting closer to her than you thought you would. I mean, you can't really dispense with sentiment in such matters, and once it enters the picture, your goose can cook pretty quickly. I knew a fellow in premed started out having an affair and ended up falling in love with the girl. He left school to marry her. I know another fellow made his girl pregnant. He's a loving daddy, delivering laundry now. I can't afford affairs that might cost me my career. Prostitutes are cheaper. Not that I don't hate going to them; I really do. But what can a man do when he knows he has no choice except to accept what's open to him? And most prostitutes are really big-hearted. I've had high-priced girls who told me to keep my money because they knew their fees would break me. I don't think it was because they enjoyed going to bed with me, either. Believe it or not, they just felt sorry for me."

Charles Roberts' experience is not peculiar to him. Many men have found prostitutes to be sympathetic to their needs. Mostly, however, they have been men whose sexual outlets differed from the norm and whom the prostitutes could pity as they would themselves.

Sex deviants talking about prostitutes, for example, will give a picture of feminine compassion that is truly remarkable. That is, provided they are true deviants and not thrill-hunters. No matter what their seeming likenesses, prostitutes can usually manage to tell the difference. And while they condemn the thrill-seekers, they are more tolerant of true deviants than society has ever been. And with less reason. They are often physically hurt when perverted men, who come to buy relief, find their weird drives leading them into channels of savagery the women do not bargain for.

Rita La Verne, who started prostituting some thirty years ago in established houses located in San Francisco's Chinatown, says, "I know lots of nuts of all kinds, types, and natures, and all I can say is, if a girl's got a heart, she can't help feeling sorry for the characters. Sure, they want you to do queer things with them, but that's because they're queer inside of them and so what can they do? But I must admit, some of them sure *are* queer. I met a couple could knock a girl's eyes out with the things they wanted her to do for them. A new girl can hardly believe she's hearing and seeing straight. Like me and the first queer I got just two days after I began in the business."

She was working one of the fanciest houses in Frisco's Chinatown in those days. The madam had built her clientele over long years. Every customer was personally known to her, and, she claimed, as dear as her own husband would have been—if she'd had a husband. She usually instructed her girls about the requests new clients might have. Sometimes she even rehearsed them so that she could be sure of perfect performances.

"But she forgot to tell me anything about this trick I'm talking about and I wasn't prepared. He was a good-looking fella of about thirty-five. If I ever saw a guy who looked like a man, this one was *it*. Then he started undressing and I got the surprise of my life. He wore women's clothes underneath his suit—silk stockings, a girdle, a slip, everything.

"Well, I was so young and innocent I thought he was trying to be cute or something. So I remembered what my madam said about customers always being right and I did what I thought this one wanted me to—burst out laughing. Well, the poor queer. That made him feel just terrible. He put his clothes on in a hurry and ran out of my room and down the stairs. I followed him, begging him to come back, but I might as well have saved my breath. He was so mad he couldn't look at me. He ran all over the downstairs hall yelling for my madam. When she came, he bawled the daylights out of her. He kept saying, 'I've never been so insulted in my life before,' and crying like a baby. I felt like a low heel. Then he turned to me and said, 'Oh, you dumb little whore, you. You dumb little whore.' He sounded just like a woman. I thought he was the queerest man I ever saw. I've seen plenty of queerer ones since, though."

One of them was a man she met soon after she came to New York and began free-lancing here. He comes to see her at least once a month, and sometimes twice, to have her sew up his chest with a needle and thread.

"I was very careful the first time he came," she explains self-righteously. "I told him he'd have to let me examine his chest for marks, because I wanted to make sure someone else had sewn him before. I wasn't going to be the first to do it."

Most prostitutes are as casual as Rita about the deviants they experience. So accustomed are they to the weird and the incomprehensible that no request can move them much.

Harlem prostitutes discuss the man named Ducky with lackadaisical good humor. Ducky lives in an expensive penthouse in midtown Manhattan and employs a butler and chauffeur who maneuver his contacts. The chauffeur, driving a black Cadillac through Harlem, shops around for girls Ducky might like. Once they are located, he asks them how they'd feel about earning a quick hundred dollars. None of them were ever known to feel any way but fine. But most of them do have questions about where they go and what they do. These the chauffeur declines to answer. He tells the girls they have to take a chance on him.

Selena May Washington, a twenty-two-year-old, willowy, brown girl, is one who took the chance. She tells what happened to her.

"He helped me into the Cadillac like my name was Queen of Sheba. He wrapped a blanket around my legs. He drove toward downtown. He never said a word from the time I got into the car till the time I got out. I didn't beat myself worrying, though. I just rode nice and easy and made believe the Caddy was mine. Before I knew it, I was in front of this drooly apartment building and a doorman helped me out of the car. I was sorry my sweet man couldn't see us. The chauffeur and I went through the door into this stunning lobby and then he helped me into the elevator that shot right up to the last floor.

"We got out and a man in a butler's uniform brought me into a room that was bigger than a dance hall. It was all dark except for one bright light coming down from the middle of the ceiling. I looked where it led and there was a big coffin on the floor and a dead man was stretched out. Wow! I started screaming. Then I noticed the dead man was smiling at me. I looked around for the chauffeur, so I could tell him to please skip the hundred dollars and let me out of this crazy house. But he was gone. The dead man opened his eyes and began looking at me. I screamed again. He started to talk. He said, 'Thank you for coming, young lady. And now I wonder if you would be kind enough to help me out of this coffin.' His hand felt very hot. I thought it would be terrible to go to bed with him, but he said I didn't have to. He pulled five twenty-dollar bills out of his pocket, gave them to me, and told me I could go home. Seems he'd got his kicks just from hearing me scream."

Sometimes prostitutes sound like women who have memorized a book on deviant sex behavior when they start talking about their customers. They have known men whose kicks, as they always put it, came from every kind of peculiar action, and they have learned to analyze and deal with them.

Almost every prostitute has had experiences with men who pay high to beat them up.

"We girls call beatings *dumpings*," says Kitty Ford, forty-two and undernourished-looking. "You got no idea how many tricks want to dump you. Sometimes they do it so hard you land up in the hospital. I don't take tricks for dumping unless I'm awful broke. Tricks pay a hundred dollars to dump girls. Sometimes more. I'd never take a dumping myself for less than a hundred. Awful things can happen to you when you get dumped. During the times I'm not too broke, I wouldn't take a dumping for a million dollars. Because how are you going to believe anything a dumper tells you? All he cares about is getting you to go with him. He'll tell you things like, 'I get my kicks out of little, teeny dumpings and I never in my life hurt a girl real bad.'

"That's what one dumper told me. Boy, you should have heard him talking. 'Honey,' he says, 'all I want to do is beat you up a little bit, and then I'll be finished. You'll have your dough, and I'll have my kicks. It'll soon be over and we'll part friends.' I kind of thought he meant what he said. Funny thing, I still think he did. In his heart I think he didn't want to dump me hard. But then, once he got started in on me, he got like there was a devil inside of him, and he just couldn't stop himself from dumping and dumping and dumping. I had that one around twelve years ago and I still got pains from what he did to me."

A few prostitutes actually specialize in taking dumpings. These may have regular customers or they may be referred to new dumpers by others who have used them. As a rule they are the least attractive of all the prostitutes, but some of them are handsome girls who are impelled by the pressures their pimps exert on them.

Marina Marlton is one of these. She is a tall redhead in her early thirties who services a clientele of twelve dumpers. All of them pay from two hundred to three hundred dollars a time, depending on what they require of her. They also take care of any doctor bills she may incur while she is with them.

"It's a terrible life," she says. "I'd never put up with it if my sweet man didn't insist. No free girl takes on dumpings. Sometimes I wish I was a free girl so I could get out of this crazy life. But since I got to have my sweet Bobby, that's the price I have to pay. He's expensive. His clothes cost me a mint. Where'm I going to get it except from the dumpers? Nobody else'll ever pay me as much. Besides, I got my life all figured. If I didn't take dumpers and make enough money to keep Bobby happy, he'd probably dump me around himself. I'd rather let the characters do it and keep Bobby feeling sweet and loving to me. You know how it is."

Most prostitutes who go in for perversions, however, even those with forceful pimps, prefer administering beatings to receiving them. Men who want to be beaten do not pay as highly as the dumpers do, but they are far more generous than most customers. Prostitutes meet a great many of them.

"Those poor jerks are all over the place," says Phyllis Mansfield, a husky, healthy-looking blonde in her fifties who is considered highly desirable by her masochistic customers. "All you have to do is walk down the street and you'll stumble over a couple of them who'll say, 'Baby, will you hit me with a whip? Will you run after me with a shoe? Will you sit on the couch and spit in my face?' The things they ask for! Jeepers! You know these guys are real

sad since so many of the houses got closed down in New
York. Every house in the good old days had special things
for them, all kinds of whips and knives and scissors for men
who liked to be cut instead of whipped. My best customer
wouldn't be coming to me today if not for the houses being
closed down."

Her best customer is a man of her own age named James
Lucas. He is tall and white-haired. He is a senior partner
in a successful New York law firm and he paints portraits
as an avocation. He agrees that he would never have started
going to Phyllis Mansfield if the formalized houses that
specialized in catering to men of his type had not been
closed down.

"Those houses were superb," he says nostalgically, "literally superb in caring for men of my type. Special girls were
assigned to us, and they were all well trained by a madam
who had a knowledge of our needs. They were of varying
types, I can tell you. Some of them were great big heavy
women like Phyllis, but not all of them. You'd be surprised
at how satisfying a well trained smaller girl can be. I pre
ferred smaller girls in those days, and all my madams used
to keep several little beauts around for me to pick from.
I really did feel at home in those houses. I've never felt so
much at home anywhere since. Where but in a house, after
all, can a man like me, whom society has dubbed immoral,
be himself?"

James Lucas claims that he began to fantasy about
women whipping him when he was a young boy.

"I still remember the first sexual dream I had. I must
have been about fourteen. I was with a queen of a woman.
I couldn't describe her accurately any more, but I remember how beautiful she was. She leaned down to me and
asked if I would care to serve as her slave. I told her yes.
Soon afterward, I felt at ease inside of me in a way I'd

never felt before. She said, 'So be it then. From now on, James Lucas, you are my slave.' Then she took her right shoe off and tried to beat me with it.

"So, you see, when Phyllis or some other sleazy prostitute whips me, I don't see her as she is. To me, she is nothing less than the queen of my dreams. If you'll pardon the melodrama, I'd like to ask by what right other people attempt to deprive me of my queen. Why is my sex life anybody's business except mine and whatever girls I gratify myself with? Incidentally, some girls are pleased to do what I ask—aside from the money."

He is not far wrong. Phyllis Mansfield speaks for a good number of her cohorts when she says, "Sure, some of us like to beat the suckers. It's fun to see them looking foolish. I guess I feel that every time I do something one of those Joes wants, I'm getting even for something another Joe did to me. Mostly I make it my business not to feel anything with the suckers. But I do with these. It's great to insult them. I guess most women wouldn't like to stand and let a fellow kiss their shoes and then kick them in the face. I love it."

ELEVEN / Sex is something else again

Most of the men who visit prostitutes would be considered normal. They are neither too young, too old, nor too perverse for other women. Nor are they lonely men who have no women of their own. Most of them, as a matter of fact, come from the ranks of the respectably married, and usually have children. They may be young or middle-aged, poor, well-off, or rich. They are workers, professional men, and businessmen. They live in the city and outlying suburbs and take good care of their families. All of them are proud of their children and most of them claim to love their wives.

When you ask these men who claim to love their wives so much why they go to prostitutes then—most of the married men are habitual tricks, not one-timers—they seem to have one common rationalization. "I just got drunk and I didn't know what I was doing." They sit in Women's Court and look into the faces of the women with whom they have been and honestly do not recognize them, because, they tell you, that's how drunk they were when they picked them up. Maybe they were that drunk, and again maybe they were not. Maybe they were so casual they never took a good look at the women's faces. Truly, the casualness of many married tricks, not only toward prostitutes but also toward themselves as customers, is amazing. Listening to them, one might think that men who were men *had* to look up prostitutes, that that, in effect, was the nature of the beast.

"I've got to get a little excitement out of life, don't I?" one young man asked confidentially. "Of course I have a wife, but what does she know about exciting a man? I wouldn't want her to know anything."

He was a very nice-looking young man too, a tall, blond, clean-cut, American-boy kind of man. He was an executive in the branch office of a large corporation in the prosperous suburb where he lived with his wife and two little daughters. He was an active P.T.A. member and a class father. He had organized and was now helping to administer a Little League baseball team in his town. He enjoyed the activity as much as any of the kids did, he said, because having good, wholesome fun with younger people had always been down his alley. He belonged to a barbershop quartet, a bunch of guys who had come through elementary and high school together. That was the kind of fellow he was, loyal to old pals. He and his buddies had entertained at all the important town functions since they were kids together.

"I'm the star with the deep bass voice," he says jokingly, "but I'm not letting it turn my head."

Typical, clean-cut American man, and he was picked up in a Harlem hallway with a smelly, old prostitute in blue jeans and a torn red sweater. By his own admission he had been in Harlem hallways before, if not with this woman, then with some others like her. As it happened, he was one trick who had not forgotten the face of his woman.

"Do you remember this woman?" The prosecutor pointed to the cringing brown girl.

"Sure enough."

The prosecutor asked whether he had known her before.

"Well," he answered jocularly, "I should say I didn't."

"How did you meet her?"

"I wouldn't say I met her exactly. You see, I was standing in this Tornado Bar up in Harlem having a little drink, when she whisked in and started giving me the business. First she asked me if I'd buy her a drink. Then she said if I wanted to get fixed up, she was ready, willing, and able. Her price was twenty dollars. I whittled her down to five dollars."

"What did you do after you agreed on a price?"

"We started going to a so-called hotel she knew about. But I'd been there before and I knew what a filthy place it was. So I figured why spend the two dollars for the room? I took her into a hallway instead and told her I'd split the room rent with her. That's where the officer found us."

The girl, an old-time prostitute and narcotics addict, was convicted. He waved at her as she left the courtroom.

Later, he said he did not really like delivering testimony he knew to be calculated to "get the old whore sent away," but he was a man who always told the truth come what may. His wife said if there was one thing she worshiped about him, it was his faculty for telling the whole truth and nothing but.

"She calls me Georgie Washington sometimes, and the kids have taken her up and begun calling me that, too. We have more fun over it. I guess the only lies I ever told her concern these whores I sometimes go to. Well, I'd call those little white lies. Wouldn't you? After all, why hurt the little woman if I don't have to?" He turned reflective. "I sometimes wonder what she'd do if she saw me with one of my sluts. Probably wouldn't believe her eyes, if I'm any judge of what my girl's like. Every once in a while I wonder if she'd divorce me if she knew. But that's laughable. Of course she wouldn't. First of all, she has a responsibility to our children. Second, she knows a woman's got to put up with a man's little shenanigans."

Peculiar as his logic seems, many married tricks maintain that the fact that they are men entitles them not only to their flings but also to their wives' utmost tolerance. They are not to be blamed for their contacts with prostitutes. No, their wives should not be blamed, either. The miserable sluts they go with are the only reprehensible ones.

Lawrence Reid, a young bakeshop owner from Brooklyn, changes whenever he talks about prostitutes from a calm little man with mild blue eyes to a fierce defender of virtuous women.

"Take all the whores in New York, for my money, yes sir, every single slut who walks the street and throw her in jail for the rest of her life." He wipes his perspiring bald head and adds sentimentally, "for the sake of fine home women like my own dear wife."

Mr. Reid, all the same, is a constant customer of the prostitutes he would throw into jail—constant and regular.

"I go out to find a girl every other Thursday night," he explains. "That don't mean I don't love my wife. I do love her. Sure. Absolutely. Didn't I just finish buying her a mink coat? If that's not love. . . . Five years ago I went out and got her a Persian lamb jacket. Beautiful."

But love is one thing, he says, and sex is something else again. A man may love his wife and still expect sexual stimulation from the women he goes to bed with—all the women but his wife. A decent man ought never to grow lustful with his own wife. He ought not to expect to wallow with the woman he has chosen to share his life and bear his children, but since wallow he must, at one time or another, he has got to find women who are filthy enough to meet him on his animal level. Then, he can be clean and considerate and respectful of the only woman who counts.

Lawrence Reid cannot remember when he first began to consider love and sex incompatible. It must have been a long time ago.

"Maybe when I was just a little kid, for all I know. We never talked about sex in our house. My mother was a pure woman like my wife, and she would have been hurt by any talk. My father was a man who kept to himself a lot. I guess I talked to the other boys in school when I got to be around twelve or so. I had my first girl when I was about fifteen. She was a pig and I felt like one when I was with her, but I had to keep going back to her, anyway. That's what I mean when I say men have dirt inside of them that they have to get rid of with dirty women—if not prostitutes, then girls like that one when I was fifteen. The only thing different about her was she didn't have a price. Outside of that, well, she'd let you do anything you wanted with her and she'd do anything you wanted for you. Filthy little tramp. They ought to throw girls like her in jail with all the other sluts.

"Yes, sir, if I had my say, the bunch of them would be behind bars. They're menaces to men. They get men in trouble. They may be diseased, but do you think that they ever look at a man like me and think what did this poor fellow ever do to me that I should take a chance on making him sick? * Do you think any of them are that decent? Oh, no. They'll take me for everything they can get, and I'm

* The problem of venereal disease is not dealt with in this book. Twenty years ago more than half of the women who appeared in Women's Court were infected with gonorrhea or syphilis. Since that time there has been a reduction in the incidence of venereal disease due to progress in the prevention, detection, and treatment of the disease. Nonetheless, one out of every six women appearing in Women's Court today is found to be infected. The problem is however not peculiar to the world of prostitution and is largely a matter for medical science.

the one's got to worry about whether they're sick or not. What good does it do me to worry? I'm no doctor, and I can't tell by looking at her whether a girl's healthy. I'd have to take every girl I went with to a hospital for testing. A businessman has no time for such stuff. What would happen to my store if I took girls around to hospitals?

"No, all I can do is go with a girl and take a chance. All right, you say, you, Mr. Reid, are a grown-up man who can take care of himself. Maybe so. Maybe so. But then I have to ask you—what's about my wife? She's not a grown-up man and she can't take care of herself. She happens to be my concern. So what's about her? Suppose I became diseased, God forbid, and infected my wife—would that be fair? Don't you believe a whore who makes a good woman sick ought to be locked up?"

He means what he is saying. Men like Lawrence Reid feel deep hostility not only to the prostitutes who service them but also to all women who do not meet their specifications for purity. Their hatred of the women they use is part of the morality they have accepted all their lives and can hardly start rejecting now. Sex is dirty to them, and that is all there is to that. If they did not condemn the "bad women," they would have to condemn themselves, or their wives, and their marriages, or the scruples that so effectively prevent them from enjoying sexual relations with the women they elect to love. This sexual shame is perhaps the greatest single factor that forces respectable married men to cohabit with prostitutes.

But these men, in a way, are among the more fortunate of prostitutes' customers. They and their wives *both* regard lack of fulfillment as right and ordained, and so there is no intellectual conflict between them.

A strange phenomenon of recent prostitution is the customer who is driven to seek paid love not by the well-known frigid wife but by the sexually demanding one. Lately the growing recognition that women are entitled to sexual satisfaction has begun to create problems for some men, and nobody is more aware of them than the prostitutes, especially expensive prostitutes servicing men in the higher income brackets. According to the more perceptive girls, these can be divided into two major types: those who move in circles where extramarital sex has become an accepted practice, and those who, sleeping with their own wives, are worried, as they have never had to be before, about whether the women find them satisfying.

The rich men who move in circles that have accepted extramarital sex are the prostitutes' favorite customers. First, they can afford high tariffs. Second, they feel no guilt about their wives and so have no need to make the girls ashamed.

"Why should I be concerned over my wife?" asks Mr. William C. Blakesee, the tall, graying, forty-four-year-old banker. "Is she concerned about me when we're at one or another of those wife-changing brawls we're always having to go to? Actually, it would be more accurate to call them *husband-changing brawls*. I think the women out our way are afraid they might be considered stupid and domestic-minded if they didn't make passes at one another's husbands. Their status with one another depends on the number of men they can annex. Literally. Next to having the biggest house and the newest cars, the rarest furs (a couple of my neighbors are sporting chinchillas and Russian sables and calling their minks 'these old rags'), they judge each other according to the number of affairs they have. I'm not exaggerating."

Mr. Blakesee would be the last man in the world to condemn his wife for the numerous affairs he knows her to have had or even for the two times he found her in bed with other men. As a matter of fact, although he is long over being in love with her, he considers her an admirable wife despite her promiscuity. She is attractive, and a good hostess.

"She does her job, which is to keep our home running smoothly, and I do mine of bringing home the bacon. Naturally we are both crazy about our children, a son of twelve and two daughters, eight and five. Aside from the kids, we're compatible enough but not romantic. Well, that's no great loss. Who wants romance at my age? If I don't get much from my wife, it's still as much as I want from her."

Mr. Blakesee seems to want more than he cares to admit, however. He seems to want warmth and a feeling that his love-making means something—to somebody. Else why would he pay a prostitute a couple of hundred dollars just to make believe it does?

Mary Lee Louis is a prostitute, one of several, whom he visits more or less regularly. She is a twenty-four-year-old slender blonde with nearsighted blue eyes. She is not nearly as attractive as his wife, or so she says, anyhow.

"I've seen pictures of her and I look like a scarecrow compared to her. But he comes to me anyway. I've got something she hasn't got for him. He told me that himself. He said, 'Honey, my wife may be prettier than you. Let's be honest, dear. She not only *may* be prettier, she *is* prettier. But you've got more sex appeal for me. Making love to you's terrific.' "

Mary Lee says she does no more for Mr. Blakesee than she does for her other rich customers.

"I do what I know they want, make believe I'm ga-ga over them. Sometimes they act like little boys playing games. Mr. Blakesee always does. He plays the cave man.

He comes to my apartment and sweeps me in his arms and holds me till he thinks he's taken my breath away. It's a howl. After he's finished making love to me, I have to tell him, 'Darling, you made me so happy I could just cry.' You wouldn't believe a grown-up man would want to play such games. But he does. Not only him. Most of the rich ones."

Mary Lee is so convinced that her prime stock in trade with her wealthy customers is her ability to act spontaneous that she recently submitted to an operation for prevention of pregnancy. She considers it an investment in her career.

"I went to this doctor and told him he had to do something for me. He said it would cost me plenty because he could get put in jail for operating on a healthy girl. I said, 'Don't let's worry about the money, doc. I'll make it back and then some.' He gave me a big deal about doctors being supposed to make sick people well and not well people sick. The hypocrite. As though he didn't know I knew he aborted every pross in town. But I kept my mouth shut and let him talk on. After he finished, I said, 'All right, doc, you're a fine man and you always do what's right. Now, how much did you say you'd charge me?' "

He charged her seven hundred dollars.

"And it was worth every cent. I can't say enough about how much my big boys appreciate it. Now I let them make love to me and act like a little innocent who never goes to bed with men but can't help herself this time because they're so irresistible."

There are plenty of high-priced prostitutes who have learned the lesson Mary Lee espouses—to mix passion with their sex. They tell you that all the big spenders, not only those who live in places where free sex is regarded as the acme of sophistication, but also those who come to them surreptitiously, demand all the pretenses Mary Lee says they do.

High-class prostitutes know that the surreptitious ones, even more than the ones who come to them openly, are driven by the devastating fear that they may be sexually inadequate. Most of them, unlike Mr. Blakesee and his cohorts, would be profoundly disturbed if their wives learned of their activities. They could not, as Mr. Blakesee could, claim tit for tat, for, so far as they know, their wives are and always have been faithful to them. But still, they need assurance and reassurance of their virility, assurance that their wives, unfortunately, are either unable or do not choose to give.

One of them, a well-known two-hundred-dollar baby, is a forty-six-year-old textile executive, C. Estis Brown. "My wife never suspects me," he says. "She meets my train at 6:20 every day, and I never fail to be on it unless I happen to have a business meeting in town. And I do mean a legitimate business meeting. I'd never visit prostitutes on her time."

Why does he need to visit prostitutes at all? He finds it hard to explain but he tries, and, in the long run, he is glad he has attempted analysis.

"My wife sometimes frightens me so much with these newfangled ideas she's picked up. I was brought up in the old school says a woman's got to please her man. But my wife thinks it's the other way: call me a fuddy-dud, but I must admit I don't consider it fitting for my wife to tell me what to do in bed. I'm just old-fashioned enough to believe I'm the one should do the telling."

Carole Long, an intelligent, young red-haired call-girl, says that she hears C. Estis's sentiments expressed every day.

"It burns them up not to be lords and masters in their own beds, and so they try to make believe they are in ours.

Personally, I have no objection so long's a trick pays enough. I guess you could say I have a real advantage over his wife. I want his money, not his love. I know my only job's to make him feel good. His poor wife's counting on him to make her feel good. I don't believe men are made that way.

"Take this hundred-fifty-dollar baby comes to see me one or two times a week. Always says he enjoys being with me instead of his wife, because when he's with her he's so busy trying to please her he hardly has time to think about himself. He's often drunk when he comes to me, and then he tells me he wishes he'd been young when his father was, or else that he'd married a wife who was exactly like his mother. He says all his mother ever worried about was keeping his father happy. I tell him times have changed, and besides, I give him a better time than his mother ever gave his father. I ask him what fun sex could have been with a woman who didn't like it? He says maybe I've got a point. But the difference between wives and girls like me is that we like what men want us to, while wives like men to do what they want. He often says that men like him ought to divorce their wives and marry prostitutes. The only trouble would be that then the girls wouldn't be prostitutes any more, but wives instead, and so the men's troubles would probably begin all over again. Especially if the prostitutes began reading Mr. Kinsey."

But the effect of the recognition of woman's right to sexual gratification ought not to be overrated, as it so easily can be. Far more important are the old ways and customs that created and go on creating the women men call *frigid* and the men women feel to be unloving.

There is not a working prostitute alive who does not have to listen to daily complaints about how cold her customers' wives are. It is not surprising that the girls' sympathies are all with the wives. Knowing men as they do, they are convinced that wives have no choice but to be cold in pure self-defense. How could any woman respond to what these men can give?

Janet Clay, who has practiced her profession for thirty years, off and on, grins a little self-consciously because she has never been able to replace the three front teeth her pimp knocked out a couple of years ago, and says in her baby whine, "What do men want from their wives anyway? It's enough the poor things got to go to bed with them, without having to act like they like it too. That's asking too much. I hear those lice talk about what they want from women, and, if I wasn't forced to make my living out of them, I'd slap them down, too. They think all they got to do is snap a whip and their wife will come. Well, a wife's no horse. Why don't they learn to make love if they want their wife to like their loving? They don't know from nothing, and none of them seems to care very much."

Court records are replete with complaints such as the following made by wives who reject their husbands sexually and hold the men to blame.

Mary Lane (tall, slender, dark-haired, dark-eyed, thirty-one): "I loved my husband very much when we were first married. Now I hate him. When he wants me, he takes me. He never stops to think that I'm human too and that maybe my requirements are different from his on a certain night. I used to try to explain to him but he closed his heart to me. He knew only one thing—I was his wife. But I wasn't his slave. Why did he always have to treat me as though I were?"

Patricia Saunders (nineteen, blond, blue-eyed, baby-faced): "I don't want to lose my husband. I love him too much. I want to make him happy more than I've ever wanted anything else in the whole world. He says I ought to be glad he wants me and I really am. I keep telling myself I ought to want him too. But I don't. I just don't. He's so rough with me. If he really loves me the way he says, why does he have to be so rough with me? I wonder if all men are rough."

Marilyn McGuire (twenty-six, five feet two inches tall, 188 pounds): "A social worker told me that I eat so much in order to make myself unattractive to my husband. She may be right. The truth is I hate having to go to bed with him. My mother-in-law says I expect too much, just because I say I think a husband ought to kiss his wife once in a while and make her know he likes her instead of just using her. I can't remember the last time my husband kissed me. He never puts his arms around me. Once I asked him to after he was through with me, and he said he didn't want to be bothered."

Prostitutes all know men like Marilyn McGuire's husband, who, once they have finished their love-making, literally do not want to be bothered. And the girls, unlike the men's wives, do not want to be bothered either.

Janet often says she wishes her customers' wives knew their husbands as well as she knows them. Then they might stop expecting kindliness or affection.

"All men are lice, like I always say. Don't count on a thing from them. Whether you're a wife or a whore, take them for all the loot you can get out of them. They got nothing to give you but money. They couldn't be kind if they tried."

Janet's statement, and she knows it underneath the bluster, is belied by many married tricks, even including some of her own.

Marshall Jeffers is one. He is an engineer in his thirties, tall, dark, and a bit too intense-looking to meet Janet's standards for male good looks. He is still very much in love with his wife after nine years of marriage, and keeps praying for the day she may find him sexually tolerable.

"I was twenty-two when we married," he says quietly. "Louise was nineteen. I think she was the prettiest, most adorable girl I'd ever known. She was very shy and I must say I loved having her that way. She clung to me at our wedding because she was afraid to face any of the guests. I felt strong because of the way she acted."

But she was shy when they were in bed together, too, shy and fearful of her husband. He kept telling her that he loved her and would sooner cut off his hand than hurt her, but she did not believe him. She said she trusted him when he asked her outright, but she looked panicked while she nodded yes. He did not attempt to make love to her during the whole first week of their marriage.

"She cringed from me when I tried to kiss her. I did everything I knew to make her want me. But nothing was any good. Eventually she came to me when I asked her, but always with a too apparent effort. I am ashamed to say that I lost my temper with her a couple of times and told her that the least a wife could do for a husband was pretend to have some feeling for him. Everything she'd ever learned at home prevented her."

Marshall Jeffers says his wife came from a fine, ultra-respectable home with stern standards for family living.

"Her mother taught her all the things good little girls were supposed to know. She learned about the obligations of marriage as my mother-in-law conceived them. She was told about the responsibilities of motherhood before she could understand words right—all but the ones involving the making of the babies. She was made to feel that a good wife was synonymous with being a good housekeeper, that if she kept her husband's home well, he would love and cherish her forever. But she was never told that he might want her as a lover. I know my mother-in-law would die at the very thought. My father-in-law too, no doubt. Sex in their house was nothing more than a dirty necessity and so they saw no reason to discuss it with their little girl. My wife today is all her parents ever hoped she would be— one of the neatest housekeepers in our neighborhood and a doting mother to the two sons we managed to have. I think the old folks would believe me mad if I told them I required something more of her and had to go to prostitutes because she hasn't got it to give."

TWELVE / Sin in Old New York

Every civilization has known the phenomenon of prostitution and has dealt with it in its own fashion according to its mores and customs. Social attitudes have changed and go on changing through the ages. Prostitutes have been exalted as the most desirable of women; they have been tolerated as necessary evils; they have been scourged, whipped, and burned at the stake. They have been fined and jailed and, in some places, their partners have too. Still prostitution has persisted through the ages.

Today we recoil at the idea of burning and whipping and wonder how past generations could have thought such methods effective. Yet, knowing full well that arrest and imprisonment never have controlled prostitution either, we close our eyes to obvious realities and tell ourselves that, someday, they will. It is not unlikely that future generations will examine the methods by which we attempt to root out prostitution with the same sense of shock and outrage that we feel on considering past ones. They may also find them comical.

Prostitution in New York, and the present community approach to the problem, can best be evaluated in the light of past events.

Sin, in the early 1800s when Broadway and Chambers Street marked the outskirts of town and Times Square was a wilderness, was no sly thing. Everyone knew that the Five Points area of the bloody old sixth ward was the place where everything went. Its most notorious street, Little Water, was lined with decaying old tenements that bore such labels as Gates of Hell, Brick Bat Mansion, and Jacobs Ladder, named for the rickety old stairs that ran up and down its outsides. Prostitutes huddled together in all those houses, living cooperatively and dividing, share and share alike, whatever money they made from their fifteen- and twenty-cent customers.

The worst building in Five Points, the one that housed more prostitutes than Brick Bat Mansion, Jacobs Ladder, and Gates of Hell all put together, was the Old Brewery that had been built in 1792 and transformed into a dwelling after it became too ramshackle to be used for its original purpose. It housed about 1,000 people and averaged at least a murder a night. The police would never go within hollering distance of it except in great force. More than seventy-five men, women, and children, mostly recent immigrants, freed Negro slaves, and prostitutes of every kind, made their home there in one great room called the "Den of Thieves." Sweeney's Shambles, two rows of connected tenements with over a thousand residents, was the second most sordid tenement in town and had the second largest number of resident prostitutes.

But the free lancers who occupied the tenements could never compete with the prostitutes who worked out of the organized houses. The Five Points houses were numerous and varied. Some of them offered weird entertainment along with the women. Kit Burns's place, Sportsman's Hall, occupied the whole of a three-story frame house on Water Street and featured, among other attractions, and in addition to young girl prostitutes, Jack, the Rat, Kit's son-in-law, who would decapitate a live mouse for ten cents and a rat for a quarter. One-armed Charley Monell, assisted by Gallus Mag, a giant Englishwoman who always kept her skirts up with men's suspenders and dragged obstreperous customers out by their ears, ran the Hole-in-the-Wall at the corner of Dover Street. Big Sue, the Turtle, a 350-pound Negro woman, ran a thirty-five-cent house for seamen and fishermen on Arch Street between Broome and Grand.

The most famous house in Five Points was kept by John Allen. He was a slender, dandified man, member of a wealthy and pious family who, around 1850, left Union Theological Seminary, where he had been studying for the ministry, and brought his young wife to Five Points. They opened a dance hall and house of prostitution staffed with twenty girls dressed in black satin bodices and bright red skirts and stockings. The daughter of a lieutenant governor of one of the New England states lived there for a while. Strangely, Allen remained a devoutly religious man despite his occupation and made a nuisance of himself by trying to convert his customers. He often interpreted the scriptures to captive audiences of musicians and harlots and put Bibles in all the cubicles where the girls took their men. On holiday nights he gave copies of the New Testament away as souvenirs.

Through the years, some of the older tenements began to crumble, and the whole Five Points area, surrounded as it was by improperly drained swampland, became known as a malarial center. It began to decline as a place of amusement and finally had to begin to reckon with a new up-and-coming sin center—the Bowery.

The Bowery achieved its first notoriety in 1826 when the Bowery Theatre was opened to the public and set a precedent for dozens of other such houses of entertainment. Prostitutes were among the theater's most ardent habitués. They swarmed the galleries, using them not only for purposes of pickup, but also as places where their relations with unfinicky customers could be consummated.

Sometime in the 1830s, a visiting English dignitary who had been taken on a long tour of the city's underside wrote home, "There is not a dance hall, a free-and-easy, a concert saloon, or a vile drinking place that presents such a view of the depravity and degradation of New York as the gallery of a Bowery theater."

The Englishman's opinion notwithstanding, many knowing people believed that the other Bowery institutions, the playhouses, concert halls, saloons, basement dives, and beer gardens, were more reprehensible than the theaters.

The huge beer gardens could seat 1,000 to 1,500 people at a time. Some of them served drinks for three cents each. Barrels stood on shelves behind the bar and their contents poured out through long lines of rubber hose. Customers were entitled to all they could gulp down in a single breath. No glasses or mugs were used. The most popular saloons provided entertainment along with the drinks—music, dominoes, cards, rifles for target shooting, and twelve- to sixteen-year-old waitresses who were willing to retire to back rooms.

All the concert halls, playhouses, and basement dives featured back rooms and accommodating young girls. They competed with the "houses of joy" whose operators were Tammany ward and district leaders.

One of the first known attempts to reform the "ladies of easy virtue" of Five Points and the Bowery began one Sunday morning in 1830. It all started because Mrs. Jonathan Starr, a rich member of the popular Free Church, did not like what she saw when Miss Julia Wainwright of

Bowery Hill strode up the church aisle in a beplumed, beribboned, dissolute green hat. When confession time came around, Mrs. Starr was the first to rise and expatiate on the debauched bonnet. She forgot in her righteous indignation to mention her own sins. The other ladies were so moved by her speech that they banded together as soon as church was out and formed a society against gay dress. They named it the Female Benevolent Society, or the Holy Club, and set to work snipping ruffles and ribbons off their clothes. They also swore to enter the home or hotel room of every woman who lived between the Battery and Washington Square and to pray for her conversion to proper apparel.

Despite its intrepid participants, who elbowed their way into houses that did not welcome them and stayed on their knees until they were thrown out, the Holy Club program was a sad failure until Mrs. Starr came forth with a new idea. Why not seek out houses where many women lived together? One prayer could then do the work of twenty.

But even Mrs. Starr's crusaders could not bring themselves to go down to Five Points and the Bowery. So they invited their husbands and brothers to membership in F.B.S. and calmly instructed them "to visit the brothels and converse freely and feelingly with the women."

Mr. Leavitt and Mr. Beebe, the first pair of man Female Benevolents, had even less success than their women had had. They suffered jeers and catcalls. In the very midst of praying on their knees, they were beaten by some champion bouncers. They went home and told Mrs. Starr that the ladies ought to do their own dirty work.

Mrs. Starr consulted Mr. Tappan, the richest and most upstanding member of the Free Church, about the problem of handling prostitutes who did not know how to behave when their betters came to pray with them. He suggested that the church buy a few buildings in the red-light areas and set up Sabbath schools that would teach the denizens not only to dress modestly but also to be well-mannered toward their superiors.

One of the first applicants for the job of Sabbath-school teacher was a pious young man from Princeton, a Mr. McDowell. He was assigned the Five Points area and had hardly been there a week when he came face to face with the horrible sight of a fellow Princetonian who had been successfully solicited by "the dirtiest of wantons." This experience convinced him that fancy dress was the least of evils and that it was harlotry that had, in reality, to be eradicated. Mrs. Starr had now met her match when it came to fervor. McDowell was so inspired that the Female Benevolents took new vigor from listening to him and cheered when he said that the Association ought to go after fancy women rather than fancy clothes. He suggested it change its name to the Magdalen Society and that he be appointed its salaried chaplain. The rich Mr. Tappan was elected chairman of the board of trustees of the new organization.

As the first move in his crusade, McDowell started a publication called "Purity and Truth." It solicited literary contributions from penitent Princeton and Harvard men who had lost their virtue to prostitutes. He then located a place where fallen women would have to listen to his preachments like it or not—Bellevue Prison and Hospital. The women who worked at hard labor enjoyed the leisure of their visits with him. They competed to tell him fascinating stories of their fall from virtue, all replete with pictures of their first seducers. Interestingly, most of them were students of the type who wrote for Mr. McDowell's journal. Now, he began to reverse his magazine's philosophy and to print more stories about ladies who had been corrupted by college students rather than vice versa.

His success at Bellevue inspired McDowell to even greater ambition on behalf of fallen women. In his first annual report, he proposed that his society undertake to sponsor a home for them. It would be called "The Asylum for Females Who Have Deviated from the Paths of Virtue and Are Desirous of Being Restored to a Respectable Station in Society by Religious Instruction and the Formation of Moral and Industrial Habits." At the asylum, McDowell declared, a prostitute could be saved for the bargain price of one dollar per week per girl. And he had himself worked out a circular which would ensure that country people as well as city folk would be induced to contribute funds to the project. It read: "Country Parents Protect Your Sons. Board A Magdalen For $1.00 A Week."

The response, aside from a few joking letters from young men who purported to misunderstand McDowell's meaning and enclosed directions whereby the Magdalens who would be sent them for their dollar contributions could find their farms, was gratifying. The first building was erected only a few months after the campaign had begun and the first contingent of triumphant Bellevue graduates was installed. Each prostitute who entered had her last name taken away and Magdalen substituted for it so that she would be sure to remember the depths of hell she had plumbed before arriving at this heaven.

But the prostitutes proved ungrateful. Although they spent their daytimes in loud praying and singing, come nightfall, they sneaked out of the asylum and repaired directly to their old haunts. It was disheartening, and conditions did not improve as the old contingents gave way to new ones. If anything, the girls grew bolder as the months wore on. In his second annual report, McDowell had to admit that only four girls had stayed at the asylum for as long as a month and only one, Rosaland Magdalen, had been converted to respectability.

Faced with such results, plus a little matter of some four thousand missing dollars which the devout McDowell could not explain, Chairman Tappan closed the doors of the asylum, sent his chaplain packing, and announced that he, himself, would take over the Bellevue visits.

The prison inmates found Tappan less congenial than McDowell. He persisted in doubting most of their stories. Yet he, not the gullible McDowell, heard and swallowed a confession that made the former chaplain's stories sound like Sunday-school exchanges.

A sweet-faced young thing claimed to have escaped from the nunnery of the Hotel Dieu in Montreal, Canada. The dreadful tale she told of the scandalous doings of nuns and priests was published, with Chairman Tappan's help, as "The Awful Disclosures of Maria Monk." Canada requested that an American-Canadian Commission be appointed to investigate the charges. After the story had been exposed as a fraud, the young girl who had told it resumed her life at Five Points where she had been born and bred, and the Magdalen Society stated publicly that it had had its full of fallen women.

After the Civil War, other areas joined the Five Points and the Bowery as sex centers. Hundreds of bagnios, protected and operated by Tammany politicos, sprang up all over the city, especially in the area from 24th to 40th Streets between Fifth and Seventh Avenues, nick-named Satan's Circus. Here there were several houses on every block that had red lanterns gleaming in their windows.

The most elegant Satan's Circus places were the seven adjoining houses run by seven sisters on West 25th Street near Seventh Avenue. The inmates of "Sisters' Row" were musical and well read. They were advertised via circulars and newspapers as "cultured and pleasing companions." On holidays they received in evening clothes and would not take patrons who did not come in formal dress. Both girls and madams, sentimentalists at heart, always gave their Christmas Eve proceeds to charity.

Much less elegant than any of the houses on "Sisters' Row" was the Haymarket located on Sixth Avenue near 30th Street. It occupied the whole of a three-story building and, although it looked a dreary place in the day, it was a dazzling place at night. Red and white lanterns blazed out of every window. Women were admitted free. Men paid twenty-five cents to enter, fifty cents to see women dance in the nude, and a dollar for a long and involved "circus."

Of the many houses in between the high-priced Seven Sisters and the lowly Haymarket, the French Madame's, grew to be the best known. The French Madame, a fat, bewhiskered old dame, advertised her place as a restaurant even though she served no food, except black coffee. Her girls demanded a dollar for their nude dances and two or three for their circuses.

Along about January of 1866, Bishop Matthew Simpson of the Methodist Episcopal Church, who had, as he later wrote, "held my nose" and made a tour of Satan's Circus, the Bowery, and the Points, stood in his pulpit and lashed out at the "city's greatest evil" and "the mad-dog politicians of Tammany Hall who encouraged it because the vicious element that profits gives votes and money to keep them in office."

"Why," he exclaimed to his shocked congregation, "are you aware that there are more prostitutes than Methodists in our city?"

The clergyman's outburst angered his congregation, but left the politicians guffawing. They said there were *not* more prostitutes than Methodists in New York. And they did nothing to remedy the conditions the Bishop railed against. Indeed, many of the most depraved dives functioned in the immediate vicinity of police headquarters on Mulberry Street and the owners, rightfully feeling secure against assault, used to joke about the locations they had chosen for themselves. Big Johnny Dobbs, whose saloon catered primarily to prostitutes, policemen and their mistresses, was once asked by a naïve outsider why so many madams and crooks had established themselves around headquarters. He answered: "The nearer the church, the closer to God." His witticism was repeated all over town.

And so, despite periodic exposés, the situation continued open and unashamed until 1892 when a new brand of reformer came upon the scene. He was the Reverend Charles H. Parkhurst, sober-looking, dark-eyed, fifty-year-old pastor of the wealthy and conservative Madison Square Presbyterian Church. One Sunday morning in February he entered his pulpit and proceeded to denounce policemen who were in league with prostitutes and racketeers, brothels that, in New York, were "almost as thick as roses in Sharon," and Tammany politicians who countenanced such conditions. He called the politicians "incarnations of the devil—polluted harpies that, under the pretense of governing this city are feeding day and night on its quivering vitals—a lying, perjured, rum-soaked and libidinous lot."

Dr. Parkhurst was immediately denounced both by the politicians and the press. His sermon was described as "vulgar—unchristian—violently vituperative." Other members of the clergy suggested that, since wickedness seemed to hold such attraction for the holy man, he ought, henceforth, to talk about Sodom and Gomorrah. Charles A. Dana, editor of the *Sun,* thought he should be driven from his pulpit. On February 23, nine days after he had spoken out, Dr. Parkhurst was haled before the Grand Jury and told to produce proof of the charges he had made. Since his evidence was vague and general, he was rebuked for his "irresponsible accusations."

A weaker man would have retired to lick his wounds, but not Dr. Parkhurst. Instead, he determined to secure the kind of firsthand knowledge no jury could scoff at. He hired a canny, hard-faced, mustachioed private detective named Charles W. Gardner to show him the city's night life. Gardner dressed him in a pair of loud flannel trousers, a brown slouch hat pulled low over the right eye, and a bright scarlet neckerchief.

"If ever a man looked the tough," he said later, "that man was the Reverend Charles H. Parkhurst."

So outfitted, the minister began his sleuthing with a visit to the dives of Five Points. In one place a young prostitute asked him to dance. An old crone in another one parked herself on his lap and begged him to call her "baby." On the Bowery, where they went on their second night out, Dr. Parkhurst plumbed the mysteries of a "tight-house," where all the inmates wore tights, and "a German house" where he was offered any one of five nearly nude girls. On a third evening the minister and the detective went through all the Satan's Circus establishments, including Mrs. Hattie Adams's expensive house, located only three blocks from the minister's own church. Mr. Gardner told the Adams girls that Parkhurst was "a gay boy from the West." The minister himself bought beer for everyone and watched a circus in which seven women, naked except for black stockings and red garters, danced, high-kicked, and played leapfrog. The extrovert, Gardner, served as frog.

On Sunday, March 13, two days after his Satan's Circus tour, Dr. Parkhurst chose as his text the ninth verse of the twelfth Psalm, "The wicked walk on every side while the vilest men are exalted." Everyone, parishioners, and the overflow crowd of visitors, knew to whom he had reference.

"I have been down into the disgusting depths of this Tammany debauched town," he thundered, "and found it was rotten with a rottenness that is unspeakable and indescribable, and a rottenness that would be absolutely impossible except by the connivance, not to say the purchased sympathy, of the men whose one obligation before God, men and their own conscience, is to shield virtue and make vice difficult. Now *that* I stand by, because before Almighty God I know it. . . ."

The Grand Jury, forced to recognize the validity of the new Parkhurst accusations, requested that the four commissioners of the Mayor's Police Board and some captains and inspectors come in and talk about the connection between the city's vice and its policemen. Although it could not gather enough evidence for a single indictment, it did find that: "The police are either incompetent to do what is frequently done by private individuals with imperfect facilities for such work, or else there exist reasons and motives for such inaction which are illegal and corrupt. The general inefficiency of the Department is so great that it is our belief that the latter suggestion is the explanation of the peculiar inactivity."

Historically, when a police department is under fire, a complete reshuffling of the Top Brass ensues. This occasion was no exception. Superintendent of Police William Murray resigned, and his successor, former Chief Inspector Thomas F. Byrnes, shifted every police captain in the city to a new precinct.

"This is the great shakeup," Byrnes told newspaper reporters.

Dr. Parkhurst, asked for his comments, smiled acidly and asked whether the Superintendent was so guileless as to suppose that a captain who had been corrupt in one precinct would suddenly turn honest in another. All during 1893 he kept hammering away at the unreformed police department, seemingly to no avail. And then it was the November election. The Legislature went Republican for a change. When it convened, it appointed a committee, headed by State Senator Clarence E. Lexow of Nyack, to examine the minister's anti-Tammany charges. John D. Goff was appointed counsel to the Committee. He was a virile-looking man with a full white beard and deep blue eyes. He was known to be an ardent foe of Tammany Hall.

Goff called Police Commissioner Charles F. MacLean as his first witness. The Commissioner, after Goff had raised a few important questions about his abundant bank account, came down with a bad case of "brain fever" that made it impossible for him to give further testimony. As the investigation progressed other police officials found themselves suffering from other strange ailments including "inability to sleep," "some confusion of ideas," "embarrassment of speech" and "actual insanity."

Soon after Commissioner MacLean was stricken, Goff began interrogating madams and brothel keepers who were reputed to have bribed policemen.

A middle-aged German named Charles Priem said that he had bought a house owned by the wife of a police sergeant. He had paid "initiation fees" of five hundred dollars to all the captains who had ever been assigned to his district, and a total of $4,300 to the men on the beat.

Mrs. Rhoda Sanford, a widow with four children, said she paid the police fifty dollars a month and bought tickets to Tammany parties and outings.

Mrs. Evelyn Bell, a pale thin woman in orchid, also

testified to the payment of fifty dollars a month for the past ten years.

Mrs. Matilda Herrman, fat and bejeweled, known as the "French gold mine" among the officers, declared that she had paid the police $20,000 in two years.

As the investigation progressed, with the interrogation of dope addicts, saloonkeepers, and gamblers, as well as madams, Goff became so popular that several reform groups and newspapers urged him to run for mayor in the next election. He refused, although he let it be known that he would like to run for recorder, an important judicial position. A fusion reform ticket was organized with William L. Strong, a liberal banker, for mayor, and Goff for recorder. Tammany ran a well-known hack, Hugh J. Grant. The campaign was heated and vitriolic. Dr. Parkhurst, the Fusion party's most voluble speaker, urged voters to realize that this election was a clear fight between Christ and Counsel Goff on the one hand, and Satan, in the person of Hugh Grant, on the other. On election day, Satan was defeated hands down, Goff securing a plurality of 53,517 votes. Before taking office, Goff continued his duties as Committee Counsel and called the Police Superintendent, inspectors, and captains as witnesses before the Committee.

Timothy J. Creedeon, the most irreproachable among the police captains, a volunteer fireman and a Civil War veteran, a teetotaler and a man who had sworn off smoking, told how he and many other captains had to pay for all their appointments and promotions.

Max F. Schmittberger, another captain, testified that from close to a thousand dollars a month he collected from the brothels, saloons, and gambling houses of his district he had to pay two hundred to his immediate superior, Inspector Alexander S. Williams. He also said that some houses could not be touched by the police because their madams had been granted immunity by certain higher sources.

Many other witnesses were called, and their stories were all the same: pay-off for protection.

The last police witness Goff called was Superintendent Byrnes, known as the Great Detective. He had accumulated some $350,000 in real estate and securities during the thirty-two years he had served on the force. Arrogantly he declared that he had "obtained more years of convictions against criminals than the detective forces of Scotland Yard, Paris, and Jersey City all put together" and then surprised everyone with the admission that the department was rotten from top to bottom. The investigation was over when he stepped down from the stand. With the whole Police Department shaken up, some people said New York, with the reformers at its helm, was a clean town now.

But on November 2, 1897, only two years after the Lexow Investigation, a Tammany candidate, Robert A. Van Wyck, was elected mayor, and men and women snake-danced through the streets singing, "Well, well, well, reform has gone to hell." The establishments that had been forced to close their doors during the short-lived respectable era opened up again with ribald song and shouting, and new houses sprang up like mushrooms all over town. The "good old days" were back with one significant change—the business that had been conducted by rugged individualists in former years began to organize now. Entrepreneurs decided that one for all and all for one could be advantageous to everybody. A force combined could be more useful to Tammany and exact more favors in return than a force divided, especially if all its members were good neighbors with great numbers of votes in their collective pocket.

The best-known prostitutional gang in Mayor Van

Wyck's New York was the Independent Benevolent Association. Nicknamed the Sam Hochstim Club for a local politico, it operated among the Jews of the lower East Side of Manhattan. All its 200 members, whose names were one of the open secrets of the day, were politicians, and its vice president was Martin Engel, Tammany leader of the Eighth Assembly district.

During its earliest operations, Frank Moss, president of the Council for the Prevention of Crime, had this to say about the Association: "They manage several clubs which are influential in local politics and which afford them the power to watch their poor women victims, to secure their hard and ill-earned money and to punish them when they are refractory.... They stand by each other and through the aid of the powerful politicians of the ward and of professional witnesses, they send refractory women to the Island [prison]."

Association members affected amazement at "the foul-mouthed Mr. Moss," and summoned the wrath of God down on his head. They said they were just a company of poor lonely men, who had formed together as a burial society. They explained that their name provided all the clue anyone would want as to their real functions. The Independent Benevolent Association, not the Association of Red Light Operators.

Actually, the Hochstim Club, controlling the traffic of women to many houses, not only in New York but all over the country, *was* originally formed as a burial society. Its members, all free-lance prostitutional operators, had been cast out of the larger Jewish community on the East Side. No legitimate Jewish organization, whether social or benevolent, would have any traffic with them, and even the associations set up to assure poor people decent burials refused to take them in. Ordinarily, the Hochstimites would not have cared. The poor Jewish society of the lower East Side was not one they aspired to enter, and, as for burial associations, they certainly did not have the same need for them as the pious men who belonged. They knew that when their time came Tammany would provide as many guests for their funerals as the most pretentious of them could wish. They were rich enough to pay for their own graves. So they remained untroubled by the exclusion, until one melancholy day when Martin's brother Sam Engel, a big-wheel politician in his own right, died and they all gathered at the funeral parlor together. They began to talk about the frailty of human life, Tammany-protected or not, and a few men expressed self-pity over their summary exclusion from neighborhood benevolent associations. One word led to another, and before Sam's body had grown cold, the I.B.A. became a reality. It incorporated under the laws of New York and, as its first order of business, bought for cash an expensive and beautiful plot in Brooklyn's Washington Cemetery.

Through all the years during which the organization functioned, meeting in the "coffeehouses" where members guzzled tea, the care and upkeep of "the plot" was the first item on the agenda. Only after that was disposed of did they go on to the mundane business of which madams needed girls for their houses.

The Hochstimites secured their girls from among the prettiest of their neighbors' daughters. They hired handsome young men, known as *cadets* in the business, who applied all their energies to seducing suitable girls. The seductions generally came easy. The girls, recently come from Russia, Austria, and Poland, had been raised on the golden dream of the golden land—America, the home of the Lady of Liberty, America whose streets were paved with money, America where Jews were considered as good as other people, America the beautiful. But it was not beautiful once they arrived. The streets were not paved with money, the overcrowded tenements were sickening places, and new Jews were called *greenhorns*. Slowly but surely, they began to give up the golden dreams they had been raised on. They began to see the poverty and the ugliness as inescapable. If America was not the golden land, what place was?

Then one day, they met the boys who wore good clothes like American men and told them they were beautiful, and all of a sudden the girls found their dreams again. No use for the fathers to beat them or the mothers to talk in woeful tones. I don't want to be a servant all my life. I don't want to sew, sew from morning until night. And when the boys asked them how they'd like to go away with them, they thought why not? They were in love, and besides, what was there to go home to?

Some girls refused to go, however. They went on dates with the cadets, accepted their hospitality, and then, at the end, remembered their parents at home and said they could not break their hearts. Then the cadets pleaded with them, offering everything, even marriage, which was easily faked in those days, and, when the cajolery failed, used stronger means. They brought them to houses on one pretext or another and left them, if not drugged or drunk, crying and screaming.

Many Jewish families, overwhelmed by this plague that had been visited upon them in the new land, worse than any misfortune that had happened in the old, cast these daughters off as dead. Some of them went through the ancient ceremonial for the dead—slashing the lapels of their clothing and sitting out seven days and nights of mourning. And always, week by week, month by month, the number of mourners increased.

And the Hochstimites grew rich as the years went on and they branched out and expanded. One group, leaving their cadets to continue soliciting the fruitful East Side, went to Newark and placed many Jewish girls in the houses there. Some went to Philadelphia and joined the Mutual Republic Club of the 13th Ward. Many settled in Chicago.

By 1900 the activities of the Hochstimites and the other prostitutional gangs had aroused an indignant city to demand action. A committee of fifteen community leaders, including William Henry Baldwin, Jr., president of the Long Island Railroad, Felix Adler, founder of the Society for Ethical Culture, Jacob H. Schiff, of Kuhn, Loeb, and Company, and George Haven Putnam, of G. P. Putnam's Sons, the book publisher, was formed to investigate prostitution. In 1902 it issued a report of its findings:

"The employees of disorderly houses openly cried their wares upon the streets and children in the neighborhoods were given money and candy to distribute the cards of the prostitutes. . . . Honest police officers who attempted to perform their duties were defied by the many cadets who openly roamed the streets or by powerful madams. A virtual reign of terror existed among the honest patrolmen and the ignorant citizens of the districts. The infamy of the private house with all the horrors arising from the cadet system did not satisfy official greed. Prostitutes began to ply their trade in tenement houses. In many of these houses as many as fifty children resided. The statistics of venereal diseases among children and the many revolting stories from the red-light district tell how completely they learned the lessons taught them. . . . Out of 1,200 hotels investigated in New York we were convinced that at least 700 were places of ill resort that revealed conditions too vile for publication."

The Committee declared that the hotel traffic had been intensified in the year 1896 by the passage of the Raines Law for New York State. It stopped saloons from dispensing their wares on Sundays, but permitted hotels, defined as places with ten bedrooms, a kitchen, and dining room, to serve liquor whenever it was ordered.

Since Sunday was a very profitable day, most saloon keepers opened "hotels" and many of them began to rent the necessary ten rooms out to prostitutes and their customers. Soon almost all the saloons had bawdy houses attached to them. The upper West Side, particularly around Cathedral Parkway and 110th Street, became overrun, although it had previously been clean of prostitution. Little Coney Island, a nest of numerous Raines Law hotels and infamous dance halls, was located there.

In its essence, this report of the Committee of Fifteen was not unlike all the other reports that had come from all the other reform groups year by year, almost month by month; but people became as indignant as though they had never heard such grisly details before. Officials responded to the public clamor and demanded police action.

They got action. Every night plain-clothes officers went out into the streets, picked women up by the dozens, and placed them under arrest. They were held along with petty thieves, wife-beaters, and drunks of both sexes. Nobody knew when trial would take place, and the so-called criminals, regardless of whether they would be judged innocent or guilty, had to stay behind bars unless they could muster what came to be known as "the station-house bond." Bondsmen charged phenomenal rates to prostitutes, often twice what they charged others. Since the police were in the habit of bringing the same prostitutes in night after night, it did not take a master mind to recognize the fact that bondsmen and policemen might be in league to fleece the women. So the reformers objected again. In 1907 they were rewarded by the creation of a Night Court that, hopefully, would combat the police and bondsman evil by offering immediate arraignments and trials.

The Night Court held its sessions at the Jefferson Market Court, under the elevated, at Tenth Street and Sixth Avenue. Although set up to try men's cases as well as women's, anyone observing the court in action might have thought that New York's only criminal activities were engaged in by prostitutes. Thirty, forty, fifty women a night were lined up before the bar of justice. The judge listened to policemen's testimony and then acted as he thought the cases warranted. He could discharge a girl with a light reprimand, or he could fine her anywhere from fifty cents to five or ten dollars; or else he could send her to jail for twenty-four hours or three years.

A few of the old-timers in their sixties and seventies who had contact with the old Jefferson Market Court are still around today. Although they talk passionately about graft and police brutality and harried judges, they have a fond feeling for "old Jeff" based, for the most part, on the practice of fining. The women with connections got off; the others went to jail. The reformers, dazzled by the unprecedented number of arrests, seemed unaware of the system's manifest unfairness. With so much police fervor, they declared, New York would soon become the cleanest city in the country.

Police enthusiasm continued and arrest records mounted year by year. Fallen women crowded the courtroom. It soon became apparent that one Court could not properly service prostitutes and other lawbreakers at one and the same time. Besides, a few reformers began questioning the efficiency of a court which operated on fines and without a fingerprint system. All of which was reason enough for

another investigation, this time of the administration of
the lower courts. It was conducted by Senator Alfred R.
Page, and it found that the reformers were right in some
of their plaints. It recommended that a new Night Court
for men be established and that the Jefferson Market Court
become the new Women's Night Court. It also called for
the installation of a fingerprint system for women convicted of prostitution, and asked that all fines be abolished
in favor of prison sentences.

Very early in its existence Women's Night Court became
a feature of New York's night life, a sort of after-theater
rendezvous.

It sought patronage with the issuance of such publicity
material as "Women's Court—Information for Visitors,"
which proudly stated, "There is considerable space for
spectators, the floor sloping from the entrance, so that all
have a clear view of the proceedings."

Shiny-faced ladies held onto their husbands' arms as they
strained to catch the stories of the painted prostitutes and
the plain-clothes policemen. The stories were all much
the same—the officers telling how they had put themselves
in a position to be picked up by the women and how they
were picked up. "She asked me to have a good time so I
asked her how much she wanted; she said fifty cents so I
went to her room and she stripped naked and then I pulled
my badge and arrested her." Most of the women, looking
hunted and scared, pleaded guilty; but a few setting themselves up against the officers called them liars. Magistrates
of the day generally took the officers' word, right or wrong.
As the then Chief Magistrate William McAdoo put it,
"How can the magistrate be expected to take the word of
one of those painted hussies as against an honest policeman?"

Few people disagreed with the Chief Magistrate's views.

One of the few was Anna M. Kross, later a magistrate who frequently presided in Women's Court, and presently New York City's Commissioner of Correction. She was a young lawyer, chairman of the Legal Committee of the Church of the Ascension.

"Unfortunately, the Chief Magistrate loses sight of the fact that no decent man would ever take the work assigned to the plain-clothes men, and that even those who have some spark of decency at the outset of their careers lose it very quickly on their jobs," she said, and went on to assail the Women's Court itself, its judicial procedure, and its rules of legal evidence as "almost a travesty on justice."

Early in 1910 those who were bucking the current found brilliant support in, of all unlikely places, the office of the new mayor, William Gaynor, a former judge of the New York State Supreme Court. Almost as soon as he took office he visited Women's Court, and as a result he abolished the prostitutional vice squad. He said its very existence was a denial of civil rights. He said that he had seen women brought beaten and bleeding into court, that he had seen them enticed by officers into offering themselves, that he had seen them framed. He said the city had no right to degrade its officers by turning them into trappers of women whose immorality it could not hope to change anyhow.

"The business of government," he declared, "is to maintain law, order, and outward decency. Uniformed policemen can doubtless accomplish this business better than decoys can."

Mayor Gaynor was too far ahead of his time to accomplish much, and, when he died in 1913, the plain-clothes vice squads were reestablished. They quickly made up for lost time. With nobody around to question their methods, they arrested more prostitutes than they ever had before. The public was pleased with them, and wishful thinkers again acclaimed New York as "a clean city."

On November 1, 1917, the Bureau of Social Hygiene published its report, "Commercialized Prostitution in New York City." Triumphantly declaring that "the commercialized exploitation of vice on a grand scale will be reduced to a minimum," it gave all credit to a new Police Commissioner, Colonel Arthur Woods.

New York [it said] has been made an unprofitable field of operation for these people, many of whom have lost thousands of dollars trying to operate despite police activity. . . . How completely the subjugation of this class has been effected is evidenced by the words of one prominent member of the former "vice trust," who, shaking his head earnestly, said in May of this year, "I'm afraid things are today and will be forever this way, as far as New York is concerned. The people are educated. There was a time when they used to say, 'New York can't get along without blood money.' That's poppycock; look at New York today. New York is done. Vice is under control."

Still prostitutes continued to pour into Women's Court *
by the hundreds. Nobody would know from observation
there that vice was "under control." And there were those
imprudent people around who went so far as to question
the validity of the report of the Bureau of Social Hygiene.
A few months after it was issued, Anna Kross wrote a letter
to Mayor John Purroy Mitchel which stated:

Prostitution has not been checked but the sporadic efforts of the police have simply compelled the underworld to resort to more secretive methods and created more need for graft. . . . The rounding up and incarcerating of unfortunate prostitutes does not solve the problem. . . . You will admit, I believe, that the underworld lives only by virtue of the fine network

* Night sessions were abolished on April 19, 1919, and Women's Court again became a day court.

of graft into which many members of the police force have frequently been enmeshed. Have you ever considered how many crimes have never been revealed? How many injustices have been done? The arbitrary power placed in our police department is the best means of covering up any and every act of the department.... I am advised that prostitution and white slavery still flourish in this community.

THIRTEEN / History repeats itself

Prostitution changed its face a couple of times in the 1920s. During the first two years it was as furtive a business as it had ever been before. The times demanded secretiveness. Contrary to popular impression, those years were grave and sober. The newspapers were full of talk of the high cost of living and somebody invented the Hard Times Party. Broadway and its side streets, victimized by the twin blights of war and prohibition, lay in sparkless ruins with all the thrill gone out, full of synthetic orange-juice stands, cheap movie houses, and unglamorous prostitutes.

Not until 1922, after people really began to overcome the clammy, postwar dread that had held them in a vise, did the city begin to find its magic again. A new kind of night life came into being that year that had as its keynotes "intimacy" and "sophisticated daring." Small cafés that called themselves clubs, full of booths, alcoves, and cozy wall-benches designed to create an atmosphere of "just us members," began to replace the brawling, sprawling saloons of pre-Prohibition days. Although they billed themselves as "sneak-speaks," anyone could easily obtain the password for entrance. Some members brought their own flasks and ordered mixings at two and three dollars for a bottle of ginger ale, but most people preferred sampling the hidden bartenders' arts. Waiters and bus boys scurried all over with trays of "soda" that left an unmistakable taint of alcohol in the air.

The swankiest cafés and night clubs in New York were owned by gangsters and were advertised as places where hayseeds could meet the fast Broadway crowd. Prostitutes were more than welcome, especially if they looked expensive. Employees all had lists of girls who preferred to have others do their soliciting, and they discussed specifics with the patrons—a girl's weight, height, and general build, her age, previous experience, her race and nationality, and her degree of passion as reported by men who had been with her. Many madams came to the cafés, some with their most attractive clotheshorses, to "do a little drum beating," according to Polly Adler, one of the most fabulously successful madams of her day.

"When I walked in [to the clubs] surrounded by my loveliest girls," she said in the recent book she wrote about her experiences as a madam, "it was a show-stopper. Soon there was a file of Polly Adler jokes which the emcees would haul out and dust off when we made our center-door fancy entrances, so along with goggling at the girls, the customers would be giggling at quips about me. Although the tabs were never less than five hundred, I felt our evenings out were a good investment. The clubs were a display window for the girls. I'd make a column or two; the latest Polly Adler gag would start the rounds and, no matter where we happened to go, some of the club patrons would follow after us and end the evening at my house. . . . As a result of all this good publicity (plus a good word of mouth from satisfied customers) business got better and better. . . ."

These were lush and palmy times for prostitutes, their madams, and underworld friends. They were admired and respected, not just tolerated. Money was king and so were you if you had it. Gangsters were heroes and prostitutes who wore minks were as envied as debutantes.

In 1925 dapper little Jimmy Walker was elected mayor and some of his backers said that he would be the best administrator in the city's history, because a man who had been in and out of so many romantic entanglements had, of necessity, to grow into a diplomat extraordinary.

In 1926 Earl Carrol gave a bathtub party that sent the press into a frenzy. He had pretty Joyce Hawley brought out in a bathtub of champagne. No wonder Polly Adler was able to say, "If I had had all of history to choose from, I couldn't have chosen a better time to be a madam."

There were many madams who became notorious in the thirties who were already big time in the twenties. Fat Jennie, the Factory, known among her girls as "Jennie with the big mouth," ran several establishments. "Old Mother Birdie" ran Birdie's House and covered her walls with framed mottoes she embroidered herself: "What Is Home Without Mother?" and "Satisfaction Guaranteed Or Your Money Back." Anna Swift, an angular, tailored, masculine-looking woman, maintained a massage parlor that catered to men who wanted to be whipped.

Houses in the 1920s were divided into "sleep-ins" and "sleep-outs." Some of the more elegant ones were combinations, with a few favored girls sleeping in and the rest on call. They charged anywhere from one dollar to a couple of hundred, and the girls and madams split fifty-fifty after deductions of expenses that included board, room, and doctors' examination fees. A few girls resented the split, but the majority felt that the madam, who had

the business acumen and took the worst chances, was entitled to whatever she could get. They were happy to be
in houses, instead of out hustling on their own.

The madams were happy, too, because they were coin-
ing money and having to turn overflow customers away. A
new phenomenon appeared among them, stimulated by
the unprecedented demand for their services—cooperation.
Every now and again, one madam or another, realizing
that she had customers enough to last her the rest of her
life, went so far as to recommend a rival. Such was the
effect of prosperity. It was the era of good feeling among
madams.

The good will radiating from the madams affected everyone concerned, including the police. Of course, the need
for bribery and graft was as great as ever, but the madams
did not resent the payments as they had in former, leaner
years. In fact, most of them paid graft generously and
many entertained policemen in their houses.

Polly Adler wrote about this period: "My apartment
became a hangout for the police themselves. On many an
evening I should have had a green light out in front as
well as the red one which tradition says should be there."

While the plain-clothes officers were hobnobbing with
Polly Adler and her colleagues, the Committee of Fourteen,
a new morality group, was conducting surveys on prostitution. It discovered that 132 out of 157 night clubs,
speak-easies, and dance studios were "definitely identified
with prostitutional activities." "These places," it stated,
"are worse than any of the Raines Law hotels of Parkhurst's day."

As morality committees had done before, the Committee
of Fourteen demanded—and received—action. Arrest
figures soared. The court was kept full of streetwalkers and
cheap dance-hall hostesses. But the important madams

continued their operations. They paid out a little more graft now that the heat was on, but they did not care because, no matter how much they had to give the police, there was still plenty left for them.

Then in 1929 the roaring twenties became tamed. People did not know what hit them after the stock market crashed. Every day the headlines told of more bankruptcies and suicides. Every day more businessmen closed their doors; but the successful whorehouse madams were not among them. On the contrary, men who had been model husbands became model patrons now. They came to have fun with the girls and to drink, and madams had their biggest profits at the bar during the months immediately after the crash.

Only the poor streetwalkers grew poorer, poorer and less discriminating. They took on men they might have turned down in better times, and they grew less careful about avoiding vice-squad officers. Arrest statistics mounted higher and higher, and the Committee of Fourteen lauded the police even more lavishly than they had done formerly.

But high arrest statistics do not necessarily go hand in hand with real vice control. In 1930, a year when impressive numbers of prostitutes were arrested and jailed, the police were faced with an exposé of graft and corruption that made the Parkhurst days look lily white. At its beginning the exposé was not concerned with prostitution. It might never have been undertaken if Fiorello La Guardia (New York's "Little Flower") had not suffered a resounding defeat in his race for the mayoralty against the suave Jimmy Walker and begun to point at the rottenest link in the whole chain of the Walker administration—the Magistrates' Courts, as it happened. He made serious accusations, which were echoed and reechoed. For months rumors about plain-clothes policemen who rode around in Cadillacs and judges who fraternized with gangsters were circulated all over town. Finally, in August of 1930, Governor Franklin D. Roosevelt yielded to the pressures civic groups were putting on him and requested the Appellate Division of the Supreme Court to investigate the Magistrates' Courts. The court granted the request and appointed Samuel Seabury, a distinguished lawyer and former judge of the New York State Court of Appeals, as referee.

Early in the investigation Judge Seabury declared that the whole Magistrates' Court system was "a mere medium for political patronage." Later on he became more specific. He told of lawyers and policemen and court employees who helped protect racketeers while at the same time they oppressed innocent people and small-time criminals without connections. He told of bondsmen, freely tolerated in the courts, who constituted a sort of clearing house between the underworld and the law. He told of bribery and fixing.

In Women's Court, where prostitutes were tried, lawyers, bondsmen, plain-clothes policemen, court personnel, and an assistant district attorney were organized into an extortion ring that operated among innocent women as well as professional prostitutes.

First there were the plain-clothes vice-squad policemen. They often framed innocent women. Sometimes they claimed that they had themselves been approached by the prostitutes. Sometimes they used "stool pigeons," the infamous "unknown men" of the police blotters. Many ingenious rackets developed around the stool pigeons.

In the Doctor's Racket, the stool pigeon posed as a patient. He entered a doctor's office while the doctor was away and demanded treatment. He placed money in a conspicuous spot and began to undress. At a given moment the officers entered and placed the nurse under arrest for prostitution.

The Landlady Racket, which victimized operators of legitimate rooming houses, was also widespread. The stool pigeon, after renting a room for himself and his wife and paying for it with marked money, brought in a prostitute. Almost immediately the police broke in, arrested the girl for prostitution, and arrested the landlady for maintaining a house of prostitution.

On October 17, 1930, Police Commissioner Edward P. Mulrooney vehemently denied the existence of the "unknown men."

"The police department," he stated, "never uses stool pigeons."

Only six weeks later, a volatile young Chilean immigrant, "Chile" Mapocho Acuna, made the Commissioner appear somewhat less than candid. Speaking from a prison cell, he declared that he had been a paid vice-squad stool for some time and he named several other men who had worked along with him Meyer Slutsky, Pinto, Harry the Greek, Chico, Harry Levey. He also detailed the lessons vice men taught their stools: give a false name and address; be prepared to have the policemen beat you during a raid; never, never go to court; and above all act as though you have never met the arresting officers.

The vice squad, with its stool pigeons, was only half of a well-defined ring that included bondsmen, lawyers, and an assistant district attorney. As soon as women were arrested, officers called bondsmen they knew and trusted. The bondsmen posted bail at usurious rates, taking women's bankbooks as their security. They then recommended lawyers who took most of what remained in the bank accounts and "fixed" the other ring members—a payoff to the assistant district attorney, who would then "go easy," and to the arresting officer, who would sugar-coat his testimony. Only the women who had no money went to jail.

The profitableness of the ring's machinations was most apparent during Judge Seabury's examination of policemen's bank accounts. Officer James J. Quinlivan had deposited $31,000 in five years, and his frugal wife had banked $57,744.67. Officer Robert E. Morris had saved over $50,-000. When asked to explained his accounts, Morris said he had won $10,000 gambling and that his Uncle George had given him $40,000 at Coney Island one day. Unfortunately, Uncle George was dead and could not back his nephew's statement.

After he had gathered evidence of corruption and of innocent women as well as known prostitutes being victimized, Judge Seabury set forth what he called the "humanized findings," the "flesh-and-blood testimonials" that would, "better than charts and graphs and reports," make the public realize how low they had permitted justice to fall.

Here are two out of twelve of those case studies as he presented them:

The Olen case

Mrs. Josephine Olen, a middle-aged married woman, of quiet respectability, ran a boardinghouse. One day, a Saturday afternoon, a man rang her door-bell and asked for Mrs. Lewis. Mrs. Olen informed him that Mrs. Lewis had moved but that a friend of hers was living downstairs. At his request she took him down and introduced him to Miss Janice. Just at this moment, the telephone rang and she left them to answer it. She was not even through her conversation when the door-bell rang again. Two men stood in the door; they showed her their badges and ordered her to take them to the same room to which she had taken the other man.

When they reached Miss Janice's room, the stool pigeon, Meyer Slutsky, had taken off his coat and vest and had planted marked money on the table. The officers, Quinlivan and O'Connor, immediately arrested the girl for offering to commit prostitution, and Mrs. Olen for keeping a disorderly house.

The two women were taken to the police station. Here one of the officers told Mrs. Olen that he would call Steiner, a bondsman, if she wished to get bail for herself and Miss Janice. She agreed and before long Steiner appeared and bailed them out.

Steiner then accompanied them home and Mrs. Olen turned over to him her bankbook which showed that she had a balance of $1,095. A lawyer was engaged to defend the women and on the following day entered a plea of "not guilty." According to Mrs. Olen, he had first demanded a fee of eight hundred dollars, but reduced it to five hundred. She also testified that Steiner said that he knew the detective that might be able to help her out, but it would cost a thousand dollars. She went to her lawyer's office. He gave her a paper to sign, which she did, thinking it was just a retainer. In reality it was an order on her bank to pay Abraham Treibitz, another bondsman, for whom Steiner worked, out of her account the sum of $1,080. She did not see her book again from the time she gave it to Steiner until after her acquittal, when another lawyer she had retained, secured it from Steiner, together with a check for $368, in rebate for the original overcharge. In other words, this false arrest cost Mrs. Olen $712, or 75 per cent of her savings account.

Weston, who had prosecuted this case, testified at one of the public hearings that the defense counsel had approached him in court before the trial and told him that he had a case in which he would like to get an acquittal. Weston said nothing. Following the dismissal, Weston testified that defense counsel paid him fifty dollars.

The Nolan case

Miss Nolan, a self-supporting woman, was in her apartment late one Saturday afternoon when Officer Abe Dicker knocked at the door, forced an entrance, struck her, and then arrested her for prostitution. She was taken to the 68th Street Station House. Here Officer Dicker, suddenly turning helpful, advised her to get a bond of five hundred dollars. When she said she did not know where to get the cash, he told her that this was unnecessary, that she could buy a bond. She was allowed one telephone call.

"Tell the person," Dicker continued, "to go to Jefferson Market Station and ask for Bondsman Lange. He will give you the bond. Tell the person going there to bring at least fifty dollars. That will be the cost."

At the same time she was informed that Bondsman Lange had a brother, an attorney, the best attorney in New York, and was advised to engage Attorney Lange to take care of her case.

In Miss Nolan's case, however, although she followed this disinterested advice, paying the prescribed bondsman an extortionate rate and retaining the prescribed lawyer, her difficulties were by no means over. At her trial, Dicker, the only witness for the prosecution, gave perjured testimony. Miss Nolan was subjected to a severe cross-examination by both the magistrate and the prosecution. Despite her repeated denials of the charge, the testimony of the janitress of her house as to what had happened, and the testimony of her character witnesses, she was found guilty.

Six months later, the Appellate Division reversed her conviction and ordered a new trial, and Miss Nolan was subsequently acquitted.

Once again, New York was scandalized. In self-defense the politicians and some of the newspapers tried to whitewash Tammany by attacking Seabury. The Judge, according to one New York newspaper, was a "wily old showman" who had given the city "a daily black eye" with his "scandals of 1931."

But public opinion was with Seabury, and before long there were resignations and dismissals both in the Police Department and in the Magistrates' Courts. Terror gripped those who had escaped Seabury's wrath. Judges were reluctant to preside in Women's Court. The District Attorney also withdrew, and until this very day has no representative in Women's Court. The plain-clothes officers sought to return to uniform duty and avoided arresting prostitutes.

Women's Court arraignments fell from 4,000 in 1929 to 513 in 1931—and the Committee of Fourteen felt constrained to take up its cudgels again. It charged that the disclosures of the investigation had resulted in an increase of prostitution. Judge Seabury replied:

"This argument is based upon the statistical fallacy under which the Committee of Fourteen operated—their theory being that as arrests for prostitution increased, the amount of prostitution *ipso facto* must have diminished. The fact is that, in all statistics of crime, it has been shown over and over that any compilation of the number of arrests is absolutely without value in the determination of the amount of crime. This is especially so under the conditions that prevailed in Manhattan, where the arrests were in many cases made by police officers for the purpose of extorting money from their victims."

In 1932, only one year after the Seabury exposé, the police resumed their program of wholesale arrests. Now, however, there was special emphasis on bringing in Negro streetwalkers. Whereas in 1929 there were two white women arrested to one Negro woman, these figures were now reversed.

By 1934 a few people were again asking embarrassing

questions of the police. Why were the poor prostitutes the only ones brought into court? What about the keepers of disorderly houses? Why weren't they ever arrested?

Anna M. Kross, now a magistrate who frequently presided in Women's Court, spoke out.

"We are proceeding through this court against the victims of prostitution rather than against the structures of commercialized vice. We see here the bankrupts of their profession—the poor, the stupid, the diseased, the friendless, the girls and women who are so unsuccessful even at this profession that they have no regular clientele but must solicit their business on the streets. We never see here the woman whose traffic in her body has brought her jewels, fine clothing, motor cars. . . . We seldom find here the exploiters of women, the procurers, seducers, disorderly house keepers. . . . Commercialized vice is as wide-spread as it was in the days before vice-crusading began. It has permeated the entire community until few apartment houses, tenements, or hotels are free of it. It has touched every neighborhood of the city. Repression has served to drive it underground and strengthen its alliance with the criminal elements of the city. Demimonde has thus become underworld."

Judge Kross knew whereof she spoke. Prostitution, in the thirties, *had* touched every neighborhood in the city. Mae Scheible, whose girls were carefully schooled in social elegance, operated right on Park Avenue; Polly Adler worked out of the heart of café-society in a twelve-room Louis Seize apartment on 55th and Madison; May Spiller ran a place on West 54th Street for rich young Benny Spiller who had advanced from small-time bootlegging in Philadelphia to big-time prostitution in New York; Cokey Flo Brown lived and worked and boarded her girls in a sedate brownstone house on West End Avenue; Ng Wong in

Chinatown trained his white girls like geishas; Dago Jean operated on West 68th Street; French Irene had an apartment on 12th Street; Babe Wagner ran an elegant and expensive bagnio on Central Park West; Douchebag Jimmy, the male madam, worked out of West 54th Street.

But most madams, unlike these prosperous ones in the thirties, operated small-scale businesses featuring one to three girls and charging a straight two dollars. In the one-girl houses, men had to take what they could get. The two-girl houses gave them a choice between a blonde and a red-head or brunette, both of them played up as "two-wayers" who would meet all requests. Madams kept their customers by changing girls every week.

"It was like a vaudeville circuit," fat old Faye Lena says today. "When a John went to a house, he never knew what he was going to find."

New entrepreneurs, calling themselves *bookers,* grew out of the vaudeville-circuit pattern. In addition to running a call service for madams, they organized a protection racket that was tied in with the bail bond business. For ten dollars a week per girl and fiteen dollars per madam, they promised bail bonds, "mouthpieces," and "fixes." Most of them were small-time racketeers like Cockeye Louis Weiner, a sixty-year-old family man who operated out of Leder's Bar & Grill on Second Avenue, or Warren Mims, known as Little Caesar, who had charge of booking white women into Negro houses.

By 1935 prostitutes' bookers, previously unknown, suddenly became news. There was a lot of talk about a bookers' headman, a vice czar. Besides, a new reform committee, a Committee of One Hundred, was formed. True to the tradition of its predecessors, it demanded action.

Tammany District Attorney William Copeland Dodge was the first who jumped to obey the call. He assigned

Assistant District Attorney Charles Pilatsky to ferret the vice czar out.

For months Mr. Pilatsky and his staff worked day and night, cajoling and threatening prostitutes, madams, and small-time bookers. They identified the vice czar as Nicholas Montana, and continued to amass evidence as to the details of his operations. In December of 1936 Mr. Pilatsky stood up before a jury and presented madams and prostitutes who knew Montana.

"What type of witnesses have we got?" he asked. "What have they to gain by coming down here to testify against this vice racketeer, this man who sits here unconcerned, with a studied poker face, looking at you day in and day out?"

Betty Hawkins, Jean De Bella, Kay Salter, Shirley Grifton, May Duval, and Ruth Ross all said that Montana had placed them in houses of prostitution. Some of the madams they had worked for also testified and told of money they had paid to Montana.

"Gentlemen, I am going to conclude by saying this to you: Gentlemen, if ever an Assistant District Attorney of the County of New York or elsewhere has ever asked twelve human beings gathered together in the jury box to do their duty, I ask it of you; I ask it of you with a certainty of purpose, gentlemen, in the object that words cannot express. I say to you, gentlemen, that the County of New York would owe you a vote of thanks that nobody could express in fitting language when you bring in a verdict of guilty, to serve notice on the vice racketeers of this County that there is no place here for them, for men of that type.

"Don't turn this man out, gentlemen."

The jury did not turn him out, and on January 6, 1936,

Judge Cornelius Collins imposed a sentence of twenty-five years in the state's prison.

"The greatest overlord of vice New York has ever known took the sentence with a smile," the triumphant young Assistant District Attorney observed.

But the triumph was short-lived. A few months later District Attorney Dodge was superseded by a special prosecutor, Thomas E. Dewey. Dewey found Montana to have been a mere errand boy for the real vice czar—Lucky Luciano.

At the time he took the prostitution business out of the hands of the small-timers, Luciano was already established as one of the top gangsters of the East. He was the head of the deadly Unione Siciliano, controlled the import of narcotics, and ran an Italian lottery and a string of horse parlors or poolrooms. Yet his name was not known. The newspapers, replete with references to Legs Diamond, Dutch Schultz, and other gangsters, never mentioned Luciano. When he was not rushing off to Hollywood or Hot Springs in his private plane, he lived opulently but inconspicuously as Mr. Ross of the Waldorf Towers, a sportsman and gambler. Everybody believed in the identity he claimed for himself, including many of the pretty show girls he took around to night-club and theater openings.

As soon as Lucky decided to syndicate prostitution, he called all the bookers together and told them they were working for him. They would continue to collect from the madams they knew. He also expected them to go out and solicit new business.

Only one madam, a middle-aged lady with squinting eyes and a long, equine face, refused to play with Lucky. Joan Martin told the Luciano henchmen who first came to see her that she had slaved many long years to make police contacts of her own and so had no need of outside protection. A few nights afterward Lucky's favorite snuff-out man and a couple of his strong-armers called to see Joan. They broke up all her furniture and told her she could report them to her police contacts or—she could book for protection. She told them she wasn't booking. A couple of nights after the furniture-wrecking party a smiling fellow with a lead pipe came. Joan had to have eleven stitches taken in her scalp. Joan's next visitor had a gun and she agreed to join when he threatened to shoot her dog.

Once all the madams were committed, the mob organized to make the promised protection a reality. It opened a central protective bureau in a hotel on Seventh Avenue with a brilliant bloodhound named Binge as director. Binge kept a steady and effective vigil for word of police raids. In 1935, a year when Women's Court arraigned over 3,000 prostitutes, only 175 syndicate girls were arrested. None of them served time in jail.

Dewey, when he struck at Lucky in 1936, was unaware of the gangster's identity. But he did know the names of some of his subordinates. He delved into their activities for many months, quietly and without any word getting around. Then, on the morning of February 1, he had syndicate executives and some of the higher-priced bookers tailed by detectives, who had orders to arrest them only when they were separated from their friends or families so that there would be no possibility of any tip-offs. At nine o'clock the next morning, he conducted the big roundup, with madams and prostitutes brought in from all the syndicate bagnios. Black Marias kept rolling up to the door of the Woolworth Building where Dewey was conducting his "singing school" on the 25th floor, and women, in every state of dress and undress, kept pouring out of them. Dewey told them that he had no wish to punish them. He promised protection to the people who informed on those who were next up the line.

"I wanted the small fry to inform on the larger," he said, "and so on up until we reached the top."

Dewey and his assistants spent many difficult days before they could persuade the ladies to talk, but gradually they began. Madams who were aggrieved over the syndicate's highhanded methods, jilted wives and sweethearts, all broke down and told what they knew. By late March, Dewey had blazed a clear path to Lucky's door. He was tried in April in the Supreme Court before Justice Philip J. McCook and sentenced to thirty to forty years in the penitentiary.

"I may not be the most moral and upright man who lives," he indignantly told the newspapermen at his trial, "but I have never been so low as to become involved in prostitution."

The Luciano exposé, combined with Mae Scheible's conviction in the same year for transportation of girls from Pittsburgh to New York, turned prostitution into a more furtive business. The police actually closed up the most elaborate houses, including Polly Adler's and Peggy Wild's. Of course, both ladies reopened the next year, but on a less extravagant scale and with most of their girls on call.

And that, the system of the call-girl, was the new *modus operandi* beginning in 1939. Many dozens of call flats sprang up all over the city. Most madams had card indexes which were invaluable in cases of suddenly enforced moves. A few hours at the telephone, some well-worded letters, and the moves made no difference.

The police had a difficult time catching up with the call-girls and their madams, and so the Women's Court became, even more than it had been before, a place for the bankrupts of the profession. Day after day, the court was filled with the poorest and sleaziest of prostitutes and the lawyers and bondsmen who still preyed on them just as they had done in Seabury's day.

In 1940 there was a new inquiry into Women's Court conducted by the then Commissioner of Investigation William B. Herlands, now a United States District Judge, and it revealed that most of the conditions prior exposés had dealt with—racket lawyers, ten of whom represented more than 100 women annually, usurious bondsmen, and plain-clothes officers who entrapped prostitutes into making passes—still existed.

It was not until 1950 that undesirable lawyers and crooked bondsmen were finally driven out of Women's Court. Improved judicial procedures designed to assure a speedy trial and Legal Aid lawyers to represent indigent defendants were responsible for accomplishing this reform. Again, reformers and newspapers, eternal optimists today as yesterday, hailed the court's cleanup as a milestone toward honest vice control. But they did not stop to think that inasmuch as the vice squad continued its traditional methods of arrest and the court was still merely a way station between the jail and the street, basic conditions were little improved.

FOURTEEN / The revolving door

What is happening in Women's Court in New York City today? If you want to know, visit the court presently located on the second floor of the modern Criminal Courts Building at 100 Centre Street. Proceedings are conducted in an imposing mahogany-walled, many-windowed courtroom designed in the best of taste and in accordance with the finest judicial standards. The magistrate presides on a mahogany bench in the front center. The witness chair is to his left, and counsel tables are in front of the bench. There is limited seating provided for interested spectators. With a view to discouraging the morbidly curious, however, these spectators' seats are separated from the court by a screen. Visit any day, Sunday included.

Outside the clerk's office

10:00 A.M.

The vice-squad officers who are to appear for arraignment or trial of the day's prostitutes begin congregating. They look like wholesome young men who could be grocery clerks, farmers, factory workers, doctors, lawyers or college professors—but not police officers. They stand around in their good-looking sports outfits, smoking and obviously enjoying the gathering of the clan. Although they talk about everything under the sun, they often revert to two favorite subjects, their families and their jobs. It is obvious even from the shortest kind of contact with them that they all have special problems with their families.

"I'm pooped," says a slender blond man in a blue shirt. "I spent all last night telling my wife that she had a better figure, dressed or undressed, than any whore I ever got. All last night. But I mean *all* night."

"Yeah," a tall, paunchy Negro squadder says. "Yeah, man." His tone reveals how well he knows the other's meaning.

All these men share their buddies' feelings, for they too have spent nights reassuring insecure and doubting wives.

"My wife says, 'Who's the blonde in your life?' I tell her, 'Baby, you're the only blonde I got. Don't you know that yet?' So she says, 'I got black hair and don't *you* know *that* yet?' Making believe she didn't get my joke, just to start a fight."

"That's nothing. You know my wife asks me, 'Tell me, Sam, how do you feel around a naked woman you never met before? Tell the truth now.' Tell the truth. What's the truth? How do I know it? I feel different one day than I do on the other. It depends on the woman, the mood I'm in, everything. But you can't tell your wife a truth like that, so I say, 'Listen, honey, I'm all for you and Pat Ward would leave me cold.' Well, if you'd seen her you would've thought I beat her up or something. She cried for hours and then she said, 'If you think that ugly little tramp's got so much more sex appeal than your own wife does, what are you hanging around here for? Go to your old prostitutes. All I ask is that you keep your two little babies with a roof over their heads.' "

"Speaking of wives," one says, "will somebody call mine up and tell her I was on a *job* till four o'clock yesterday morning?"

Almost everyone volunteers to call because no one knows when he might need a similar favor. A woman who, today, is as understanding as any vice officer could possibly require may become a jealous wreck tomorrow.

After a while the wife tales begin to pall and grow more serious than their tellers intended—if you love your wife you can't really be facetious about her hurts, wrong or right, justifiable or not, and so, much to everyone's relief, somebody changes the subject. He starts joking with a dark heavy-set man, Rex Lever.

"Sexy Rexy," he says easily.

Rex Lever is humorless on the whole and that may be why he takes more kidding than the rest of the men. "Aw, come off it," he says.

But the man who started the bandying does not want to come off it. Today, of all days, he has a good reason for making a butt of Lever.

"Sexy Rexy," he repeats. "Sexy for any grandma over sixty-five."

He is referring to a sixty-five-year-old grandmother who, at three o'clock yesterday morning, linked her arm in Rex's and forced him to accompany her home. In the taxicab she hailed and helped him into, she kept saying, "I can hardly wait. What you do to me! Oooh, I can hardly wait!"

Now Rex is sorry that he ever yielded to the impulse to share the incident. "That dame," he says, "if I ever see her again, I'll run like hell." And, because he wishes to make a dent in the levity, he says, "Now my wife when I told her. . . ." And there they are right back where they started from. They are bound to come back to it sooner or later anyhow. That is the way it has got to be with men on jobs like theirs.

Inside the court clerk's office

9:00 A.M.

The clerk's office is a dingy, light-green room in need of a paint job. Roberta Jackson, the assistant court clerk, types complaint sheets as the officers dictate them. These contain, among other points of information, the women's behavior as the officer is supposed to have observed it.

At 3:10 A.M. on Wednesday, April 25, according to Officer Johnson, Esther Lowery, 52, got into his automobile at Union Hall and South Road, Jamaica.

"She asked if I wanted to do a little jazzing," he told the court clerk. I said, "How much?" "Two dollars," she said. "Do you French?" I said. "Not for two dollars," she said. "Four dollars for French. O.K. for four dollars for a Frenchy?" "I told her O.K."

At 12:15 P.M. that same Wednesday, Officer McKee is supposed to have gone to a Brooklyn apartment and into a bedroom where one Louisa Alvarez, 23, "did offer to commit a lewd and indecent act with deponent, demanding and receiving the sum of $5 therefor and was disrobed for the commission of said lewd and indecent act. The officer also said that, when he revealed his identity, the woman told him, "I would never take you for a cop."

And so the stories go, one like all the others, except for minor details.

At 2:45 A.M. Joyce Crocker, 32, engaged Officer Cohen in conversation, offered him a "good time" for ten dollars, brought him to her apartment and, before he pulled his badge, disrobed "down to her garter belt and stockings."

At 5:00 A.M., Officer Eggers, contacted by a shill, went

to the Hotel Westly where Selma Rose, 29, "for the sum of $50 did disrobe naked and offer to commit an unlawful act of sexual intercourse."

At 10:15 P.M., in Officer O'Brien's car, parked in Central Park, 57-year-old Clarice Clay "did offer to commit prostitution with deponent, demanding and receiving the sum of $2 therefor and did thereupon open the fly of deponent's trousers for said purpose."

At 4:20 P.M., Officer Brady went to a massage parlor on East 55th Street and was shown into a bedroom where thirty-one-year-old Sally Sullivan told him, "Take off your clothes. The man outside takes all the money."

In the prisoners' cage

9:00 A.M.

The first prison van arrives from the House of Detention where arraigned women are kept until trial day and convicted women are kept until sentence. They are brought into a caged area directly outside the courtroom.

The newcomers flock together, sitting close and taking comfort in the nearness of body to body. But the old-timers sit nonchalantly and begin, after a while, to hold court like oracles of old, telling the new ones what to expect, making predictions: "You'll walk, honey, wait and see— but you, I'm sorry to say, you won't walk—and you, oh, there's a long sentence in your future, I can see it now, and you'll get hysterical, cry like a little baby, but it won't help, nothing'll help you any more, dearie, and, if I'm telling a lie just spit in my eye and call me liar." They talk about the judge's personality, this one being "easy, a dollbaby, a honey-chile and a judge with a heart as big as all Harlem." All the same, they give the warning old-timers have given newcomers since the court was first opened: "If it's a cop on your case, forget it; guilty or innocent, you might as well plead guilty. A John's a different story."

They talk about the matter of legal counsel and how to handle it. Use Legal Aid, they say. Legal Aid lawyers are as good as private ones any day, even if they do service you for free; and they're on your side; they care what happens to you, they really do. Why, a couple of months ago, there was a pretty little gal in court put up some fight for all the women she defended and, every time she lost a case, she looked like someone'd just got through kicking her in the face. That little lawyer gal cared what happened, and that's more than you can say about some of those private sharks. Your money's all they want; and if you're not loaded, you can drop dead in front of them and they wouldn't bat an eyelash. Well, all right, the new girls say, so suppose the private lawyers aren't worrying about you, they still have tricks of the trade, don't they? Oh, tricks of the trade, the old ones think, you little innocent, if you only knew how little they're worth in a court like this, you wouldn't be worrying about tricks of the trade.

Lucy Marinelli, a big, fat woman with gray-streaked hair and a blind eye, says you know what you can do with all lawyers, Legal Aid included. She's going to plead her own case today and she wants everyone to witness her triumph.

"I can't lose, because God's on my side. The Greatest Judge of all, so what I care about that little man in his big chair and all them dirty, lyin' cops put together?"

Missy Jones Lincoln, a sixty-year-old stick of a woman, wags her wiry head and shouts, "Hear, hear. Stand up and preach loud this mornin'." Missy has a salt shaker. She got it from the prison kitchen by dint of her superlative cunning, and she plans to use it selflessly, for the good of all the women awaiting trial. She calls the shaker her "fount" and the salt her "holy water," and she intends to anoint all the girls as they go into court. Then the judge will *have* to let them walk. Contemplating it, she rocks back and forth and makes a little song of her faith. "Oh, you sweet shaker, you. Oh, oh. Oh, you sweet shaker, you. Oh, oh. Oh, you sweet."

Other women in other places might hoot at such a superstition as Missy's. Here they would not dare. Here they have faiths of their own and some of them are just as odd as Missy's. There is a tubercular-looking blonde of twenty-three, who keeps caressing an *I Like Ike* button someone gave her during the last campaign. She talks to Mr. Eisenhower the way Lucy Marinelli talks to God.

"Let that judge make me walk, Mr. Eisenhower. I'm on your side. Won't you be on mine?"

Now that they are seated and conversing, the girls' nervousness is an appalling thing to watch. Even the old-timers, for all their bravado and oracular airs, grow tense as trial time approaches closer. One slender little girl with a lame leg keeps walking up and down, up and down, until an elderly, motherly type gets up and throws a plump arm out to catch her.

"You won't help anything by walking, honey. You're like an expectant father."

There is another odd one in court today, a pretty, coquettish girl. Yesterday when she was arraigned, this elegant creature called herself French Camille, spouting French at the judge, telling him, "You weel be so kind to forgeeve my 'orrible *Anglais*," fluttering her false eyelashes, holding her hennaed head higher than any girl in court.

Today she sits isolated and known now for what she is, a man in woman's clothes. Who could have suspected it? Let no one ever say again that clothes don't make a woman. French Camille might never have been revealed at all if it had not been for the doctor at the House of Detention. She received the shock of her life, and promptly ordered Camille into solitary confinement. As a matter of fact, she did not know whether to keep her in the women's jail or send her to a men's prison, and now here she is in Women's Court and nobody knows whether she will be tried with the other prostitutes or sent to a court for others of her sex. She looks unconcerned, as though she has no care, and her head is still held high. She talks to no one and nobody talks to her. Some of the women would like to talk but they don't. They glance at her, but surreptitiously, and they grow embarrassed when they catch her eye. Unfortunately, some of the police officers are not so polite as the prostitutes are. Having heard about the curiosity, they come into the cage, even though it is against regulations, and look at Camille. Now they bring the pretty young Legal Aid attorney and stand guffawing as they point out the curiosity. She shrugs her arm free from that of the man who is holding it.

"Let me out of here," she says. "I won't be a party to anything like this." Outside the cage she sits down on the visitors' bench and talks to one of the newspapermen. "God," she says, "I thought I'd get used to this place after a while. But now I don't think I ever will. It doesn't matter how often you've been here. You still see something every day that makes you want to cry."

Two more vice squadders go into the cage after the Legal Aid attorney goes out. One says, "I've seen plenty of dressed-up fags but I'd swear this one was a woman."

"Well, I don't know," the other one answers. "If my wife had legs like that. . . ."

And French Camille suddenly loses her accent and lashes out in plain Brooklynese, "Yeah? I'll knock yer block off if ya don't get outa here, ya pair of lousy, no-good bums."

In the prisoners' cage

    9:00 A.M.

The new girls who have been picked up during the night are sent to the cage to await arraignment. Some of them, like the girls awaiting trial, are old-timers and they gravitate toward their friends.

"Hey, what're you doing back so *soon?*" a trial girl asks a fat, crooked-heeled arraignee who wears a gold-chained lorgnette pinned to her greasy cotton dress.

"Same as you. Same as you," she says, smiling and showing four gaps where her top front teeth ought to be.

The trial girl is just about to make an answer when Nola, a small slender girl with huge black eyes, screams and falls writhing on the floor. The lady with the lorgnette kneels down and tries to hold her, but Nola keeps rolling away from her. A policewoman runs out of the cage and comes back with two policemen. They grab Nola and hold her pinioned by her arms and legs.

"Poor kid," one says, "she needs a fix bad."

"Yeah," the second one says, "I hope she can hold out till the doctor gets here."

The doctor will come at ten and give her a shot. She will regain her equilibrium after a while and be able to stand before the judge and hear the charges against her.

In the probation office adjacent to the court

    9:00 A.M.

The two probation officers, Jean Lovett and Irene Miller, are at their desks. There are many people sitting on the benches and flowing over into the hallway, women who have been placed on probation and are here to report their doings, and friends and relatives who have come to plead for their own: "If you give her one more chance I promise you. I know what you're going to say.

I know all the times she's been in before, but this time it's going to be different, something tells me . . . my heart tells me it's going to be different now. Give her a chance, one more that's all, and if she flubs this one too, we'll both wash our hands. What do you say? Well, sure I guess I couldn't really wash my hands, but one thing I will promise you, cross my heart and hope to die, no matter what happens you'll never see *me* here again. If you just give her this one more chance. I'll never, never bother you as long as I live, and may God strike me dead if I do."

A man well-known to the officers sits across from Miss Lovett's desk. He has been to see her on the average of once every six months for the past three years, for that is how often his wife has been picked up for prostitution. He is a small, anemic-looking brown man with burning eyes and a low, soft voice.

"My poor girl. Them po-lice is still pickin' on her. Can't you stop 'em, Miss Lovett? I tell you what, those Gestapo boys might's well come over here. The American po-lice treats you just the same. My wife came out lookin' for me. She was just walkin' down the street when they picked her up two times in one month.

"I feel like takin' a gun and shootin' myself because I can't take care of my own wife better. When I come out of the Army, doctor says, 'Boy, you got a little case of psycho-neurosis. Don't let nothin' worry you.' Don' let nothin' worry me. I near have a fit when I think of my girl. You should've seen me try to cook yesterday and them three little chillun lookin' up and sayin', 'Where's ma done gone, daddy?' Right before I seen them, a neighbor told me, 'Your wife's been arrested.' "

He wants Miss Lovett to tell the judge his wife's a good woman and to give him his honest word that she'll never return to Women's Court again if he lets her go this one more time. If the probation officer can't intercede with the judge, he wants her to arrange for him to see his wife, so that he can tell her how much he loves and needs her and so she will know there is one person who believes her innocent no matter what proof the policeman has been able to muster against her this time. But, Miss Lovett, much as she would like to, can't arrange for him to see his wife, for she knows from previous experience that the woman doesn't want to see him. The last time she tried to arrange a meeting, the wife, slender, slovenly, overly made up, bounced her head so that her bell earrings tinkled and said, "Only good thing about prison's I don't have to look at Jimmy for all the time I'm in. Hurray! Hurray!"

Finally Miss Lovett manages to get the man, still muttering about the Gestapo and American po-lice, away from her desk. A tall, emaciated, toothless woman takes his place. She tries not to cry but the tears come in spite of her.

"My daughter don't belong here," she says. "My husband's to blame. You ought to get him and put him in jail, not her. A little girl like that, she don't know what she's doing when her father's so mean she's got to get out of the house. The girl never had a home like other children."

Today Miss Miller's duties are pleasant compared to Miss Lovett's. She is seeing the women who, having been placed on probation, are here to report their progress. They are also supposed to present the pay slips they have garnered on their jobs and many of them, as Miss Miller would expect, don't have any slips to show. But they are full of enthusiastic stories about what successes they are in legal employment. One girl, a voluptuous bleached blonde in her middle twenties, proudly presents a series of slips from a Coney Island side show.

"I got a profession now," she says. "I'm a fire-eater," and

adds, "Please don't think I'm showing off when I tell you I'm good, I really am."

But there is one girl who, alone, out of all who are collected here, is hostile and angry. She is a slender, blue-eyed blonde of twenty-three, chic even though her clothes seem inexpensive. At her trial, three months earlier, she said she was framed, and when the judge put her on probation she told him that, if he were fair-minded, he would let her go home, and put the officer who arrested her on probation. Every time she sees Miss Miller she persists in repeating her story.

"What happened is this. I went to the Blue Doll lookin' for a hostess job. The woman that owned the joint told me, 'You're a pretty kid but a hostess needs more than looks. Let's see how you get along with the men. I know some cute kids who can't get a tumble and some plug-uglies who can just electrify the boys. What about you, kid? Are you the electrifyin' type? I'll give you a knockdown to one of my regular customers and find out.' Then she introduced me to this boy, Bim, who was sitting at the bar. He started buying me drinks. I must have had around four or five, and then Bim had to go home and he leaned over and introduced me to the fellow beside him. I knew the boss was watching me and, after Bim left, I was afraid she'd think I couldn't make time with men. So I moved over to this other fellow and started turning on the charm. We sat at the bar for a couple of hours drinking. He must've bought me four, five drinks.

"After a while he said I was gorgeous and he'd give anything to go to bed with me. He asked me what I'd take. Well, I was afraid if I told him no soap right off he'd get up and leave me and the boss'd think I was no good at holding men. So I decided to con him along and said a hundred dollars. Was I surprised when he offered me seventy-five. My husband's in jail and I have a baby and I don't know when I last saw seventy-five dollars all in one lump, so, being drunk as I was, I told him yes. We got out and into a taxi and then he pulled his badge and arrested me."

In the police officers' room

9:00 A.M.

The Johns begin to collect in the vice squadders' office, dingy and pale green like all the other rooms attached to this court. There are four Johns in court today. They sit far apart on the wooden bench, not talking or looking at one another, divided half and half, two comfortable witnesses and the others here against their wills.

A slender, blond young man named Terry Smith sits at the far end of the bench. He has a pink, smooth baby face. Last week, when the police officer followed him to the room to which he had taken his three-dollar crone, he found Smith beating her with his shoe. Now, Terry is wondering whether he will have to describe the incident to the judge. Is it a criminal activity, and will he be punished when the court finds out? The officer, when he arrested the woman last week, told him, "Look, buddy, there's nothing to worry about; all you are is a witness against the whore; nobody asks witnesses questions they don't want to answer."

"Well, suppose I don't want to answer anything about the woman either?" he asked the officer, and the officer said, "Well, if I were you, pal . . . ," not fiercely, not even unkindly, but anyway, you'd have to be a fathead not to understand his meaning, and so, naturally, here he is today, waiting his turn to testify against the woman.

The other unwilling witness is about forty, tall, dark, and beefy. The girl the officer caught him with is one he has known for several months. He works until midnight for a trucking firm and has been used to meeting her after work, maybe twice or three times a week. His wife is an invalid and so he goes to this girl.

It was more than just the sex. Sometimes he would take the girl out drinking. She was a gay companion and good in bed, too. Once in a while, lying there after he'd had her, he'd fall a little bit in love with her and wish she were his wife. Not really, though. After all, his wife, for all her faults and difficulties, was a good, pure woman, while this one, well, she wasn't the best girl in the world, the most moral, that is. Hadn't she let him pick her up in a bar? They'd got drunk and gone back to the beat-up room she lived in and she'd undressed with no urging.

As for the money, yes, he had given her money, just as the officer had seen him do in the bar that night he picked them up, but he wasn't really paying for sex. At the beginning he had just given her presents, a pair of pearl earrings, fake, of course, since they cost all of two dollars, a couple of pairs of nylon stockings, a two-ninety-eight bottle of toilet water. Well, then, one thing led to another, and after a couple of weeks with her, he began giving her money instead of presents, as much as he could spare, ten dollars one week, another five, another nothing. She never asked for anything, and she acted pleased with whatever he gave her.

Was she a whore? He didn't know. Maybe yes, maybe no, depending on how you looked at her. Of course, men were her only source of income, since she didn't work and had no husband to support her. He knew for a fact that she had at least two men in addition to him, maybe more. One paid her rent and the other took care of food and clothes. She told him she had no feeling for either of them, and, believing her despite himself, he used to think it would be

wonderful if he could tell her to ditch them and say, "From
now on I'll take care of everything and you just stay home
and wait for me to come see you, hear?"

What a crazy dream for a man with an invalid wife on
a truck driver's salary. Of course, the cheap little tart didn't
need any luxuries. Even though there were three men
taking care of her and sharing her favors, she still wore
sleazy clothes and lived in a shabby little room with just a
bed and a chest of drawers in it. Poor kid, she didn't ask
much from any of her men. No wonder she hung around
bars all the time. Poor kid, huh? If she was such a good
girl as he tried to make himself think she was, why didn't
she go out and get herself a job instead of sitting around
waiting for the crumbs men gave her from off the tables
of their wives? Oh well, what did he care, as long as he got
his and his wife Gladys never knew what was cooking.

As long as he got his. That was what he told that officer who picked him and the girl up. The officer was a
nice-looking young fellow and pleasant to talk to. He
remembered noticing him in the bar before he'd gone with
Lorette. He was sitting at the next table with a cute-looking
little chick. He was making some play for her. Well, sure,
he was doing his job, the girl must have been a pro, but it
looked like more than a job the way he kept putting his
hands on her. It looked like he was enjoying his job. Say,
there was a job for a man with an invalid wife to have all
right, all right. Maybe he'd ask that officer how a fellow
could get to join the force. They'd grown real chummy,
once he had finally agreed to testify against Lorette.

At first the officer had had to threaten him and say he
guessed he'd have to have a little conversation with Gladys.
That scared the life out of him. He told the officer how
sick his wife was, on her back all day and all night and a
little touched in the head the way an invalid gets to be after

a while. Suppose, he'd asked the officer, threatening in his turn, suppose she's crazy enough to turn on the gas and kill herself after you finished talking to her, what then? "She's your wife," the officer had said, "and your worry, not mine." Well, Gladys *was* his worry, and she'd always been a pretty good wife to him before she got sick. He owed her a lot more than he did Lorette.

And that's the reason he's here today. He sits and worries his knuckles and hopes he won't have to see Lorette face to face at her trial. If she looks at him with those big black eyes of hers. . . .

In the courtroom

10:00 A.M.

The judge has gone to his chambers, combed his white hair, and put on his robe. He has taken his place on the bench and is ready to sentence the convicted women. The probation worker, standing beside him, is there to aid him with advice based on her knowledge of the girls.

10:05 A.M.

Mary Jean Louis, a muscular frizzly-haired girl of twenty-four, and the Legal Aid attorney who defended her at trial stand before His Honor. He confers with the probation worker who points to her arrest record, ten arrests that began five years ago when Mary Jean was nineteen.

"You were in this court less than a month ago," the judge tells Mary Jean. "You came before me and I gave you a thirty-day suspended sentence. I also gave you a warning. Do you remember what I told you?"

Mary Jean falls on the floor and begins to beat her head. "Oh, Jesus, help me. Jesus, stand by me, Jesus. Help me, sweet Jesus. Don't get angry. Give me a chance. Jesus, oh Jesus."

The judge motions to a couple of officers to pick Mary Jean up off the floor. He says, "You came before this court ten months ago and you were given four months in the workhouse. You served your sentence and came right out and started walking the streets again. You've been in and out of this court ever since. Now, I've got to give you another thirty days."

Mary Jean looks horrified and as though she cannot believe her ears.

"Thirty days," she screams out, "thirty days. I'll have to lay down and die before I do that, Your Honor. I just can't do it. I ain't got all my health about me." She falls to the floor again, stiff and immobile. "Oh, Jesus, oh, Jesus, don't get angry. Oh, Jesus." She flails out at the two officers who lift her up, and then walks back to the cage between them trancelike and still muttering, "Oh Jesus, oh Jesus." Once there, however, she makes a flying leap for her girl friend. "Whoops, honey, all I got was thirty days and all the time I expected ninety."

10:15 A.M.

Louise Daischer, a small, slender twenty-four-year-old blonde in a black dress that was outdated when someone gave it to her a couple of years ago, tries to smile as she stands up for sentence, but she is terrified and looks it. The judge whispers, "Don't worry," more to himself than to her, and examines her record. She, her husband, and young baby lived with her parents in Bridgeport, Connecticut. Her parents and husband evidently had the usual in-law difficulties and one day the two young people picked up and came to New York. They left the baby with its grandparents.

Once in the big city, Louise's husband said, "I'll get a job now and I'll keep it. You wait and see."

And she, loving him, said, "Sure, baby."

But he looked down at himself, shabby suit, worn shirt, tieless, and he thought, "Nobody'll give me a job the way I look." One thought led to another and he told her how he felt.

"Please, baby. Just a couple of times so I can look decent when I apply for a job. Then I'll get hired on a good one, and we'll have our family together again in our own home."

She approached three men. Two turned her down. The third asked her price. "You'll have to ask my husband," she said. So then he pulled an officer's badge out of his pocket and arrested her and her husband. After her trial the judge remanded her for full investigation.

Now, her mother and father stand in court, two shabby little people, the mother in run-down-at-the-heels shoes and a pancake hat. Father and mother hold their daughter's hands, stroking them and crying.

Her father addresses the judge. "She's a good girl, Your Honor. Its' only that Michael. . . ."

Her mother shushes the father and says, "He's all right. Just a boy with bad luck."

"You want your daughter home?" the judge asks.

"Do we want her home?" the mother repeats. "Oh, Your Honor, yes, yes."

The judge turns to Louise. "No one can blame you for what your heart made you do. But it is important that you learn to use your head from now on. Remember, young lady, your body is not for sale. And now, since I know that you are not in the habit of soliciting men, I am going to suspend sentence. Take her home, mother, and watch out for her. Good luck to you both."

10:30 A.M.

Rena May Miller, a tall, gangling sixty-one-year old woman with bleached blond hair, stands to receive her forty-second sentence in twenty-five years.

"Can I say something, Your Honor?" she asks.

The judge nods.

"I don't want to tell you your business. I just think I ought to get a S.S. I should've got a break or something when I was a teen-ager. I'm tired of going to jail. I'm too old. I'm too old. When I was younger, I could do it."

The judge gives her thirty days.

"All right," she says, "but what good's it going to do?"

10:40 A.M.

Mary Ryan for sentence. Jean Silver for sentence. Greta Johnson for sentence. All three are old-timers with a total of 102 arrests among them. All receive thirty days in the workhouse and take their sentences with equanimity, because they know that any other judge would have been harder on them. Only Greta Johnson says:

"Please, Your Honor, if you put me on probation, I promise to do my part and reform, so you'll never see me in this court again."

The judge looks at her arrest sheet for a long time.

"You," he says sadly, "could write a book on probation, you've had it so many times."

11:10 A.M.

Seven women are arraigned before the judge. The court officer reads the charges against them and informs them of their rights—the right to communicate with relatives or

friends, by letter or telephone free of charge, the right to
the aid of counsel at every stage of the proceedings and
before any further proceedings, and the right to an ad-
journment to procure counsel. He then asks them how they
plead, guilty or not guilty. Five of the seven plead not
guilty.

11:30 A.M.

Trials begin. There are eleven scheduled. The women
are tried under the vagrancy statute, Section 887(4)(a) and
(c) of the New York State Code of Criminal Procedure.

Clause (a) defines a vagrant as "a person who offers to
commit prostitution." In practice this is the clause invoked
when a girl solicits or approaches a plain-clothes police
officer. It is considered that in order to effect a valid arrest
the officer must be the person solicited; should the officer
solicit the girl, the sense of the statute has been deemed
inapplicable.

Clause (c) defines as a vagrant a person "who loiters in
or near any thoroughfare or public or private place for the
purpose of inducing, enticing or procuring another to commit lewdness, fornication, unlawful sex intercourse or any
other indecent act." It is this clause which is used when a
girl is arrested in the company of her John.

11:30 A.M.–1:00 P.M.

Trials of Tina Roder, Sylvia Jones, and Maria Debusa.

All three women are old-timers as their previous records
(fifteen arrests for Sylvia Jones, eighteen for Tina Roder,
and thirty-nine for Maria Debusa) reveal. All three plead
not guilty, and Maria Debusa maintains that she is as "innocent as the day I was born," but the judge finds them all
guilty.

1:00–2:00 P.M.

Court adjourned for lunch.

2:00 P.M.

Trial of Hilda Ellison, represented by Legal Aid Society. Officer John Mowry, complainant.

Officer Mowry is one of the handsomest men on the vice squad, six feet, one inch, black hair, blue eyes, and a shy Irish smile. But he is a newcomer and, according to some of his fellow officers, "still wet behind the ears." Today his lack of experience is glaringly apparent as he takes the stand against Miss Ellison and swears to tell the truth, the whole truth, and nothing but the truth.

"At about eleven-thirty A.M.," he says, "the defendant smiled and said hello. I smiled and said hello and continued on my way. On 55th Street, I saw the defendant again. She smiled at me again. She said, 'Where are you staying?' I said, 'In the hotel here.' She said, 'What do you do?' I said, 'I'm in the plumbing business. I'm a designer.' Then we went to a delicatessen and she asked more of what I was doing. She suggested that we go up to my room. I said, 'Wait a minute. I want to get one thing squared away. Are you doing this for love?' She smiled and said, 'What do you think?' We entered the hotel, got into the elevator, and I pulled my badge and arrested her. When I arrested her, she said, "Please don't take me in. I won't do it again.' I said, 'Oh stop, I've seen you around the hotel plenty of times.' She said, 'When?' I said I worked nights. She said, 'I know some girls who used to do this. I never understood how they could expose their bodies to strange men.' "

Miss Ellison's lawyer begins questioning Officer Mowry.

"Were you actually registered in the hotel?"

"No."

"Did this defendant at any time put a hand on your person?"

"No."

"Did she ever say she was going to commit an act of intercourse?"

"No."

"I haven't yet heard from this officer that the defendant was going to commit an act of prostitution," the attorney tells the judge. "There has been no overt act, no exposure. Where is the act, the offer? And the offer is a primary ingredient you have to spell out. If that is the People's case, defendant moves to dismiss on the ground the People have failed to make a prima facie case."

The evidence is obviously insufficient, and the judge has no choice but to dismiss her case. She leaves the courtroom making a face at Officer Mowry on her way out.

"I been in this business too long to be caught by the likes of you, rookie," she says.

Officer Mowry is embarrassed to have his colleagues witness his failure. But they are comforting. They assure him that, in a few weeks, as soon as he begins to absorb vice-squad techniques, he will have one of the best arrest records in the squad. He's bound to with his looks. He says his looks don't worry him. He knows he can get the girls all right. He is only concerned because he can't seem to figure out what makes good trial evidence. The others tell him that all that was wrong with his Hilda Ellison case was that he grew impatient. He should have made her set a price, or better yet, taken her to a room and gotten her to disrobe. He's a lucky fellow, incidentally, because Bill Breen will be testifying today and Bill is, far and away, the brightest star of the whole vice squad. He never comes to court with insufficient evidence.

2:30 P.M.

The four prostitutes brought in on indirect arrests are called for trial in quick succession. All the Johns, including the truck driver whose friend, Lorette, is on trial, testify exactly as you would expect them to. The truck driver is the most ill at ease of the four. His voice is very low, and he keeps his head down in the hope that he won't have to see Lorette. But she looks straight at him and, during one unguarded moment, he finds he's got to meet her eye.

All four women are adjudged guilty.

3:30 P.M.

Trial of twenty-five-year-old, red-haired Rhonda Swan, represented by private counsel, Officer Bill Breen, complainant.

Officer Breen takes the stand confidently. A man with his reputation ought to be sure of himself. He is in his thirties, a dark, swarthy man in sport clothes, not particularly handsome or dignified, and yet there are those who say, put Bill in a derby and banker's gray suit, fill his pipe up with good tobacco, give him a light, and just watch the pros come flocking to him. They always think he's a bank president or a Midwestern industrialist. Truly he has no equal in the business. There used to be an officer who could compete with him, a dumb-looking cluck named Robert Smith who always went out in a hick suit, pants too short and too tight, jacket too long, umbrella in rain or shine, and a *Farmers' Almanac* conspicuously under his arm. He could put on a Southern drawl, too. He brought women in by the dozens. But he is no longer on the force and so Bill Breen's record is unequaled; and he is as good on the stand as he is in the field.

The Police Prosecutor, conducting the case for the People, begins Mr. Breen's direct examination.

Q.: Officer, on April 23, 1956, at 12:30 A.M., at 760 Riverside Drive, did you arrest the defendant in this case?

A.: I did.

Q.: Will you tell us the circumstances which prompted you to make the arrest?

A.: I met the defendant about 11:55 P.M. on the southwest corner of Seventh Avenue and 55th Street. She smiled and said "Hello" to me. She said, "What are you waiting here for?" I said, "I have an appointment but I may have been stood up." She said, "Would you spend twenty-five dollars?" I said, "What do I get for that?" She said, "A good time." I said, "Do you French?" She said, "Not usually. But I will for you. I like your type." We took a cab up to her apartment where she stripped, all but her bra.

"Now you see how to get evidence," Officer Mowry's buddy whispers admiringly. "Breen don't stop till he gets all kinds of evidence and gets a girl on every count, so he's got to win his case."

The defendant tells a totally different story from Breen's. She says: "I came down to the House of Chan to have some Chinese food. After I ate, I had to phone a girl friend and said I'd meet her on 59th Street. At 55th Street I meet this officer. He was standing there laughing. He said, 'I'm cheating.' I said, 'What do you mean?' He said, 'I'm cheating on my wife.' I never heard of such a thing. I said, 'If your date turned you down, come on and have a good time.' When he said he would spend twenty dollars, I figured maybe he would take me to the movies or something. He asked if we could go to my apartment for a cup of coffee first, and I thought since he was going to treat me so nice, I might as well take him. I was surprised when he told me he was a cop. All the time he looked like a fag to me."

This woman, Rhonda Swan, is an old-time prostitute.

Having been in the court before, she knows that the words "good time" do not necessarily constitute an offer to commit prostitution. And so, the officer, if he wishes his case to stand, cannot afford to rely on such flimsy evidence. Therefore, where she says "a good time" he specifically says "French" and that, coupled with her exposure, assures him of a conviction. The Judge has difficulty in dismissing Officer Breen's case for lack of sufficient evidence. He finds the woman guilty, as Officer Breen has known he would.

4:00 P.M.

Trial of fifty-two-year-old Aline Wright, represented by Legal Aid Society, Officer Lou McDowell, complainant.

Officer McDowell, a gentle, scholarly-looking man with glasses, arrested Aline at the Hour Glass Bar on Second Avenue. He said she had sat on the bar stool next to his and had "roamed my body with her hands. So after a while, I asked her if she'd like to have a good time and she said, 'Sure.' I asked her how much she wanted, and she said anything I wanted to give her. I said, 'None of that. You set your price now, so I'll know you won't be dissatisfied.' She said, 'Would you like to give me ten dollars? And I want you to take me to the Shelburne Hotel.' "

When Aline Wright, a stout, matronly woman in brown orthopedic shoes, takes the stand, she says the officer's story is true on the whole. She can only differ on the description of her motivations.

"Your Honor," she says in a reedy voice, "I wish I could explain how I felt that night. I was lonely because I had a big fight with my son-in-law over the baby; he says I spoil him. My daughter agreed with her husband, and I thought they didn't want to see me any more. I got no friends of my own so I felt terrible. I went into the Hour Glass. I was never there before, because I'm not a drinking woman.

When I saw this officer my head was spinning. He was so nice. I told him about my daughter. He said he was sorry for me. He said I had a nice figure and didn't have to worry about my daughter's family. I could get myself a man. I don't know, I wanted to touch him then, so I did. Your honor, my husband died nineteen years ago and I never had a man since then. Sure, I said yes when he wanted me to go with him." She does not recollect having asked the officer for money, although she admits she might have. As for the Shelburne Hotel, she smiles and says, "Look me over, Your Honor, sir. Do I look like a woman they'd let in the door? I was dreaming when I told him to take me to the Shelburne. Judge, can you blame an old woman for dreaming one time in her life?"

The Judge finds her not guilty.

4:20 P.M.

Trial of Eleanor Jones, represented by Legal Aid, Officer Lawrence Gerda, complainant.

Officer Gerda, a small dark man in his late thirties with a bald, bullet-shaped head, takes the stand. He states on direct examination:

"On April 23, at ten o'clock in the evening I dialed TR 4-1200. I said, 'Eleanor Jones?' A voice answered, 'Yes, that's me.' I said, 'This is Milt. Jimmy the peddler told me to call you.' She said, 'What does he peddle?' I said, 'Rubbers. I met him on the dock.' She said, 'Do you know the address? It's 330 West 85th Street, Room RA.' Defendant opened the door when I knocked. I said, 'How much?' She said, 'Five dollars.' Then she started to disrobe. She removed a blouse and skirt and just had a slip on."

When Eleanor Jones, a fifty-five-year-old, dark-brown woman with a long nose, a low forehead, and small, squinting eyes, takes the stand in her own behalf, she claims that

the officer framed her. Her testimony on cross-examination
follows:

Q.: Were you in your slip when the officer arrested you?

A.: Yes, sir. I went to go to the bathroom in my slip and
   brassiere when this officer come along and was standing in the hall.

Q.: Where is the bathroom in relation to your room?

A.: Out in the hall. Way down.

Q.: How many people do you share your bathroom with?

A.: Nine.

Q.: Men and ladies both?

A.: Yes. Mixed.

Q.: So you went to the bathroom in your slip and bra?

A.: Yes, sir. I know it ain't respectable, but I had to go
   bad. (Turns to judge) I'm a churchgoing woman and I
   got a married daughter. I got no call to be bad.

Q.: Have you ever been convicted in this court before?

A.: Yes, sir.

Q.: How many times?

A.: I don't know. My mind's going round. I can't remember a thing.

Actually she does know how many times she's been in—
thirty-four. What good will it do such a one to be sentenced
yet another time? But the judge feels he has no choice and
must find her guilty.

   4:40 P.M.

Court is adjourned.

FIFTEEN / There but for the grace of God

And so the judge, sometimes much against his will, sentences some women to jail. What is prostitutes' jail in New York? What is jail in New York? What is jail anywhere, and what do we hope it will do for a woman? If you are a person who feels a great gulf between yourself and one who has been sentenced to prison, then you cannot imagine what she goes through while she is there. But if, when you see or read about her, you can think for a moment that there, but for the bitterness deep inside, there, but for the little kink in the mind, there, but for the accidental circumstances, there, but for the grace of God, go I, then you can have some perception of what it means. You can glean a little of how terrifying it can be when the iron gates first lock you away from the world you know.

Every woman who has ever gone to prison, regardless of how tough she appears, will remember to her dying day the first hours of incarceration, the sick, numb feeling and the overwhelming fear, always more prevalent in women than men, that she may break down and go insane. Or the agony of jealousy that comes with the pictures she cannot thrust out of her mind—her man in another woman's arms and her child growing fond of somebody else. She wants to scream and beat the walls down, and the only reason she does not give way to herself is because she is afraid they would ship her off to some padded cell if she did.

And it makes no difference, when it comes to bearing tribulations like these, whether the prison she is in has been humanized or whether it has not. The fact is that a prison is a prison, and life on the inside, tolerable or not, is no substitute for freedom. Punitive-minded citizens need not fear—there will never be a woman in her right mind who will *choose* to go to prison no matter how merciful it may become in the future. Any prostitute from Maine to California, regardless of whether she has experienced the best or worst of prison facilities, will tell you so, unequivocally, and from the heart.

New York has two official prison facilities where prostitutes are sent, along with other sentenced women, from disturbers of the peace to murderers: Westfield State Farms in Bedford, New York, and the House of Detention for Women on Tenth Street and Sixth Avenue in New York City. In addition, the court may send young girls with hopeful prognoses to the Villa Loretta in Peekskill.

The Villa Loretta, providing a spiritual atmosphere and offering an opportunity for wholesome living under optimal physical conditions, renders a valuable service. But it is equipped to handle only small numbers of very young girls, and so we do not include it in our consideration of official institutions. But anyone who holds young prostitutes to be irredeemable would do well to talk to its staff and examine its records. They would find a different picture from that at either the House of Detention for Women or Westfield State Farms.

Westfield State Farms, a reformatory located amid rolling farmland outside New York City in Bedford Hills, New York, takes girls from sixteen to twenty-one and, when it seems desirable on occasion, women up to thirty. The physical atmosphere is pleasant on the whole, offering a tremendous contrast, in its exterior, to the House of Detention. Inmates live in cottages, each one having her own tiny room which she can decorate to her taste. They eat and prepare their food and have a large part of their social life there.

In some ways Westfield State could appear to be a very austere school as well as a prison, for it offers academic and vocational instruction: typing, stenography, English, art, music, beauty culture, laundering, baking, sewing-machine operation. There is also a recreation program, basketball, baseball, volleyball, and a home-dug swimming hole. There is a well-equipped hospital on the premises having, in addition to the usual facilities, a cheerful nursery where mothers who have borne their babies in the institution can keep them until they are nine months old.

No doubt about it, Westfield's approach could, if it were in reality as effective as it sounds, take a girl a bit out of herself and make her know she is still a person. Maybe it could even help to check a little of the bitterness that caused her to be committed in the first place.

But Westfield's approach is more a theory than a reality today despite the knowledge and compassion that Henrietta Additon, superintendent of the institution, and herself a distinguished pioneer in prison work, brings to her position.

After all, Miss Additon, like every other superintendent in the country no matter how enlightened, must rely upon the officers who staff her institution. Officers are the ones who meet the women every day and have immediate authority over them. They are the ones who have to make prisoners feel like human beings instead of numbers. But where does one find officers with the will and ability to do such a job, women who are themselves healthy enough? In our institutions by and large, at Westfield State, the Women's House of Detention, in any prison in this coun try, this is a serious problem. Why should we expect to find them there? After all, people who are happy and adjusted do not deliberately seek to shut themselves away from the world.

"All our officers got to be a little touched in the head," Wanda Green, who has been committed for three months now and, by dint of a bad temper coupled with a strong muscle, has become a recognized leader, explains. "They're bigger jerks than us girls. They could be on the outside looking in and yet here they are. Crazy."

Some of the women are not as kind as Wanda when they analyze their officers. They say they are there for one of two reasons and no other. Either they are sadists who find outlet for their power drive in jail, or they are homosexuals who come to meet young girls under conditions which make them practically unrejectable.

They say about the ones they call sadists:

"One officer, she don't even speak. She wants you to know from her look what she wants you to do. God help you if you don't."

"This officer always tells the girls if they were smart, they'd never have got caught."

"You don't know how mean officers can be till you get visitors. Then they sit right in the middle of you and look like you and your visitors was dirt."

"Sometimes there's lots of colored girls in the hospital and this nurse makes the remark she wasn't there to serve no niggers."

"The doctors. They don't like to believe you're sick. One can't see; can't hear. If you get an aspirin, you get a long speech about how you must be fooling about the headache because us girls are always trying to kid the big shots. Then she might lock you in your room. Better than take all that, forget it."

Their stories about the ones they characterize as homosexual are less personal. Most of them talk about the looks of officers and speculate on what they must be doing with "other girls."

"You ought to see Miss Blank," says twenty-two-year-old Gilda Johnson who spent almost two years at Westfield and is in court now awaiting a new sentence to the House of Detention. "What a creep! She looks so much like a man it ain't even funny. The girls call her Blankey Boy. She has plenty to do with the girls. I hear she just decided to wear a little lipstick, but nothing helps. Some of the others don't look so bad as her, but they do the same things."

If you listened to prison women, you would think there was not a sexually normal officer in the whole sad, strange prison world.

Although it is certainly not true that every one they stand ready to accuse is a lesbian, some officers doubtless are. This place they have chosen to live in is, in the last analysis, manless, and so if their interests and feelings had not been centered on women, whether overtly or not, they might never have elected to come there at all.

Despite what they say about their officers, there are few Westfield women, however, who actually claim to have had relationships with them. What they say, when you pin them down, is that officers who are themselves homosexual are more tolerant of lesbian relations among the women themselves.

Actually we have known for a long time now that homosexuality, inspired by officer tolerance or not, is not an infrequent concomitant of single-sex institutional living, whether the institution be a jail or a boarding school. It is merely that the special needs of delinquent women, who do not have the other outlets that boarding-school girls have, add intensity to their relationships and doubtless make them last longer. Besides, prostitutes, many of them having experienced casual homosexuality on the outside, are particularly prone to accept such relationships here as conveniences which they will shed more or less easily when the time comes.

There are those who engage in lesbian activities because they crave affection, as every normal woman does, and because their normal cravings have been denied for too long. Then there are the ones who avoid loneliness by becoming part of somebody else. And, of course, there are all the women, who, having sold themselves to men for so long, are now selling themselves to women for the cigarettes and candy that pops keep their moms supplied with here. What has sex ever meant to them anyhow?

No, a new prostitute's greatest danger from being institutionalized lies not so much in learning about the ways of lesbian love, nor even in acceptance of its standards and mores. The danger lies in the reinforcement of the prime pattern she has been sent here to correct—a revulsion against authority born of bitterness and self-pity and nurtured by inadequate people who are not so much sadists as they are small-minded people who are smug in their notion that black is black and white is white, and that women who have once tangled with society are a different breed.

In the long run it is this basic insensitivity of the staff that services most of our institutions that can negate the value of the most socially oriented program and send many of the women out of the best of current institutions angrier and more resentful, worse than they were before.

This is not to say that some prostitutes have not abandoned the "life" after being at Westfield State Farms.

Miss Additon has in her files many letters that would indicate that girls have found new lives for themselves. But one can offset the letters many times over by considering the vast number of women who, having served their sentences out at Westfield ten, fifteen, twenty years ago, were arrested soon after they came out and have continued to be police and court cases until today.

The case of Catherine Lowe is typical. In March, 1941, having been released from Westfield in January of that year, she was arrested for prostitution and given a suspended sentence. In April she was arrested again and given another suspended sentence. She managed to stay out of the courts in May and June, but came in again in July and was sentenced to thirty days at the House of Detention. She was picked up again on December 26, 1941, for unlawful possession of drugs this time, and given a sixty-day sentence. After that, she was not heard from until 1943. Here is her arrest record from that date:

5/19/43	Disorderly Conduct (Jostling)	Magistrates Court	Workhouse 5 Days
5/24/43	Disorderly Conduct (Jostling)	Magistrates Court	Workhouse 5 Days
5/28/44	Prostitution	Magistrates Court	Sentence suspended
8/22/44	Prostitution	Magistrates Court	Workhouse 6 Months
8/ 3/45	Burglary	Felony Court	Dismissed
12/10/45	Prostitution	Magistrates Court	Workhouse 6 Months
7/ 9/47	Unlaw. Poss. of Drugs	General Sessions	Workhouse Time Already Served
11/13/47	Petit Larceny	Special Sessions	Penitentiary 1 Year

8/31/48	Unlawful Sale of Heroin	U.S. District Court So. Dist. of N.Y.	U.S. Reformatory for 3 Yrs. (Discharged 7/21/50)
10/11/51	Prostitution	Magistrates Court	Workhouse 60 Days
4/19/55	Vio. Sec. 3305, Public Heath Law	General Sessions	Workhouse 90 Days
11/ 6/55	Unlaw. Poss. of Drugs	Special Sessions	Workhouse 90 Days

Catherine Lowe does not easily talk about herself. She usually stays by herself, reserved and imperturbable. Unlike other women in her business, she does not like to think of what brought her to her present pass nor will she permit herself any sentiment about people she may once have loved: her divorced husband and the two children, almost grown now, who live with him; her dead father; her mother who has been in a mental hospital for the past ten years; her brother who kicked her down the stairs of his home one time. If you tried talking to her about them all and listened to her and watched her, you would think the woman had no feeling in her; but if you happened to stumble on the subject of her early experience at Westfield, then you would see a different person with all the imperturbability broken through.

"Oh God," she says, "I can't tell you how horrible it is. A training school for every mean, rotten thing you can think of. And the young girls having to go there! It kills me to think about them. I know they're finished after a year or two there. Like I was. Oh God, the poor kids! I worry about them. They aren't like me. They can still be saved if you treat them right. But not at Westfield. Never at Westfield. You can't save girls by sending them to hell, and Westfield is plain hell. The only worse place I can think of is the House. That's worse. Worse than Westfield and worse than hell."

Everybody who knows it feels the same way about the House of Detention, located in the heart of Manhattan on Greenwich Avenue and West Tenth Street. It is a modern escape-proof building originally designed to be merely a place of temporary detention. A bastillelike structure, it serves today as a place of detention, a workhouse, and a penitentiary. It is a loathsome place, guaranteed to make women who already feel estranged know that from now on there must be bad blood between them and the world that has sent them here.

They come straight from court, in the hot metal vans that have the look of cages, feeling, many of them say, like animals in a zoo. They pass through the heavy steel gate in single file so that the uniformed male officer can count noses, one, two, three, four. You're just a number now, baby—and nobody is around with either the time or inclination to ease the depersonalization. One, two, three, four. After a while, with days and nights blending into one another the way they inevitably do in prison, the most energetic women will grow lethargic and indifferent, but now, just in from the outside, the lethargy, the welcome dulling cannot have begun yet. Women are alert to everything during these first hours in jail. They are still pained from the arrest process and saying good-by to loved ones. These may be pimps and other prostitutes, but they are loved ones all the same and precious to them, especially now. They want to cry even though they know tears may lead to breakdowns.

"To those who are in prison," Oscar Wilde wrote in *De Profundis*, "tears are a part of every day's experience. A day in prison on which one does not weep is a day on which one's heart is hard, not a day on which one's heart is happy."

A first day at the House of Detention is one to turn women's hearts hard so they may never weep again.

They sit around for long hours together and await their formal admission procedures: the young prostitutes who may be first-timers; and the madams who don't consider jail so bad as long as they find new recruits there; and the dope addicts, overcome by the pain of their withdrawal, and looking, some of them, like living death; the lesbians; the murderers; and the crazy women who will end up in mental hospitals once they get weeded out. They grow hungry and thirsty while they sit around but nobody cares. The officers who are responsible for them during their first hours, assuming they reacted to their misery, are too busy to do anything to alleviate it. There are only a few of them on duty, and each one has her own rigidly defined function.

First, there is the shower officer who forces them to undress, takes their own clothes away, sees to it that they take showers and get their prison clothes—one pair of black oxfords with cuban heels, two pairs of much-mended ankle socks, three cotton dresses, two cotton slips, two pairs of panties, and a couple of bras. Practically all the bras are flat and useless. No corsets or girdles are issued.

There is not a sadder sight than some of the obese prisoners who, if nothing else, have been managing to keep themselves looking decent on the outside, confronted by the first sight of themselves in prison issue.

"I always knew I wasn't much," Molly Sands, a two-hundred-pound streetwalker in her early forties, says. "But now, every time I look down at myself, I think I'm less than nothing. I've been here two months now and I'm getting used to myself, but you should've seen me when I first came. I bawled like a little baby. The officer said, 'Well, what's the matter with you?' I said, 'I know I'm a fat horse and all, but maybe, if you got me a better bra, one that would really hold me in, I could get to looking decent. This way I'm disgusting.' She looked me up and down and she said I was right about being disgusting all right, but she never mentioned a word about getting me another bra. I asked her please. I said, 'You're a woman. You ought to know how another woman would feel about looking like I do." She said I should've thought of being a woman before I got myself locked up. That's as much as she knows about it. She says the clothes are not the worst things about being in jail. Maybe not to her. To me they are. I'll never forget looking at myself the first day. I told myself, 'What's the use of going on with this life anyways when you were born to be an ugly duck like me?' Yeah, the clothes are the worst, all right. Unless you want to count the doctor's examination. That's really the worst. You know, I had lots of awful things happen in my life and some made me feel dirty, crawly-dirty. But nothing ever made me feel like that first doctor's examination did."

By the doctor's examination she means the pelvic examination which all new prisoners receive. Every woman knows how unpleasant a pelvic examination is at best, but nobody can know what it is for House of Detention inmates unless they have seen it administered. It is an indignity that no woman should have to be subjected to.

Huge groups of women wait around until the doctor arrives, flustered and hurried because she is under pressure. She summons them into her office by twos or threes and takes one on the examining table while she orders the others to strip. She gives no recognition to the natural fears women have at such times, nor would she have time to offer any reassurances if she did. She grabs a speculum which has not been prewarmed for comfort and jams it into the girl on the table while the other two look on. Then she wipes her with a cotton swab wet with sanitary solution, inserts a device which ejects a local treatment, hands her a piece of cotton for "mopping herself up," and urges her out of the room.

A strange thing about Americans—we who pride ourselves on our chivalry—we often wound forsaken women and for no good reason. We forget our gallantry where they are concerned and often treat them less considerately than the men of their group, not only by what we do *to* them but also by what we do *not* do *for* them. Here in New York, for example, we send vagrant men to Hart Island, a rehabilitation center in the country, while we send vagrant women to jail. And that jail, the House of Detention for Women.

Two girls occupy a small cell that has two tiny windows heavily screened on the outside for maximum security. Each girl has her own cot, usually with a broken spring. Cells also contain a wash basin and a toilet with a metal cover. There is a shelf with room for several hooks attached to the wall. Two clothes hooks hang from the shelf. The cell is heavily barred from ceiling to floor. The bars, three inches apart, are morbidly painted in pastels and never fail to give the women a laugh.

"Ain't we the fancy schmancies? Pink prison bars yet."

Women's cells are constantly cluttered with their possessions, such as they are: three slices of bread on a window sill; an old milk container with commissary jam in it; a deodorant jar full of peanut butter; a pink cold-cream jar and a bottle of toilet water looking vulgar and out of place here. Clothing is crowded together in heaps, or else, having been washed, is pasted against the walls with the hope it won't have to be ironed.

The House, in addition to its cells, three floors for girls awaiting trial and three and a half for permanent prisoners, contains a thirty-bed hospital, a chapel where different religious groups hold services and Alcoholics Anonymous and Narcotics Anonymous hold meetings. It has a small library, a so-called beauty shop, with a couple of stoves, to enable Negro women to do each other's hair, and a roof which is the only outdoors a woman will know all the time she spends there.

The prison program is extremely simple.

6:30. A.M. Lights on, and those who want showers had better scramble for them. Most women refuse to rush and wash up in their cells. Some of them don't wash at all until the others, offended by the odors on their blocks, gang up and make them.

7:15. Breakfast.

8:00. Long-term girls, fortunate enough to have work assignments, report to the laundry, or the sewing room, or the kitchen. Short-term girls, including the majority of prostitutes, go back to their cells and sit around, either on their cots or in the outside corridors, until lunch.

12:00. Lunch.

12:30–3:30. Short-term girls may sit around their cells or be assigned to clinic, beauty shop, recreation roof, etc.

3:30–4:00. Count-up time, with all women due back in their cells.

4:00–6:00. Women may sit around their cells or corridors.

6:00–6:30. Dinner.

6:30–9:00. Women may sit around their cells or corridors.

9:00. Lights out.

And so the days merge into the nights, one like all the

others, and the monotony becomes the most important
thing to reckon with. Meals become exciting, not for the
food but the company.

"The food's slop all right," fat, old, toothless Birdie
Bryan explains with rare good humor. "I put sugar on
everything, meat, potatoes, just to get a little taste in it, but
all the same I sure look forward to meals. They're something to do."

The commissary truck that comes onto the corridors
selling luxury items (candy, cake, cold cream, perfume)
is anticipated, especially by the girls with money, almost
as much as mealtimes are. They socialize at commissary
just as they do at mealtimes, and the truck's coming has
the added advantage of enabling those who feel starved in
jail "to build myself up." Prison women buy unbelievable
quantities of candy, cake, and jam.

If one were to rank prison activities according to their
popularity, one would probably find that fighting followed
closely after mealtimes and commissary. Nobody knows
better than the women themselves what inspires them to
the fights they always engage in so passionately—plain, unadulterated boredom.

A woman stays in the shower longer than the others
think she should and a couple of them get mad at her. A
woman tells a joke and her cellmate doesn't seem to appreciate it. One woman disapproves of another's grammar
and doesn't mind fighting to defend her opinion.

Most fights that have no more motivation than these
are generally loud and boisterous, and, although they
would frighten an outsider who witnessed them, the women
do not take them seriously. The fights they worry about
are the ones with deeper bases. One woman steals another's
girl with bribes of the chocolate and cigarettes those with-

out money would sell their souls for. The defeated one says she'll kill her if it's the last thing she does, and everyone knows she means what she says.

More important than the individual fights in jail are the group fights based on who women happen to be and whether they are high or low in the House's hierarchy.

Prostitutes are considered the lowest of the low by every one except other prostitutes. Yet they, if they happen not to be addicted themselves, say that dopies are lower than they. The small minority of addicts who have never been on the streets resent the prostitutes and believe they are the last women in the world who ought to feel free to throw stones. And both addicts and prostitutes stand together in their condemnation of abortionists. Doubtless the only ones who are not held in contempt by one group or another at the House are murderers and women in for grand larceny.

But the contempt, resulting as it often does in violence, must not be misjudged. Prison is a great leveler, and so no matter what she may say or do, underneath, every woman from murderess to prostitute feels a vast sympathy for all the others, and if ever there is an incident between an inmate and an officer, everybody stands together in loyalty toward their own. They also stand together when they know someone to have been hurt by an outsider. Murderess, thief, or addict, a woman could cheerfully kill some prostitute's pimp, when day after day passes with her holding vigil at the window and him never showing up to wave hello at her, or when he has agreed to come to see her on visiting day and she has spent hours readying herself for nothing.

Those are the times when women need kindness from their own and they get it in ample measure, all disagreements forgotten. The best thing about prison life is the warmth with which prisoners envelop one another when it is most necessary—not just during the terrible times, but also at times that might seem to an outsider to be happy ones, mail and visiting times, for instance.

Mail and visiting hours are not always happy times in prison. Often they bring women who are trying to forget back to themselves and make them conscious of what they have lost on the outside. They read their letters ten, twelve times a day until the pages get dirty and dog-eared and torn. Every piece of bad news or puzzling information, that they could doubtless take in their stride on the outside, sends them into hysterics here. Middle-aged women cry like babies during mailtime and are always sure to be gathered close to somebody's bosom and held until they are comforted. Mailtime in jail is painful, but never quite as painful as visiting time.

Visiting time. The prisoners dread it as much as they look forward to it. Inmates see outsiders in either of two visiting areas. The one for sentenced women is a bare room containing only a long table with several chairs. Visitors sit on the left side and inmates on the right. All contact is supervised by an officer who sits at the head. Dope addicts and women who are still awaiting trial receive their visitors in a dark, eerie, maximum-security room. The women stand in steel booths equipped with telephones and communicate with their visitors who stand on the other side and watch them through heavy glass peepholes. They can never touch each other.

It is hard to say who suffers more during visitors' hours —prisoners or visitors. The visitors are appalled and the prisoners know it. Visitors try to discipline their faces so as not to show their feelings but they seldom succeed. Most of them who come are women, for it is a rare pimp who will show his face when his girl is in jail. Sometimes they are friends from the business, and they suffer more than other people because, seeing their friends, they think, in fact they *know,* some day soon it will be themselves in there. Sometimes the women's mothers come to see them. They are often self-conscious and humiliated to be in such a place, and they feel guilty. It may be a long time since they have seen their daughters, and now they think what a place to be seeing them in. So they laugh and they talk about mundane things as if they had seen the girls only yesterday. But they look sick and beaten underneath all the laughter and talk, with eyes begging their girls, "Don't blame me. Not my fault, not yours either maybe, but still not mine." In their way the people who smile and laugh are as hard to watch as the ones who break down and have hysterics. They hate to see the time go by, and yet they are glad when the officer comes around shushing people and telling them their time is up. They are glad and yet they are sorry, too. So much to say and so little time to say it in. If they feel resentful, as some of them do, and show it, then they are sorry as can be. If they do not show it, though, there is something inside them that hurts because they do not.

These are only some of the reasons why visiting times, although they keep the women going, are such agonizing experiences. But agonizing or not, they are necessary, not just because prisoners have a right to see the ones they love, but also because, unless they see outsiders once in a while, the long-termers, and to a lesser extent the short-termers, lose all touch with the reality of the outside world.

Because Anna M. Kross, Commissioner of Correction, is aware of the need for prisoners to maintain contact with the outside, she has introduced a service whereby kindly-disposed people, most of them bright, well-educated women, come to see and talk with inmates at regular intervals. Although they have come under criticism from some sources, there is no question but that Friendly Visitors render a valuable service at the House. So lonely is prison life that the women, even those who act hostile, feel grateful.

Mary Anderson, in her sixties, an old-timer who has been in and out of the House of Detention "more times than twice the fingers on both my hands," has this to say about Friendly Visitors:

"They come and talk like they're interested in you. They never treat you like dirt the way the officers do."

In some ways, Mary Anderson's comparison between officers and Friendly Visitors hits at the very roots of why the House of Detention, like Westfield and other institutions, could not ever change a prostitute's psyche. Friendly Visitors never treat you like dirt. Officers do. Again, as at Westfield, the women feel the reason officers treat you like dirt is simple to understand: being sadists, they enjoy hurting you. And, again as at Westfield, once you get to know the officers, you realize they are less sadists than smug, small-minded people. Many of them are lacking in formal education and have little or no intellectual understanding of the drives toward antisociality. Incidentally, the best-educated officers and, therefore, the most aware in many ways, are Negroes, among whom there are a goodly sprinkling of college graduates.

At heart, House of Detention officers are the same as any group of people any place, some good, some bad. It is just a pity that the bad ones are in a position to do so much harm to human beings who are in such desperate need of help.

Actually, the women's major complaints about personnel are directed more against the medical staff than the officers. They feel that the doctors are more brusque than the worst old-time officers. The validity of such an accusation is difficult to check, but one thing is undoubtedly true: if the doctors are the least kindly people here, they are also the most put upon. They work long hours and receive an incredibly low salary.

This, then, is the prison for ordinary prostitutes: overworked, underpaid doctors who cannot be expected to be interested in their charges; inadequately trained officers; an occasional bright spot offered by some friendly visitor; a manic-depressive alternation on visiting days; and over everything, the devastating boredom of having nothing to do.

Prostitutes with problems outside the norm learn a different House of Detention, however. They learn of the cooler and the tank. The cooler is the place where disturbed or hysterical girls are sent to be cooled off, and the tank is the place addicts go.

Tony Robinson, a registered nurse with a brassy voice and bleached hair going dark at the roots, has experienced the cooler many times during the thirty or so sentences she has had for prostitution and narcotics addiction. Between jail sentences she has been a Bellevue mental patient because she suffers from periodic depressions during which she tries to kill herself. Before she was arrested the last time, she attempted suicide with an overdose of morphine. She recovered from the overdose at Bellevue and was taken straight to the House of Detention while still in a highly depressed state. She could not hold rational conversations either with her cellmates or her officers and claimed she saw snakes.

"I knew how sick I was," she says today, "and having been through it before, I knew if they gave me some Thorazine I might keep myself under control. They laughed at me for trying to prescribe for myself, even though I am a registered nurse. They believe that once a woman's hit jail, she's forgotten everything she ever knew professionally. Needless to say I never got my Thorazine. As a matter of fact, I never got to see a doctor. I never received any kind of treatment. They just stuck me in the cooler where I couldn't annoy anybody if I tried and let me stew in my own juice. If I yelled and screamed, they didn't need to worry since they couldn't hear me anyway."

The cooler is entirely isolated from the rest of the jail so that inmates like Tony Robinson won't, as one staff member puts it, "annoy other people." It consists of three cells, two of them lined with heavy wire mesh and one containing the usual tile walls. Each cell has a sink, an uncovered toilet, and a mattress on the floor. There are no sheets on the mattress. Girls lie in the cooler for days at a time without any attention from anyone except the officer who slips their food through the heavy barred doors. If they eat the food, all right, but nobody cares whether they do or not. Tony, depressed as she was, did not eat a bite for three days. Sometimes sick women become sicker in the cooler and nobody knows it. Many of them do not have the energy to scream their pain, and those who do know they will not be heard anyway. Every generation of prisoners can tell you of women who have died while in the cooler, and although their stories are mostly fiction, some of them are fact. To see the cooler is to know that even if women do not die there, they well might.

The tank for accommodation of drug addicts, the vast majority of them prostitutes who have no other way of supporting their habit, rivals the cooler for the distinction of carrying the name "hellhole of the house." Its cells are an affront to human decency, unbelievable in the New York of this day and age. They have the look of the cooler cells, only there are more of them, dirty, smelly places with the same uncovered toilets and unsheeted mattresses on the floor, and with solid steel doors that contain tiny holes through which the women may be observed.

Drug addicts are all herded into the tank regardless of how they feel. Young girls, old women, first-timers, old-timers, prostitutes, pushers or peddlers, it makes no difference here. Nor does it matter if a girl or a woman happens to be one who voluntarily went to the court and asked to be hospitalized for the cure of her habit. That's right: she may have read the law that offers the city's hospital facilities to any addict requesting them, and, after having engineered her own commitment proceedings with the high hope of hospital care, she finds herself in a penal institution and in the tank instead.

For the tank in the House of Detention is the only "hospital" women addicts in New York, whether under arrest or self-commitment, ever get to know. They may be sick unto dying, overcome by the tortures of withdrawal, in the very middle of the twitching and the retching and the sweating and the diarrhea—still the tank is their "hospital."

As soon as a girl has had an enema and been examined in all her body orifices so that the authorities can be certain she has no more dope on her, she is herded into the tank along with all the others for the beginning of her cold-turkey cure. She will doubtless be too weak, during the early days of withdrawal, to know what is going on around her. She will lie in her bed in the vomit and diarrhea nobody bothers to tidy up. After a while, she will get out of bed and join the other tankers who sit around the corridor alternating between sweating and shivering and huddling as close to the radiators as they can get. Day or night, they wear the filthy wrappers in which they sleep.

The house physician rarely visits the tank. Once in a while a nurse comes to administer simple medications, vitamins and intravenous injections, but more often, weak as they are, the women are prodded into wakefulness and forced to make the trip to the hospital. The stronger women have all they can do to get there and the weaker ones never go at all.

A day in the tank would devastate an outsider. Here, more than in any other part of the House, man's inhumanity not so much to other men who have erred as to women who have is sickeningly apparent. There is a vast difference between the way we treat female addicts and the way we treat males.

Male addicts on Rikers Island, while they are given the cold-turkey cure just as women are, are placed in the prison hospital as soon as they arrive. They are permitted to smoke and there are facilities for their comfort.

"Why the difference?" old time addict Miriam Shay asks. She is a former schoolteacher, a tall, skinny woman in her early forties who was fired from her job when she first got the habit some ten years ago and has been prostituting ever since. She still retains a semblance of the prim, proper look she must once have had. She says, "If men addicts are sick people who need hospitalization, why aren't women? I've never been to Rikers myself, of course, and I'm sure addicts aren't treated as humans there any more than they are here, but at least they are put in the hospital. If you want to cure addicts, you've got to do a lot more than put them in a hospital; but at least Rikers is doing that. Here, at the House, the cure's a nightmare. How can a nightmare help a woman? I'll tell you what every cure I've had has done for me. It's made me start whoring again with a vengeance because I had to get the stuff quick so I could get over being haunted by the experiences I had while I was in. You can really become obsessed by such sights as I've seen in the tank.

"I've seen women in such pain that they try to hang themselves. I've heard them yelling in the night when they knew nobody would come to help them. I've had one girl ask me to sing 'When the Lights Go On Again' while she tried to kill herself."

SIXTEEN / If it weren't so tragic

Incarceration never "cured" a prostitute—never did and never will. Prostitution is basically a social, a medical, and a moral problem. The penal approach to the problem is at best but a feeble attempt to repair damage done in early childhood. Why, then, do judges go right on sentencing women through an endless revolving door? Don't they know the folly and futility of it all? Of course they know. But what can they do? The law is the law, and the public approves of it.

Judges who sit in Women's Court often receive letters about prostitutes that are hostile, vicious, malevolent beyond imagination.

"If I had my way they'd all be hung by the neck till they died."

"I'd like to see them stay in jail forever."

"Those women don't deserve to live."

Recently, a judge, presiding at the trial of a hundred-dollar call-girl and her madam, received a newspaper picture of the two women that bore the caption, "Ex Model Breaks Down on Stand," and a letter signed simply "Citizen." Under the picture, Citizen, casting a blow on the side of the angels, had printed two obscene words in large red letters. The letter stated:

My dear Judge
   Just look at these phoney pictures
   "Poor innocent" whore too damned lazy to go to work—
   Whorehouse madam making money off lice like that—they ought to be put out of business and out of the world. Well, what are you going to do?

Letters of this kind are the regular concomitant of any publicized prostitution trial; and so are titillating newspaper articles, calculated to please the prurient, and branding women as guilty before they are even tried. If you were to ask newspapermen why they write as they do, they would tell you, "This is what the public wants. It wants to see such women punished."

But why? What drives people toward an urge for punishment? Ask them if you will. Tell them how useless jails have been historically when it comes to reforming prostitutes, and they will ask you: "How can you let such women go unpunished?" You might say, "Are they hurting you that you should want to see them hurt in return? Are you being threatened? When they take men to bed for money, who are the losers except themselves?" At the end, after you have made your most persuasive arguments, they will look you in the eye and reply: "It's justice."

But the obligation of a judge of a criminal court is not merely to administer justice but also to dispense charity.

Psychiatrists who have studied the motivations of the urge to punish say this talk of impersonal justice is more often than not an outlet for people's repressed aggressiveness. As Henry Weihofen, professor of law at the University of New Mexico, says in his recent book *The Urge to Punish:* "No one is more bitter in condemning the

'loose' women than the 'good' women who have on occasion guiltily enjoyed some purple dreams themselves. It
is never he who is without sin who casts the first stone."

Is it not likely that people cast their own sins, their
own miseries, guilts, and hatreds along with the stones they
throw? This is not to say that prostitutes, cheapening as
they do a drive that ought to be associated with a love that
is sacred, and reducing it as they do to a mere business like
any other business, a commercial calculation, are pretty
or nice. But what right do the rest of us have to become
so furious with them? These broken women who sell their
bodies are their own worst enemies, not ours. And those
who wish to see them treated as a menace to society ought
to look into their souls and gauge their reasons.

So ought the law. It is time to put the hostile public
in its proper place and to stop dignifying its thirst for
vengeance and instinct for hate. It is time lawmakers, instead of following in the wake of a misguided public,
assumed the responsibility of providing leadership toward
understanding. Perhaps then we will see that people are
not really as bloodthirsty as they seem to be. It may be
that the hostile public is only the voluble public, the
crackpot fringe, and that most people, far from requiring
retribution when they have not been hurt, would be
pleased to find a way to help women whose lives are so
sad and sordid.

Truly, prostitutes are the derelicts of female society.
Housewives who enjoy their husband's love and respect,
mothers who bear their children in wedlock, girls who
expect to be wives and mothers some day are richer in
the ways that count than the most successful prostitutes
in town. Can we really carry malice in our hearts for the
poorest among us—empty, bewildered misfits our culture
helped create? They have *chosen* to live in their weird

world—only a few have been pushed into it—because, terrible as it is, it seems less painful to them than living in the normal world in which they feel they do not belong.

Why do they feel they do not belong in the normal world? What were the crucial events of their lives that led them, in the end, to make such bitter rejections? Where and why did their parents fail them and where did the whole community? When did they start developing the hostility toward society that is characteristic of all prostitutes? What were the gaps in our preventive and rehabilitative processes that, let's face it, helped make them what they are today? What about the children's courts and institutions for neglected and dependent children and juvenile delinquents which had many of them during their more or less formative years? What about the community approach to drug addiction, so important in any consideration of prostitution in our time?

What about our mores and customs? Our patterns, in every segment of society, for marriage and family living? Our feeling about minority peoples?

All these factors have gone into the making of prostitutes' amorality.

Prostitution has its roots deep in the fabric of society. The basic unit of society is the family. Just so long as society is so far from being perfect, just so long as so many families are inadequate materially, emotionally, spiritually, and otherwise, just so long are we likely to have the phenomenon of prostitution. The answers are not to be found in more vigorous police enforcement or sterner justice. Some prostitutes who are still very young can be aided by a more modern therapeutic program. But the fundamental answers to the problem are to be found primarily in an improved society, a society that will give greater recognition to its dependence on God and will more adequately provide for the humblest of His children.

Once we realize these almost self-evident truths, we must also know how farcical our primitive justice is and has been through the years. No wonder prostitutes are as much with us today as they always have been. We continue in our blindness and stupidity to attempt to legislate morality. The criminal law should be based upon the moral law. It does not follow, however, that all moral offenses should be designated as crimes. The purpose of the criminal law is to maintain and safeguard the common good. Moral offenses, such as prostitution, that do not under most circumstances militate against the common good, should not be made part of the criminal law. The present law dealing with prostitution is an expression of detestation of such acts by the public. But such a motive is not sufficient reason for making them crimes, mortal sins though they are. Further, the existing law depends for its effectiveness upon a system of police espionage and entrapment, which is itself detrimental to the common good. When will we learn that morality is the business of the home, the school, and the church—but not of the state?

Such blindness and stupidity is, of course, not peculiar to New York, or indeed to the United States. English law, although less harsh, is equally farcical. It proscribes "soliciting and importuning to public annoyance" (at least one man must be observed by the arresting officer to *look annoyed* at a woman's approach). The usual fine for the offense is forty shillings (approximately $5.60). While many London streets remain overrun by prostitutes, the courts are kept cluttered with women who know they must take their turns at being arrested and periodically paying the nominal fine. There, as here, the court has degenerated into a solemn absurdity that brings the whole law into disrepute.

Recently a Committee of the Home Office in London began a study of the subject of the law in relationship to prostitution and homosexuality. At the request of this Committee, the late Bernard Cardinal Griffin, Archbishop of Westminster, commissioned some seven Catholic clergymen and laymen to prepare a report presenting to the Committee of the Home Office a reasoned account of Catholic moral teaching on the subject. The group included a professor of moral theology, a parish priest, a queen's counsel, a psychiatrist, a psychiatric social worker, and a welfare officer. The chairman was the Catholic Chaplain to London University. Its report set forth the following principles, among others, as being applicable to prostitution:

"It is not the business of the State to intervene in the purely private sphere but to act solely as the defender of the common good. Morally evil things so far as they do not affect the common good are not the concern of the human legislator."

"Sin as such is not the concern of the State but affects the relations between the soul and God."

"Attempts by the State to enlarge its authority and invade the individual conscience, however high-minded, always fail and frequently do positive harm."

"It should . . . be clearly stated that penal sanctions are not justified for the purpose of attempting to restrain sins against sexual morality committed in private by responsible adults. They . . . should be discontinued because:

    (a) they are ineffectual;

    (b) they are inequitable in their incidence;

    (c) they involve severities disproportionate to the offense committed;

(d) they undoubtedly give scope for blackmail and
    other forms of corruption."

These principles are, of course, as applicable in New
York City as in London. Did not our own Mayor Gaynor
give us much the same counsel almost half a century ago?
Has not our own police and judicial approach through
history been shown to be ineffectual, inequitable, severe,
and corrupt? And are they not, to a greater or lesser degree,
the same today as they used to be? Take the vice squad.
Its very being is an immorality and a shame. We are forc-
ing the guardians of our society to play a filthy game of
entrapment and are making spies, decoys, and stool pigeons
out of them. Yet, hypocritically we dare to affect surprise
and indignation when some of the dirt rubs off and one of
the recurring investigations reveals the corruption that
the informed know has always been characteristic of the
vice squads. Do we really have a right to expect basic
decency from men to whom we give such degrading jobs?
And whom are we trying to fool with the notion that
prostitutes, these pitiful women, as easy to catch as fish
in a stocked pool, need *agents provocateurs* to track them
down? This does not mean that we ought to tolerate open
and notorious solicitation. On the contrary. We ought to
require our uniformed police to approach this aspect of
the problem with greater determination. Fewer women
would walk the streets if they were faced daily with men
whom they knew to be officers. And we would have very
little need for recourse to arrest and the resultant proceedings that take place in Women's Court. In the words of
Mayor Gaynor: "Uniformed policemen can doubtless accomplish this business better than decoys can."

Why do we not stop the mockery—with our courts as
well as our police force? Because prostitutes do not belong
in court and should not be on trial, the proceedings in

Women's Court are a veritable farce. How can there
be a fair trial on so important an issue, when it is re-
peatedly reduced to a question of veracity between an
accused person and a police officer? If you were a judge,
would you find it easy to call the guardian of the law a
liar? And so it is that, while in other courts defendants
are presumed innocent until they are proved guilty, here
it often seems to be the other way around.

Does this mean that "decent" women are often sent to
jail? Most probably not. Today, we believe that few police
officers would descend to framing "decent" girls. But one
can hardly escape the impression that many of them act
on their moral certainty of a woman's guilt, that they do
not hesitate to invent the evidence on which she would
have to be convicted, and that, in effect, they behave as
judge and jury as well as arresting officer and *agent pro-
vocateur.*

Incidentally, "moral certainties" are not always in accord
with the truth and especially not in the weird world prostitutes inhabit. Take the small matter of anonymous tips
on which plain-clothes men base many of their arrests.
Can they always be sure of the motivations of such in-
formants? Plain-clothes men would probably answer that
the women they get, whether or not they are guilty of
the specific offenses with which they are charged, are
certainly prostitutes. They would probably go on to say
that the question of whether a prostitute is guilty of a
specific offense on a specific occasion is basically academic.
But—is it? Can we trust our police always to protect the
innocent if they do not respect the rights of the guilty?
Are we not sacrificing our prerogative to that trust just
so that we may catch large numbers of prostitutes whom
we know we can never help?

It would be laughable if it weren't so tragic.

Glossary

This glossary was prepared by Maria Leach, student of American dialects, folk speech, and slang, and member of the American Dialect Society.

The terms included here (all used in the book) represent a small sample of the special lingo of the world of prostitution, as used by prostitutes and pimps, police, lawyers, and journalists. Many terms from drug-addiction argot are included and defined in the meanings in which they impinge upon or overlap the language of prostitution. A number of general underworld slang terms are also given in the special usages in which they occur in the text. It must be remembered that many of these words are used in other argots with other special significances. For verification of some doubtful meanings, Eric Partridge's *Dictionary of the Underworld* (London, 1950), and *Really the Blues* by Mezzrow and Wolfe (New York, 1946) were consulted.

alkies Persons addicted to alcohol; alcoholics.

alreet All right: Harlem term.

baby A prostitute's customer.—**a hundred-dollar baby** A man willing to pay $100 for a girl.

barnyard hen A run-of-the-mill girl in a pimp's stable as distinguished from his favorite or head chick.

beat the lip To talk nonsense.

beat the rap To outwit the police or the court; to avoid conviction of a criminal charge.

bluenosed Conventional; puritanical.

booster A shoplifter.

boosting Shoplifting.

broad A girl or a woman.—**racket broad** A woman engaged in any underworld racket; specifically, a prostitute.—**square broad** A girl or woman who lives according to the conventional social code; specifically, any woman not a prostitute.

bull A plain-clothes officer; a detective.

bust An arrest: by extension from drug-addiction lingo, in which a **bust** is a raid on a drug-users' parlor.

cadet A young man hired to seduce girls for a whorehouse: a term of the 1890s.

call-girl A prostitute available by telephone.

chick A young girl.—**head chick** The favorite girl in a pimp's stable.

circus An exhibition of sexual, orgiastic acts, originally performed for customers of a whorehouse; now any such exhibition.

clink Jail.

cokies Cocaine addicts.

cold turkey Sudden and complete withdrawal of a drug from an addict: a drastic method of cure. The term is classified as medical and journalistic slang.

con To talk encouragingly and enticingly; to build up confidence.

cooler A group of soundproof cells where hysterical and depressed girls are confined "to cool off."

copesetic Satisfactory; fine and dandy.

cow A prostitute; one of a group of girls in a pimp's stable. See *horse, 2.*

cruise To solicit; entice; pick up.—**Did you cruise a bull?** Did you solicit an officer?

daddy-o 1. A pimp. 2. A customer, or a prospective customer.

dark meat A Negro woman; specifically, a Negro prostitute.

dicty Snooty; stuck-up.

dump To beat.

dumper A man who gets sexual excitement from beating a girl. The term is probably an extension of **dump** (prison slang) to knock down; attack.

dumping A beating.

exotic dancer A provocative dancer such as a strip-tease artist.

fag Short for **faggot,** a male homosexual.

fix A hypodermic shot of a narcotic.

fix To give a hypodermic shot of a narcotic.

fleabag A dirty old prostitute; also a dirty rooming-house or hotel.

freebies Girls who are sexually promiscuous, giving their services free of charge, usually without soliciting; "amateurs."

French, Frenchy Fellatio; fellation: an aberrant act performed with the male sexual organ and the mouth.

get some fish To solicit and get some customers.

head A drug user or addict.

hincty Stuck-up; high class; snooty.

hincty little ofay Snooty little white (girl).

hooked So addicted to a drug as to suffer excruciating physical pain without it.

hopped up Exhilarated by a drug.

horse 1. Heroin. 2. One of a group of girls in a pimp's stable. See *cow, stable.*—**new horse** A new girl taken on by a pimp.

hot-bed hotel A hotel in which the rooms are rented over and over for an hour or less.

hustle To solicit as a prostitute; to "work the street."

hustler A prostitute.

jazz Sexual intercourse.

jive The jargon or special language of swing music and swing musicians, plus New York Negro slang plus drug-addiction argot: a secret and special lingo, incomprehensible to "the squares." Hence **jiving,** by extension, has come to mean kidding, talking meaninglessly or insincerely.

John A prostitute's customer; specifically, the anonymous witness (her customer) who testifies against her in court.

joint Formerly, a low drinking saloon; now, any night club.—**real joint** One frequented by underworld personnel, especially by pimps and prostitutes. One that is *strictly tourist* caters to sightseers and thrill-seekers.

jolt An injection of a narcotic drug.

jostler A pickpocket.

junk A narcotic drug; drugs collectively.—**junked up** Exhilarated by a drug.

junkie A drug addict: usually one addicted either to morphine or heroin.

kick 1. The thrill, satisfaction, or reaction from taking a drug. 2. The drug itself.—**on the same kick** On the same drug.

King Kong In the South, illegal moonshine whisky; in New York, corn whisky.

life, the The world of prostitution.

lush A drunk.

main line The large vein in the arm into which a narcotic drug is injected.

main-liner A drug addict who uses intravenous injections of the drug.

matinée A man who visits prostitutes in the afternoon and still gets home on time.

me-me Chinatown term for sweetheart or prostitute.

mom The girl who takes the female role in a lesbian relationship.

mouthpiece A lawyer.

ofay A white person: pig Latin or back-slang formation for *foe*.

outlaw A prostitute who does not have a pimp.

pad A bed, bedroom, or apartment.

pop The girl who takes the male role in a lesbian relationship.

popping See *skin-popping*.

pro or **pross** A prostitute.

punk A teen-age boy.—**punk kid** Worthless and displeasing teen-age boy.

pusher A retail peddler or seller of narcotic drugs.

racket 1. Any underworld means of livelihood; an illegal scheme or enterprise; specifically, prostitution. 2. A system for establishing and maintaining homosexual relationships.

rat To inform to the police or the authorities.

roll To steal from.—**to roll a lush** To steal from a drunk.

sing To inform to the police or the authorities.

skin-popping The injecting of a narcotic drug under the skin.

sniff To inhale powdered heroin or cocaine.

square One who lives according to the conventional social and moral code; specifically, anyone not in the prostitution racket; anyone not in the know.

square guy Any man not involved in "the life," i.e., the world of prostitution; anyone not involved in a racket.

squealer's mark A cut with a knife from forehead to lower lip.

stable A pimp's group of girls.

stuff Narcotics in general.—**on the stuff** Using or addicted to a narcotic drug.

sweet man or **sweet daddy** A prostitute's pimp.

tank A group of cells having solid steel doors with peepholes, in which drug addicts are confined during the cold-turkey period.

trick A prostitute's customer.

tumble Notice or recognition.

walk To be released from legal custody; to go free.

when push comes to shove If worse comes to worst.

white meat A white woman; specifically, a white prostitute.

wife-in-law A prostitute related to one or more prostitutes by association with the same pimp.

yen Craving; specifically, the agonized craving of an addict deprived of his drug.

About the Authors

Before becoming Chief Magistrate of the City of New York, Judge Murtagh served as Assistant Attorney General of the State of New York, Special Assistant to the Attorney General of the United States, and Commissioner of Investigation of the City of New York. Of his judicial work, Judge Murtagh writes:

"The Magistrates' Courts of the City of New York are some fifty-odd courts of so-called criminal jurisdiction. They deal with a variety of problems, the more important of which are basically social rather than criminal in nature. The first of these problems to engage my attention in 1950 was the subject of *Cast the First Stone*. I spent many months presiding in Women's Court and eliminating many of the conditions that had been the occasion for scandal in past decades—the activities of members of the bar preying on prostitutes, the activities of bondsmen who independently and in concert with lawyers were victimizing defendants, and unnecessary delays in the trial of cases. It was not, of course, very long before I realized that these conditions that have been so often criticized in the past were merely the indicia of something fundamentally wrong, namely, the community approach to the problem of prostitution."

Sara Harris's background and talents provide an excellent complement to Judge Murtagh's experience. She was graduated from New York University and did postgraduate work in sociology at the University of Chicago, the New School for Social Research, and the University of Mexico. Mrs. Harris has been associated with such institutions as the New York State Training School for Delinquent Girls, the Chicago State Hospital, the Chicago Urban League, and the Health Council of Greater New York. She is a gifted and successful professional writer. *The Wayward Ones,* a novel, was published in 1950, and she is the author of *Father Divine, Holy Husband* (1953), and *Skid Row, U.S.A.* (1956). The last book, a study of derelicts and vagrants, was the occasion for her meeting with Judge Murtagh.

M